Race and the Origins of Progressive Education, 1880–1929

Race and the Origins of Progressive Education, 1880–1929

Thomas D. Fallace

TEACHERS COLLEGE | COLUMBIA UNIVERSITY
NEW YORK AND LONDON

Published by Teachers College Press, 1234 Amsterdam Avenue, New York, NY 10027

All rights reserved. No part of this publication may be reproduced or transmitted in any form or by any means, electronic or mechanical, including photocopy, or any information storage and retrieval system, without permission from the publisher.

Copyright © 2015 by Teachers College, Columbia University

Portions of Chapters 1 and 2 were adapted from "Recapitulation Theory and the New Education: Race, Culture, Imperialism, and Pedagogy, 1894–1916," 2012, *Curriculum Inquiry, 42*(4), 510–533. Copyright John Wiley & Sons. Used with permission.

Portions of Chapters 2 and 5 were adapted from "Race, Culture, and Pluralism: The Evolution of Dewey's Vision for a Democratic Curriculum," 2012, *Journal of Curriculum Studies, 44*(1), 13–35. Copyright Taylor and Francis. Used with permission.

Library of Congress Cataloging-in-Publication Data is available at loc.gov

ISBN 978-0-8077-5651-5 (paperback)
ISBN 978-0-8077-7377-2 (ebook)

Printed on acid-free paper
Manufactured in the United States of America

22 21 20 19 18 17 16 15   8 7 6 5 4 3 2 1

Contents

Acknowledgments	vii
Introduction	1
Progressive Education and the Theory of Recapitulation	3
Major Arguments	5
Methodology	6
Terminology	8
Overview of the Book	9
1. Roots	**13**
Social and Intellectual Transformation	15
Anthropology	17
Sociology	19
Psychology	22
Economics	27
History	29
2. Recapitulation	**34**
Recapitulation for Proto-Progressives	35
Teaching Native Americans and Southern Blacks	38
Imperialism and the New Education	44
Pre-1916 Dewey	47
Recapitulation and the New Education	53

3. Reform — 59
- Experiments in the New Education — 60
- Origins of the Social Studies — 64
- Social Efficiency — 69
- Race in Textbooks — 74

4. Racism — 83
- From Neo-Lamarckianism to Eugenics — 84
- G. Stanley Hall and William Bagley — 93
- Edward Thorndike — 97

5. Relativity — 103
- Cultural Relativity — 104
- Cultural Pluralism — 108
- Post-1916 Dewey — 112

6. Refashioning — 124
- Child-Centered Progressives — 125
- Administrative Progressives — 128
- Sociological Deficiency and Cultural Pluralism — 134

Epilogue — 145

Notes — 149

Bibliography — 171

Index — 185

About the Author — 200

Acknowledgments

The research for this book was generously funded by a grant from the Spencer Foundation. I am very grateful for its support. Portions of the manuscript appeared earlier in "Recapitulation Theory and the New Education: Race, Culture, Imperialism, and Pedagogy, 1894–1916," and "Race, Culture, and Pluralism: The Evolution of Dewey's Vision for a Democratic Curriculum." I thank John Wiley & Sons and Taylor & Francis for permission to reuse this material. Many scholars provided feedback, criticism, suggestions, and encouragement while writing this book. Johnathan Zimmerman and Shannon Sullivan read early portions of the manuscript and helped me clarify my terminology. Their positive responses to the project led me to believe that I was on the right track. Ronald Evans, LaGarrett King, Jim Garrison, and Mary Ann Stankiewicz suggested additional sources for my narrative and argument. Christine Woyshner provided very detailed line-by-line feedback on my first few chapters that helped me clarify and strengthen my argument throughout. I know that Professor Woyshner was very busy with other projects, so I greatly appreciate her time. I was very fortunate that, perhaps, the leading scholar in the country on race and education in the early twentieth century, Zoe Burkholder, happened to be my neighbor. Professor Burkholder read the entire manuscript, met with me on multiple occasions, and provided enthusiastic support and insight into the book. Her timely feedback was greatly appreciated, and it was a pleasure to get to know her through this project. I am grateful that when faced with the choice of reading the first few chapters or the entire manuscript, Johann Neem elected the latter because, as he put it, he would "learn more." Professor Neem's insatiable intellectual curiosity served as an inspiration, and his feedback on the manuscript strengthened it greatly. At William Paterson University, I thank Dean Candace Burns for her recognition and support of my research, and Priscilla Stevens for helping me with the paperwork related to the grant. Brian Ellerbeck and the production staff at Teachers College Press were extremely efficient and helpful. Finally, my wife, Victoria Fantozzi read the entire manuscript, while working on her own research, chairing her department, and raising our kids (with my help). After ten years of marriage, I am more impressed by her with each passing year.

I never write on weekends or evenings, so there is no need to thank my children, Quinten and Linus; they experienced no neglect as a result of this project. However, while I was writing this book my boys, five and two, repeatedly stripped down to their underwear, launched themselves off furniture, hurled projectiles across the room, and generally acted savagely. They helped me see the appeal of the theory of recapitulation, which equated young children with the stereotypical depiction of premodern wild men and women. One day on a playground, when several boys including my own spontaneously picked up sticks and began using them as weapons, a mother turned to me and suggested, half-jokingly, that such behavior must be innate. Indeed, this was the belief at the turn of the twentieth century, not just of mothers, but of leading scientists, theorists, and educators. Although literal belief in the theory of recapitulation was mostly abandoned by World War I, its racist and ethnocentric legacy continues to affect our society and schools to this day.

Introduction

In 1906 an African man named Ota Benga was taken from the Congo, transported to the United States, and housed in an exhibit at the Bronx Zoo in New York. Benga, a Pygmy, was displayed with some scattered bones in the monkey house beside an orangutan. Beneath his cage the following was written: "From his native land of darkness/ To the country of the free/ In the interest of science/ And of broad humanity."[1] The implication of the exhibit was that Benga had more in common with the orangutan on his side of the fence than he did with the New Yorkers on the other side of the fence who came to view him. As shocking as this may seem to twenty-first-century readers, this conclusion was fully consistent with much of the social science research at the turn of the twentieth century. As leading German biologist Ernst Haeckel explained in 1904: "[Reason] is for the most part only the property of the higher races of men; among the lower races it is only imperfectly developed.... Natural men (e.g., Indian Vedas or Australian negroes) are closer in respect of psychology to the higher vertebrates (e.g., apes and dogs) than to higher civilized Europeans."[2] Haeckel was the author of the influential biogenetic law that ontogeny recapitulates phylogeny—that is, the anatomical and psychological development of the individual retraced the evolutionary history of the human race. Haeckel's theory was an extreme, literal example of deep-seated belief in Western thought, that all the races of the world could be placed upon a single linear scale of development, that people of color represented earlier steps in the evolution of the human race, and that all social differences were in some way directed by the evolutionary history of each race. Thus, according to Haeckel and most other social scientists, the orangutan and the African Pygmy represented two concurrently living, sequential steps toward the White race, which had evolved from apes to savages to barbarians to civilized man in a linear process of development. As a result, most scientists considered Benga anatomically, psychologically, and sociologically deficient because he represented a previous step toward modern civilization.

Three years later and several miles away across the Harlem River, John Dewey of Columbia University delivered a brief but remarkable speech that directly challenged the assumptions underlying the exhibition of Benga at the Bronx Zoo. In 1909 at the National Negro Conference, Dewey defiantly declared "there is no inferior race, and the members of a race so-called should each have the same opportunities of social environment and personality as those of the more favored race." Dewey insisted that the slight differences among the races were much smaller than the differences among the individuals within each race. As a result, Dewey argued, the idea of dismissing an individual because of his/her race was an "injustice," and he insisted that all humans should have "a full, fair and free social opportunity."[3] Dewey's audience that day later evolved into the National Association for the Advancement of Colored People (NAACP), and Dewey would be a founding member of the organization.

On the surface, Dewey's address on race appears to repudiate the very conception of racial hierarchies underlying Benga's capture and display at the zoo. This is largely correct because Dewey's philosophy of pragmatism rejected the inherent or essential value of anything, including racial types. That is, Dewey rejected the idea that certain individuals or social groups had a latent potential to achieve or not achieve a certain sociological level based on their anatomical makeup. Dewey's philosophical rejection of static essences and latent potentials distinguished him from many of his peers such as Haeckel, who believed that allegedly inferior races could not overcome the latent potential of their heredity. Dewey's philosophy was color-blind in the sense that individuals' sociological level was not linked to their inherent worth. Rather sociological level was a contingent outcome of people's interaction with a mediating social environment. Nevertheless, for Dewey, these mediating social environments could be arranged along a single continuum leading from savagery to barbarianism to civilization. In fact, Dewey made numerous references to the sociological stages of savagery, barbarianism, and civilization throughout his most famous writings.

For example, in 1911 Dewey argued that the lessons of past societies "absolutely must be transmitted to the succeeding and immature generation if social life itself is not to relapse into barbarism and then into savagery." In *How We Think*, Dewey averred that were it not for education, "the story of civilization would be writ in water, and each generation would have laboriously to make for itself, if it could, its way out of savagery." Likewise, in *Democracy and Education,* Dewey explained that students should understand, "the entire advance of humanity from savagery to civilization has been dependent upon intellectual discoveries and inventions."[4] For Dewey, White Euro-American society just happened to be at the forefront of progress, but it did not necessarily need to be; history had just turned out that way. Non-White savage, primitive, and aboriginal groups such as Benga's African Pygmies just happened to represent earlier stages in the linear path of human progress, not because of their inherent or essential worth, but simply because history happened to have left them behind. Dewey's conception of contingent stages of sociological progress formed the framework for his curriculum at the famous Laboratory School at the University of Chicago (1895–1904), and it informed many of his pedagogical theories.

If we contrast the pragmatic ideas of Dewey with the biologically deterministic ideas of Haeckel, they diverge sharply. Dewey believed that education could transform any individual regardless of race into a modern, civilized democratic citizen; the individual simply needed to be exposed to the ideas and methods of civilization at an early age. Haeckel, on the other hand, believed that heredity and anatomy limited the potential of individuals from certain racial groups because non-Whites were more like instinct-driven animals than they were like a civilized human. However, when we step back and view their ideas from a broader perspective, we can see that Dewey and Haeckel disagreed about the cause of the sociological deficiency of non-White savages such as Benga. They also disagreed about whether or not the sociological deficiency of non-White savages could be overcome. However, they agreed upon the basic fundamental assumption that non-White individuals such as Benga were developmentally and sociologically deficient. In other words, both Dewey and Haeckel agreed that Benga's lifestyle represented an earlier stage of development that had been surpassed by the civilized. They both accepted that the lifestyles of Whites and non-Whites represented different degrees of social worth, with Whites representing a more sociologically, intellectually, and ethically superior form. Ultimately, despite their fundamental and important divergence on the issue of heredity and anatomy, both Dewey and Haeckel believed in different versions of the theory of recapitulation.

PROGRESSIVE EDUCATION AND THE THEORY OF RECAPITULATION

The theory of recapitulation was the belief that the development of the individual retraced the development of the human race. To put it other ways, it was the theory that the stages of psychological development of the individual corresponded with the stages of sociological development of social groups, or that individuals passed through the same linear stages through which societies pass—specifically, the stages of savagery, barbarianism, and civilization. Contemporaries believed that some individuals, mostly White, developed fully, while others, mostly non-White, did not. The theory of recapitulation was inherently ethnocentric and racist because it depicted people of color as inferior and inchoate, as prior steps toward the more ontologically developed Euro-American. Yet, the theory of recapitulation made a pervasive impact on educational theory and curriculum between 1890 and 1929—the formative years of progressive education—and the influence of the theory could be found even decades later. This book traces that history.

Progressive education was a heterogeneous movement to reform American schools for a modernizing world brought on by industrialization, urbanization, shifting demographics, and the expanding reach of scientific research into social issues. Progressive education began in the 1890s and lasted until the 1950s, when it experienced a backlash by numerous critics calling for a return to rigor in the U.S. curriculum. The essence, extent, and definition of progressive education have been one of the most disputed topics of the last half-century.[5] Despite disagreement over the origins, nature, and impact of progressive education in American schools, general consensus exists that the idea of child-centeredness was in some way at the ideological core of the movement. For example, historian Arthur Zilversmit identified the desire "to create schools in which children would find a nurturing environment that would allow them to develop their individual capacities" as the single most defining feature of the movement. Diane Ravitch named "the idea that the methods and ends of education could be derived from the innate needs and nature of the child" as one of four major aspects of progressive education. Furthermore, Herbert Kliebard identified "the assumption that the natural order of development in the child was the most significant and scientifically defensible basis for determining what should be taught" as one of four major ideological currents of period.[6] Although progressive education cannot be reduced solely to child-centeredness, the idea is indisputably at the philosophical core of the movement, especially in its early years. The simple idea that the child rather than the teacher or textbook should be the major focus of the classroom is, perhaps, the single most enduring educational idea of the era.

Child-centered pedagogy emerged in the eighteenth and nineteenth century from the innovative ideas and techniques of European philosophers Jean-Jacques Rousseau, Friedrich Froebel, Johann Heinrich Pestolozzi, and Johann Herbart. Drawing upon their ideas, Marie Montessori, Colonel Francis W. Parker, and John Dewey further developed practical applications of child-centered pedagogy in their innovative schools in Italy and the United States.[7] Thus, by the turn of the twentieth century, child-centered pedagogy emerged as a powerful international idea espoused by some the world's leading educators. However, child-centered education became a national movement in the United States with the introduction of the new education in the 1890s, which morphed into progressive education after World War I. The new education, historian Patricia Albjerg Graham explains, was "directed toward the poorer classes whose members, both native and foreign born, were crowding cities that were booming with industrialization." Progressive education, Graham argues, was directed toward affluent, middle-class "parents concerned about the quality of education existing in the public schools" and was characterized by "child-centeredness, individual expression and creativity."[8] The new education was exemplified most famously by the platoon system of Gary, Indiana—an experiment championed by Dewey and his daughter Evelyn in their 1915 book *Schools of To-Morrow*. Referred to as the Gary Plan, the curriculum involved a two-platoon system in which mostly immigrant students studied academic and industrial content in shifts. Progressive education, on the other hand, was exemplified most famously by the hands-on, cooperative learning of Dewey's Laboratory School at the University of Chicago, Marietta Johnson's Organic School in Fairhope, Alabama, and other private and suburban school experiments depicted in Harold Rugg's and Anna Shumaker's 1928 book, *The Child-Centered School*. I provide further explanation of the many facets of progressive education throughout the book as they relate to race, but in general I define the new or early progressive education as the ambitious movement to reform American society by better preparing children for the modernizing world through relevant, hands-on learning that catered to their individual differences. Because the new education essentially became progressive education, I use terms early *progressive education* and *new education* interchangeably.

MAJOR ARGUMENTS

My book aims to make three significant contributions to our understanding of the origins of progressive education and its relationship to race and the theory of recapitulation. First, I demonstrate the pervasiveness that the ethnocentric and racist theory of recapitulation (the belief that the development of the individual recapitulated the development of the human race) had on the earliest advocates for the child-centered new education. Although some historians have addressed aspects of the impact of recapitulation theory on educational thinkers, their focus has largely been limited to the so-called child study advocates such as psychologist G. Stanley Hall and the American followers of German philosopher Johann Herbart.[9] Most historians have depicted the theory of recapitulation as an isolated idea that had limited impact on other leading progressive educators. My study demonstrates that the influence of the theory of recapitulation extended well beyond Hall and the Herbartians to all the early architects of the new education such as Colonel Francis W. Parker, John Dewey, Lester Frank Ward, William Torrey Harris, Charles Judd, William Bagley, Charles Eliot, Irving King, and many others. The application of the theory of recapitulation to educational reform did not originate with Hall, nor was it limited exclusively to Hall and his followers. Instead, the theory reflected a set of beliefs about race that was shared by Hall's entire generation. The theory of recapitulation had an impact on classroom practice, teaching materials, and textbooks between 1880 and 1929. I argue that the ethnocentric theory of recapitulation was the leading framework for explaining racial difference in the early years of progressive education, and it served as a major rationale for the introduction of child-centered pedagogy in American schools.

Second, exploring the underlying racial assumptions of the theory of recapitulation allowed me to determine the racial views of progressive educators prior to 1916, before high-profile national debates emerged about racial difference, intelligence testing, and eugenics that brought the issue of racial diversity in American schools to a wider audience. In general, the literature on race and ethnicity prior to 1916 has either focused on the education of non-Whites, the impact of the eugenics movement on education, or educational developments that occurred during and after this date.[10] Historians tend to frame the debate on race and education simplistically as one between scientific racists such as Haeckel and cultural pluralists such as Dewey. In addition, scholars have been relatively silent on the racial views of progressive educators prior to this time. However, scholars' dynamic positions on race and their relationship to proposals for educational reform framed the debates on race and culture that took place in 1916 and beyond. My study focuses primarily on the understudied pre–World War I period. As a result, I demonstrate how views on the education of racial and ethnic minorities evolved significantly and in nonlinear ways between 1880 and 1929, before scientific racism retreated among most scholars in the United States, and the Great Depression alleviated scholarly concerns for racial degeneration by shifting attention toward issues of economic inequality.[11]

Third, my study traces both constancy and change in the thinking on race between 1890 and 1929. I argue that during these years there was a major shift in viewpoints on racial difference, from a belief in the biological-anatomical inferiority of non-Whites to a belief in the sociocultural inferiority of non-Whites. Yet despite this significant change, progressive educators still depicted people of color as ontologically inferior, as somehow less formed beings representing an earlier, lower lifestyle inappropriate for Euro-American civilization. For example, writing in 1925, educational psychologist William Bagley asserted: "The brightest European child reared from birth by a group of Pigmies [sic] would appear as a moron or worse if later transported to a highly civilized and cultured environment."[12] Like Dewey, Bagley believed students' abilities diverged largely because of differences in education, environment, and experience, not because of innate or hereditary characteristics. In fact, Bagley's assertion appeared in a book attacking the deterministic views of psychologists arguing on behalf of the biological-anatomical inferiority of certain individuals and groups. Yet, even when Bagley denied that Pygmies such as Benga were biologically determined to remain in a state of savagery forever, he nevertheless believed that Benga's lifestyle was less developed because the Pygmy represented the sociological-psychological equivalence of a "moron" in the civilized world. This belief in the ontological inferiority of people of color justified American imperialism abroad in the 1890s, and supported the political and educational disenfranchisement of non-Whites in American society in the 1910s, 1920s, and beyond. It also established a cultural deficit, or pathology, model toward the education of students of color that remained largely unchallenged until the 1970s.[13] In general, this study seeks to fill a hole in our understanding of how race influenced the origins of progressive education, and to consider the ways in which this reform movement intentionally and unintentionally perpetuated racial inequality in American society.

METHODOLOGY

A major reason for the scholarly neglect of the racial views of early progressive educators is that scholars prior to 1916 rarely addressed race directly. To unravel the hidden views of these historical actors, I approached the topic through the lens of intellectual history. As historian Arthur Lovejoy explains, the history of ideas assumes that there are:

> implicit assumptions, or more or less unconscious mental habits, operating in the thought of an individual or a generation. It is the beliefs which are so matter of course that they are rather tacitly presupposed than formally expressed and argued for, the ways of thinking which seem so natural and inevitable that they are not scrutinized with the eye of logical self-consciousness.[14]

Most of the scholarship on progressive educators has focused on the significant divergences in the social outlooks of figures such as sociologists Herbert

Spencer and Frank Lester Ward, educators John Dewey and William Torrey Harris, and educational psychologists such as G. Stanley Hall and William Bagley.[15] However, instead of outlining the differences among these scholars, my study focuses on how these figures shared "tacitly presupposed" beliefs about the sociological worth of non-White groups. As leading British child study advocate James Sully wrote in 1895: "As we all know, the lowest races of mankind stand in close proximity to the animal world. The same is true for infants of the civilized races."[16] Not only did Sully explicitly and succinctly state his belief in the theory of recapitulation, but more significantly he presented it as something "we all know." The theory of recapitulation was not something that needed to be explained thoroughly or supported with extensive evidence because it was a "tacitly presupposed" belief shared by the entire intellectual community. My narrative presents dozens of examples of how well-known and lesser-known social scientists, educators, and textbook authors drew upon the theory of recapitulation in their suggested programs for how to prepare children for their role in the modernizing world. I demonstrate that almost all of the significant proponents of reforming the American curriculum believed in the theory of recapitulation—that the development of the individual retraced the sociological history of the human race, and that non-White social groups represented an earlier, inferior status. Prior to World War I, scholars did not view culture in relativistic terms, as something that everyone had in different forms. Rather, they viewed culture as something that social groups either had or did not, or had to different degrees. Social groups were judged hierarchically against the standard of Western civilization. In this sense, the term *savage* was racially coded to mean undeveloped, dark-skinned, child-like, non-Christian. The early architects of what came to be known as progressive education shared this understanding. I argue that the very idea of child-centeredness that played such a central role in the progressive education movement can itself be traced in part to the theory of recapitulation. As one anthropologist reported in 1900:

> The view that the individual more or less distinctly repeats at least the chief stages in the development of the race, both mentally and physically, has been accepted as the cardinal doctrine of the newer theories of education which in the form of "child study" have made their influence felt in America and the old world.[17]

Furthermore, as one visitor to Dewey's famous Laboratory School explained, "The study of American Indians . . . is taken up . . . for the purpose of utilizing that identity of interests which anthropologists tell us exists between the child and primitive man."[18] The theory of recapitulation was both adopted and reinforced by the leading social scientists of the period. Reform-oriented scholars such as Frank Lester Ward and Dewey employed the theory of recapitulation in their major works, despite their pivotal role in shifting the discourse on race from concern for the biological-anatomical deficiency of non-Whites to the sociocultural inferiority of non-Whites.

TERMINOLOGY

Racial language during this period was constantly shifting. As a result, I paid close attention to my own terminology as well as the evolving terminology of time. Scholars in the late nineteenth and early twentieth century did not consistently employ the term *theory of recapitulation*, although some did. Rather, they called it *the genetic method, the historic method, recapitulation*, or they simply referenced the stages of sociological development casually through the terms *savage* and *barbarian*. Nevertheless, they all shared the belief that the development of the individual retraced the history of the human race. Although I use the term *theory of recapitulation* throughout, in reality there were many *theories* of recapitulation; scholars espoused numerous iterations of the idea, some taking it more literally than others. However, in general the leading scholars and influences of early progressive education shared four basic beliefs. First was that all societies of the world could be placed upon a linear scale of development leading through the sociological stages of savagery, barbarianism, and civilization; second, that all individuals of the world pass through the same linear stages of psychological development; third, that these sociological stages somehow aligned with the psychological stages; fourth, that non-White individuals and societies were stuck in an earlier sociological-psychological stage as living fossils representing an earlier lifestyle that had been abandoned by the civilized.

The term *culture* was equally problematic because its meaning changed rapidly during the years covered in this book. To some, aboriginal social groups such as Benga's Pygmies had no culture, and so the term was never applied to groups that were believed to be in the barbarian and/or savage stage. To others, social groups such as Benga's Pygmies had an earlier, embryonic, less developed form of culture. For example, in the quotation cited earlier, Bagley contrasted the lifestyle of Pygmies with the "highly civilized and cultured environment" of the United States, implying that Pygmies either had no culture or they had a less developed form of culture. Not until the mid-1910s did some social scientists begin to use the term *culture* in the sense that it is now understood—as a relative, dynamic, context-bound, collective way of making meaning of the world. In an attempt to navigate this shifting terminology, I avoid using the term *culture* and *cultures* unless absolutely necessary. Instead, I use the term *social group* to refer to what we would now call cultures, and *sociological stage* to refer to the perceived steps toward the development of White lifestyle. In addition, I use the term *sociologically deficient* to depict the contemporaneous belief that non-White social groups represented an earlier, ontologically less developed lifestyle.

Furthermore, I tried to avoid relying too heavily on the dichotomous language that has characterized much of the literature on the racial views of progressives, such as eugenicist versus pluralist, scientific racist versus cultural relativist, and/or efficiency versus humanist progressives because the views of early progressive educators were inconsistent and messy.[19] For example, educational psychologist William Bagley publicly changed his mind twice on the issue of the role of heredity in education in response to emerging discoveries in biology. Dewey made dozens of references to the ethnocentric stages of sociological development in his early and middle years, but he abandoned much of this language after World War I as he focused more upon pluralistic cultural interaction as a major component of his philosophy. In addition, different scholars' views on recapitulation and heredity did not necessarily dictate their views on social progress. For example, G. Stanley Hall was the strictest recapitulationist of his generation because, like Haeckel, Hall subscribed to the literal—that is, anatomical—version of the theory. Yet, counterintuitively, Hall was a critic of European imperialism (he specifically opposed the genocidal Belgian policies in the Congo that led to Benga's display), a supporter for the education of African Americans, and an advocate for the sensitive treatment of American Indians. Furthermore, African American scholar Kelly Miller was identified by his White peers as a "radical" for his idea that Blacks ought to have full political and social equality. Yet Miller endorsed eugenics and tried to apply the theory to improving his own race. In general, scholars such as Dewey and Ward have, perhaps, been given too much credit by historians for their egalitarian views on race and culture, when in fact they still believed in the sociological deficiency of non-White social groups.[20] Conversely, eugenicists and biological racists of the time have, perhaps, been contrasted too starkly with egalitarians like Dewey, when in fact virtually all scholars of the period shared the four basic assumptions of the theory of recapitulation outlined above. That is, they all believed in the sociological deficiency of most people of color.

Finally, I avoid applying the term *pseudo-science* to describe many of the racial theories employed between 1890 and 1929, even though by current standards these theories were based on inconsistent, weak, and erroneous empirical grounds. From the vantage point of the present, the theory of recapitulation was overtly racist, self-serving, and even a little bit ridiculous. Looking back, it is easy to see how science was used by White scholars and policymakers as a tool to exploit and oppress vulnerable groups. Yet, at the time, scholars took these theories seriously as *science*, and even those who challenged and opposed racial hierarchies did so in the spirit of scholarly collegiality and scientific objectivity. In other words, the architects of progressive education saw no distinction between *pseudo-science* and *science*, and so, in order to better capture their intellectual world, my narrative also makes no distinction. "[T]he responsibility of the historian or sociologist who studies racism is not to moralize and condemn," historian George Frederickson explains, "but to understand this malignancy so that it can be more effectively treated, just as a medical researcher studying cancer does not moralize about it but searches for knowledge that might point the way to a cure."[21]

OVERVIEW OF THE BOOK

The first chapter, "Roots," traces the intellectual context from which the new, or early progressive, education emerged. I demonstrate how the leading social scientists of the nineteenth century held the basic assumptions of the theory of recapitulation, which reinforced the inferiority of non-White groups. Specifically, I document this constancy in racial views in the disciplines of anthropology, sociology, psychology, economics, and history from the late nineteenth to the early twentieth century. Although twentieth-century scholars challenged the basic epistemological views of the scholars of the previous generation, they largely adopted their racial ideals as embedded in the theory of recapitulation. Many of these scholars authored textbooks specifically aimed at teachers and high school students. Collectively, they formed the intellectual context that engendered the new, or early progressive, education.

In Chapter 2, "Recapitulation," I explain how scholars and policymakers used the theory of recapitulation to justify racially segregated schools and to rationalize a differentiated curriculum aligned with the perceived instincts of each racial group. Scholars used many of the ideas that appeared in early progressive schools in the United States to teach non-Whites under U.S. control. I demonstrate how early experiments in progressive education; the education of Native Americans, Southern Blacks, and foreign non-Whites in the U.S. territories of Puerto Rico, Hawaii, Cuba, and the Philippines; and the pre-1916 educational ideas of John Dewey shared an underlying conceptual framework grounded in the theory of recapitulation.

In Chapter 3, "Reform," I explore how some of the most successful and prominent early progressive educational reforms such as the Laboratory School at the University of Chicago, the Committee on Social Studies report that launched the field of the social studies, and the pervasive and influential idea of *social efficiency* are all related to the theory of recapitulation. However, the theory of recapitulation began to lose its explanatory power as progressive educators shifted their focus from educating non-Whites to anxieties about teaching the children of White immigrants who were flooding American cities and schools. I also trace how the theory of recapitulation informed the contents of children's literature and popular middle and high school textbooks.

In Chapter 4, "Racism," I address the impact of the rediscovery of Mendelian genetics on educational reform. I again document the constancy of the idea of racial hierarchy among leading progressive educators such as Edward Thorndike, G. Stanley Hall, and William Bagley, even as the theory of recapitulation began to lose its scientific backing, because the theory was replaced by statistical models of intelligence, heredity, and racial differentiation.

In Chapter 5, "Relativity," I document how anthropologist Franz Boas and his associates forged an alternative perspective on race that was grounded in a relativistic, contingent approach to culture and racial identity, and scholars such as W.E.B. Du Bois, Carter Woodson, Horace Kallen, and Randolph Bourne outlined a new inclusive ideology of cultural pluralism. Drawing upon these new ideas, Dewey expanded and revised his own views on race and culture during and after World War I.

Finally, in Chapter 6, "Refashioning," I demonstrate how leading progressive educators in the 1920s rejected the "cultural relativity" position of postwar Dewey and the Boasians and maintained their belief in the sociological deficiency of people of color. In the Epilogue, I present some of the enduring effects of the racial views of progressive educators, such as the idea of child-centeredness and the deficit approach to students of color.

It will not surprise anyone who has studied this period that scholars writing over a century ago were ethnocentric and/or racist, and that their racism directly and indirectly found its way into their work. However, with this book I am suggesting something more than this. I argue that because the theory of recapitulation was a major rationale for child-centeredness, ethnocentrism was built into the early years of progressive education itself. Child-centeredness and education for individual difference, which to this day represent major aspects of the progressive approach to education, emerged directly from the theory of recapitulation. Ultimately, the idea that teachers should nourish a child's natural and instinctual curiosity never disappeared. However, educators have largely forgotten that child-centered pedagogy emerged from the pervasive ethnocentric belief in the mental equivalence of White children and non-White adults.[22]

CHAPTER 1

Roots

The idea that non-White individuals and societies were less developed than their White counterparts began with the philosophical theory of the Great Chain of Being as first espoused by Plato and Aristotle. As a result of this philosophical foundation, throughout Western history most educated men held a conception of the universe as, according to intellectual historian Arthur Lovejoy, "an infinitive number of links ranging in hierarchical order from the meagerest kind of existents, which barely escape non-existence, through every possible grade . . . , to the highest possible creature."[1] The Great Chain of Being took on its racialized character during the age of exploration and age of imperialism during which Europeans came into contact with non-Christian, premodern hunter-gather societies.[2] The term *savage*—which was consistently employed to describe non-White hunter-gatherers—not only suggested non-White, but also non-Christian. The publication of Charles Darwin's *On the Origins of Species* and *The Descent of Man*, as well as preexisting evolutionary theories of sociocultural development, gave further credence to concepts of racial competition and struggle, with savages and barbarians at the bottom of the developmental scale. "At some future period, not very distant as measured by centuries," Darwin predicted in *The Descent of Man*, published in 1871, "the civilized races of man will almost certainly exterminate and replace throughout the world the savage races." Darwin viewed such competition among societies and the displacement of lower races as inevitable.[3] Darwin and other evolutionary theorists consistently depicted White societies as evolutionary winners and non-White societies as evolutionary losers in the race for survival and dominance, and non-White races were depicted as savage antecedents to civilized Western races. As Darwin affirmed, the "Western nations of Europe, who now so immeasurably surpass their savage progenitors, . . . stand at the summit of civilization."[4]

In 1878 in his book *Ancient Society*, anthropologist Lewis H. Morgan codified the principle stages of human development more formally as lower savagery, middle savagery, upper savagery, lower barbarism, middle barbarism, upper barbarism, and civilization, with accompanying descriptions of each stage. Morgan's hierarchical language was adopted by virtually every social scientist of the period when depicting racial and ethnic groups. In this book, Morgan noted that "The history and experience of the American Indian tribes represent, more or less, nearly, the history and experience of our own remote ancestors"—an ontological and methodological assumption that he shared with his peers.[5] Likewise, in his 1881 book *Anthropology*, British anthropologist Edward Burnett Tylor confirmed Morgan's three stages of sociological development. He defined savagery as the way of life in which "man subsists on wild plants and animals," barbarianism as the state in which societies "take to agriculture," and civilization as having "the art of writing . . . which binds together the past and future in an unbroken chain of intellectual and moral progress." Tylor explained that "civilization in the world has grown up through these stages, so as to look at a savage in a Brazilian forest . . . may be the students' best guide to understanding the progress of civilization."[6] Leading anthropologists agreed that savage, non-White aboriginal societies represented a less developed, earlier stage of sociological development that White societies had surpassed.

In addition to these leading anthropologists, German biologist Ernst Haeckel proposed the biogenetic theory that ontogeny recapitulated phylogeny—that is, that the development of the individual recapitulated the history of the anatomical development of the human race. Haeckel's recapitulation theory provided scientific support to the notion that individuals progressed through stages similar to societies', although this general idea had been around for centuries. His theory also reiterated the view that non-White societies and individuals were ontologically less developed than their White counterparts, because they represented an earlier stage. Haeckel's recapitulation theory was based upon two mechanisms—terminal addition and condensation—that were closely aligned with neo-Lamarckianism, or the theory of the inheritance of acquired characteristics. According to Haeckel, as an organism gained new traits, those traits were terminally added to the end of the ontogenetic sequence as a new stage, and previous stages in the developmental sequence were condensed to make room for the additional stage. As a result, this process was dependent upon an organism passing its acquired characteristics on to its offspring via the germ-plasm, a precursor to genes.[7] Although Haeckel's mechanism for the anatomical development was disputed, it nevertheless confirmed the general belief that all humans developed linearly along the same pathway. Haeckel's anatomical theory of recapitulation supported the idea that the White child was the developmental equivalent of a non-White adult.

By the end of the nineteenth century, there was a biological and anthropological framework to envision the world as a single scale of human development. The findings of the newly professionalized social sciences supported four basic "tacitly presupposed" understandings that reflected the Great Chain of Being and the theory of recapitulation. First, all the societies of the world could be placed along a single, linear path leading through the sociological stages of savagery, barbarianism, and civilization; second, all the individuals of the world could be placed along a single, linear path leading through specific psychological stages; third, these psychological stages more or less recapitulated these sociological stages; and fourth, non-White populations such as Africans, most African Americans, most Native Americans, East Asians, and aboriginal Australians were stuck in an earlier sociological-psychological stage of development. Thus, most social scientists considered savages the sociological and psychological equivalent of children and vice versa. Although significant differences existed among scholars about the mechanisms of racial differentiation and evolution, virtually all social scientists subscribed to these four basic beliefs.

In this chapter, I not only demonstrate how the leading social scientists of the nineteenth century held the basic assumptions of the Great Chain of Being and the theory of recapitulation, but more significantly, I demonstrate how these basic assumptions remained unchanged as the generation of early-twentieth-century scholars sought to challenge many of the philosophical assumptions of the previous generation. In other words, although early-twentieth-century scholars challenged the basic epistemological views of the scholars of the late nineteenth century, they uncritically adopted their racial ideals as embedded in the Great Chain of Being and the theory of recapitulation.[8] Many of these scholars authored textbooks specifically aimed at teachers and high school students. Collectively, they formed the intellectual context that engendered the new, or early progressive, education.

SOCIAL AND INTELLECTUAL TRANSFORMATION

Between the end of the Civil War and the beginning of World War I, the United States underwent a rapid social, cultural, and economic change, a point espoused by nearly every educator, social scientist, and reformer of the period. The nation shifted from an agrarian to an urban-industrial society, transforming from what historian Robert Wiebe called face-to-face "island communities" to a corporate, bureaucratic world governed by a "new middle class" of white-collar professionals.[9] Immigrants from Southern and Eastern European countries arrived in large numbers, adding tremendous stress and anxiety to the existing cultural order. Public school enrollments rose significantly as well, leading to changes in the role and purpose of elementary and secondary schooling. Historians and social scientists professionalized and placed their faith in scientific training and methods to identify and solve any and all social problems, including educational administration and learning theory. They created professional organizations to exert their influence more effectively. The National Education Association (NEA) was founded in 1857; the American Historical Association was founded in 1884; the American Economic Association was founded in 1885; the American Psychological Association (APA) was founded in 1892; the American Political Science Association was founded in 1903; the American Anthropological Association was founded in 1904; and the American Sociological Association was founded in 1907. These organizations met annually and issued journals to disseminate their latest scientific findings.

During these years, Americans and Europeans completed a centuries-long process of conquering the aboriginal populations of the world. Between 1880 and 1914, most of the world beyond Europe and the United States was divided up among Great Britain, France, Germany, Italy, the Netherlands, Belgium, Germany, and the United States. By World War I, there were no independent states left in the Pacific, and only a few independent states remained in Africa. Driven by a need for raw materials, expanding markets, international competitiveness, and a desire to civilize and Christianize the backwards peoples of the Earth, the major European powers developed from nations to empires. The contacts these Western nations had with the non-White aboriginal populations reinforced their preconceived notions of racial dominance.[10]

In addition to this professional mobilization and imperialist expansion, an epistemological transformation took place during this time: a transition from an epistemology of latent potentials and static essences to an epistemology of contingency and growth. Intellectual historian Morton White described this ideological transition as a "revolt against formalism," and philosopher Eric Bredo described it as a shift from describing the world in terms of "essential differences between given objects" to conceiving "of organic and cultural forms in functional terms as emergent within a continuing life process."[11] That is, the new generation of scholars whose careers crossed into the twentieth century approached knowledge as functional, open-ended, and context-bound. Knowledge was not waiting beneath the surface, floating in metaphysical space as eternal truths or static essences waiting to be discovered. Instead, knowledge emerged through interaction with a specific context, and was contingently tied to that context for its validity.

Even prior to the publication of Darwin's *Origin of Species*, nineteenth-century scholars offered numerous theories of social, cultural, and biological evolution. However, these theories were composed of grand narratives and closed systems that sought to explain everything in the universe in terms of transcendent and/or metaphysical laws. For example, leading nineteenth-century thinker Herbert Spencer reduced the entire universe to a single teleological law of movement from the homogeneous to the heterogeneous, a grand theory that informed his views on sociology, economics, political science, psychology, and education. The "increase in heterogeneity so brought about is still going on, and must continue to go on," Spencer explained in an 1857 essay, "and that Progress is not an accident, not within human control, but a beneficent necessity."[12] Appreciating the full implications of Darwin's theory, philosopher John Dewey, psychologist William James, economist Thorstein Veblen, historians James Harvey Robinson and Frederick Jackson Turner, sociologist Albion Small, and anthropologist Franz Boas attacked Spencer's notions of static essences and closed systems. In their place, they suggested that all knowledge was contingent, socially mediated, open to revision, and tied to specific contexts and purposes. In place of essences, they offered history and growth.

Dewey outlined this paradigm shift in his 1909 essay, "The Influence of Darwinism on Philosophy." He explained how, prior to Darwin, philosophers were engaged in determining the eternal and essential nature of things. Even when recognizing the growth and evolution of an entity, the objective was to discover its "fixed form and final cause," thus ascribing a latent potential and static essence to what was actually always in a state of constant flux and contingent growth.

"The influence of Darwin upon philosophy," Dewey insisted, "resides in his having conquered the phenomenon of life for the principle of transition."[13] As Dewey explained a few years earlier in a set of essays on the evolution of ethics, most social scientists were in the business of trying to determine the essence of a thing by tracing it back to its original, pristine form, or trying to determine how the latest form of a thing was the most real. Dewey dubbed the first approach the *materialist* and the latter approach, the *idealist*. The *materialist* approach assumed that "early forms of a historical series are superior to later forms," and, inversely, the *idealist* approach assumed that "various members of the series . . . [possess] different degrees of reality, the more primitive being nearest zero."[14] Thus, Dewey and his pragmatic peers denied the idea that either earlier or later forms were more real than the rest of the series; instead, the reality was the entire series itself. Unlike most other historicist schemes of the time, Dewey's historicism denied that earlier forms of reality contained a latent potential for later forms. This applied not only to societies, but also to the mind. As Dewey later explained in *Democracy and Education*, "Instead of latent intellectual powers, requiring only exercise for their perfecting, [impulses] are tendencies to respond in certain ways to changes in the environment so as to bring about other changes."[15] A particular social context was needed to draw out the potential of a person, society, or species, which was not necessarily latent, but instead was activated by the same social context as previous iterations of the form. One philosopher, Robert Brandom, described this Darwinian epistemological shift as a second Enlightenment. As Brandom explains:

> For the original Enlightenment, explaining a phenomenon (occurrence, state of affairs, process) is showing why what *actually* happened *had* to happen that way, why what is actual is (conditionally) *necessary*. By contrast, for the new pragmatist enlightenment, it is possible to explain what remains, and is acknowledged, as contingent. . . . That kind of understanding whose paradigm is Darwin's biology is a concrete, situated narrative of local, contingent, mutable, practical, reciprocal, accommodations of particular creatures and habits.[16]

This paradigm shift from latent potentials to contingent growth had an immediate impact in the disciplines of anthropology, sociology, psychology, economics, and history. Each will be explored in turn.

ANTHROPOLOGY

Anthropologists in Britain and the United States were primarily concerned with studying the history and evolution of humankind. As a group, anthropologists unequivocally supported the Great Chain of Being and the theory of recapitulation. They drew upon several sources. First, they read and interpreted the firsthand accounts of non-White aboriginal societies in Africa and the Americas that were authored by explorers and adventurers. Second, they often visited these non-White aboriginal societies themselves and wrote their own firsthand accounts. Third, they measured the skull and brain sizes of different racial groups and studied the fossil remains of prehistoric humans. Fourth, they traced the development and spread of languages. Based on these ethnographic and pseudo-scientific studies, anthropologists constructed racial classification systems and evolutionary flow charts. The major debate among American and British anthropologists over the course of the nineteenth century was whether the cultures of the world could be traced to a single human origin (i.e., Adam and Eve), or whether non-White groups constituted distinct, degenerate, or alternative races. Those who believed in a single human origin were called monogenists; those who believed in multiple races were called polygenists.

The leading racial theorist in the United States during the post–Civil War era was zoologist Louis Agassiz. He was a polygenist and a recapitulationist, writing, "The brain of the Negro is that of the imperfect brain of a 7 month's infant in the womb of a White."[17] By the end of the nineteenth century, most anthropologists in the United States and Britain overturned Agassiz and agreed that all humans belonged to a single species and that, despite biological and instinctual differences, divergences among social groups was best explained by culture. The main proponent of the culture idea was British anthropologist Edward Burnett Tylor, whose 1871 book *Primitive Culture* was a classic in the field. The book consisted of comparisons and contrasts between the behaviors of savage and civilized groups. "The comparisons between the savage and civilized religions," Tylor explained, "... brings into view, ... a deep-lying contrast in their practical action on human life."[18] Tylor affirmed the theory of recapitulation, concluding that the "history of civilization teaches, that up to a certain point savages and barbarians are like what our ancestors were and our peasants still are, but from this common level the superior intellect of the progressive races has raised their nations to heights of culture."[19] Here, Tylor speculated not only that all races could be placed in a single, universal scale of development, but also that early White ancestors were the sociological equivalent of non-Whites in the present. He specifically named "American savages" and "African barbarians" as the kind of premodern social groups he was addressing, a lifestyle that he declared was uniformly present in the "lower races from Kamchatka to Tierra del Fuego, and from Dahome to Hawaii."[20] Drawing upon his affirmation for the theory of recapitulation, Tylor presented a persuasive monogenist position that the world consisted of one human race, and that societies differed in degree of culture, not in kind. As mentioned above, proto-anthropologist Lewis H. Morgan identified seven distinct stages of sociological development ranging from lower savagery to civilization. His seven stages confirmed a scientific classification system that was reprinted in sociology textbooks of the 1890s. Morgan insisted that his sequence of stages was "historically true of the entire human family, up to the status attained by each branch respectively."[21] In addition, Morgan confirmed the accepted belief of the time that only White social groups had progressed beyond barbarism.

As the nineteenth century progressed, anthropologists attained a higher status among other social scientists investigating the biological continuity between humans and animals. Proponents of the new psychology, new sociology, new history, and new education approached their subject through an evolutionary lens. They often cited and drew upon the latest research of anthropologists, who confirmed the theory of recapitulation in their work. For example, throughout his book *Primitive Culture*, Tylor compared "the state of things among children and savages," asserting that the two were psychological equivalents.[22] Likewise, anthropologist W. P. McGee, who was head of Bureau of American Ethnology, compared the growth "from infancy to maturity" of Whites to growth from "lower races to the higher, [or] from the earlier culture grades to the later."[23] Furthermore, leading British anthropologist Alfred C. Haddon also argued that the child "repeats in its growth" the development of the savage "from which civilized man had so recently emerged." Evidence for this correspondence, Haddon reasoned, could be seen "in the singing games of children [which is] a persistence of savage and barbaric practice."[24] The beliefs that non-White societies represented a previous step toward the civilized White culture, and that non-White adults were the psychological equivalent of children represented first principles that were assumed to be true by virtually every anthropologist at the turn of the twentieth century, until Franz Boas and his students challenged these ideas in the early twentieth century (see Chapter 6).

SOCIOLOGY

The two leading sociological theorists of the late nineteenth century were Herbert Spencer and Lester Frank Ward. Curriculum historians tracing the origins of progressive education almost always contextualize their discussion in the divergent beliefs of these two leading thinkers.[25] Spencer was a leading social Darwinian who espoused a *laissez-faire* approach to economics and public policy. He coined the phrase "survival of the fittest." Ward, on the other hand, was a proponent of government intervention and social welfare. Ward was one of the first advocates of using education as a means of social, economic, and cultural uplift. Yet, despite these major differences, the sociological theories of both Spencer and Ward relied on the recapitulation theory. Both made numerous references to the universal sociological stages of savagery, barbarianism, and civilization, and both specifically referenced non-White social groups as occupying the precivilized stage. For example, in *First Principles*, Spencer argued that all societies moved along an identical linear process of growth from a state of homogeneity to greater and greater heterogeneity. "The change from homogeneity to heterogeneity is displayed equally in the progress of civilization as a whole and in the progress of each tribe or nation," Spencer explained, "and is still going on with greater rapidity." This universal law could be proved, Spencer insisted, by studying "existing barbarous tribes" because these tribes represented a period of transition from a lower to a higher sociological stage.[26] So, according to Spencer, premodern societies represented earlier steps toward more the developed civilizations and could be studied to gain insight into earlier forms of Western culture. In addition, Spencer suggested that this continuum of social development could serve as a guide for curriculum. As Spencer explained, "The education of the child must accord both in mode and arrangement with the education of mankind, considered historically."[27]

Ward directly challenged the deterministic social views of Spencer. While Spencer believed that the purpose of discovering social scientific laws was to live in accordance with them, Ward believed that the purpose of these laws was to know them in order to direct them toward the social good. Whereas Spencer believed that education and social welfare interfered with the natural order of things, Ward enthusiastically supported public interventions on behalf of the less fortunate. While Spencer believed that the characteristics of races were innate and immutable, Ward believed that the social inequality of races was largely the result of environment and education. Despite the significant differences from Spencer, Ward nevertheless employed the savage-barbarian-civilized sociological scale to depict cultural difference and believed that education represented a distancing from savagery. For example, in *Dynamic Sociology*, Ward expressed how education represented an "assault on savagery," because it separated the civilized from the lesser social forms. "The mark of a barbarian is not the language he speaks, . . ." Ward insisted. "It is his rude intellectual development, his narrow range of views, his rough treatment of others." Ward concluded that "Everything that distinguished a savage from a civilized man can be directly or indirectly traced to differences in education."[28]

Ward argued that unless people were fully assimilated to civilized society, they could still be in state of arrested social development, the sociological equivalent of a barbarian or savage. "In every large city," he explained, "there exists throngs of barbarians,—nay savages," who would be "far better adapted to Zulu-land or the Figi Islands." Although Ward recognized "differences in brain development" between savages and the civilized, he considered the cultural level of individuals to be a contingent outcome of their education, not of their inherent worth. This was a more egalitarian view of non-Whites than most sociologists of the period held. Nevertheless, Ward specifically identified the non-White cultures of "Zulu-land" and "Figi islands" as representing the sociologically deficient savage cultural type.[29] Ward considered the human intellect to be a contributing factor in the evolution of humankind. "In human society," Ward argued in *The Psychic Factors of Civilization*, ". . . the soul is the great transforming agent which has worked its way up through the stages of savagery and barbarianism, to civilization and enlightenment." Beyond these generic stages, Ward identified three specific stages of sociological growth: autocracy, aristocracy, and democracy. As he explained: "Most European countries have passed through the first two of these stages into the third. Some may be considered as still in the second, while most half-civilized, barbarous, or savage nations have not emerged from the first."[30]

Although Ward did not explicitly link his sociological stages to the psychological stages of the child as many biologists and anthropologists had done, he nevertheless pointed to the failure of psychologists to take a recapitulation approach to mind. "In biology it is becoming recognized that the beings inhabiting the earth . . . have been raised to their present estate through a prolonged series of developmental steps," wrote Ward, "but in psychology it is still the practice to deal with the mind as something independent of the past."[31] Ward was critiquing the faculty psychology that viewed the mind as a series of static faculties waiting to be activated and strengthened like muscles. Drawing on the new psychology, Ward argued that the mind needed to be reconceptualized as active and evolving. Although Ward did not explicitly outline a recapitulation theory, he quoted Haeckel, author of the biogenetic law that ontogeny recapitulates phylogeny, at two points in *Psychic Factors of Civilization*. Several years earlier, in *Haeckel's Genesis of Man*, Ward specifically praised Haeckel's recapitulation theory and reflected upon its possible application to sociology.[32] However, the overall purpose of Ward's *Psychic Factors of Civilization* was to outline a psychological theory of human evolution based upon his sociological stages, so in a general sense Ward's text supported the recapitulation theories of the new education that were emerging in the 1890s.

The sociologies of both Ward and Spencer had advocates in the United States who adopted the language of sociological deficiency when referring to premodern, aboriginal social groups. Franklin Giddings, a disciple of Spencer's and one of the most influential sociologists of the early twentieth century, made repeated references to savage life in his 1896 textbook, *Principles of Sociology*. In this text, he identified the common crowd mentality of "the child and savage" and specifically identified the non-White groups of "Blackfellows of Australia, the northern Eskimo of Greenland, [and] the Amazonian Indians of Brazil" as examples of "low savage tribes." Although he recognized that "we cannot be sure that the lowest savage societies of the present day exactly reproduce all the features of primitive communities," Giddings nevertheless considered such comparisons to be based upon "reasonable assumption." In fact, he used these assumptions throughout his text, such as when he identified the sexual promiscuity among present-day "Innuits, Tahitians," and "once among the Aryan peoples."[33] Thus, according to Giddings and most social scientists, the present-day non-White societies such as "Innuits" and "Tahitians" represented the sociological equivalent of the earlier White "Aryan" groups, reinforcing the belief in the ontological inferiority of these non-White groups.

Sociologists on the other end of the spectrum espoused similar views on the sociological deficiency of non-Whites. Albion Small was the most influential American sociologist in the reformist tradition of Ward. Like Ward and Dewey, who was Small's colleague at the University of Chicago, Small took a more egalitarian view of non-White groups and considered their inferior status to be result of their environment and education, not their biology. As Small wrote in his text *General Sociology*, "All Men, . . . from the most savage to the most highly civilized, act as they do act, . . . because of variations in the circumstances of their environment, both physical and social."[34] Here, we can see that Small rejected the inherent or biological inferiority of the savage, but nevertheless accepted the sociological inferiority of the savage and placed him on a linear scale of development in accordance with the theory of recapitulation.

The theory of recapitulation not only provided a hierarchical conceptual framework for the interpretation of racial and national groups, but it also served as a methodology for studying the development of the civilized world. As influential French sociologist Emile Durkheim argued in his classic *The Elementary Forms of Religious Life*, to study "something human . . . we must begin by going back to the features that define it at that period of its existence and the show how it gradually developed, gained in complexity, and came what it is at the moment under consideration."[35] This approach was an example of what Dewey referred to at the *materialist* approach. Durkheim's study examined the religious practices of aboriginal Australians, who were believed to represent the earlier "totem" sociological stage in the history of humankind. In other words, to determine the true nature of the origins of religious beliefs, Durkheim needed to go "back" in time to a society in an earlier stage of sociological development represented by existing non-White cultures. A few years earlier in *Ethics*, John Dewey and James Tufts identified the "totem group" specifically as "North American Indians, Africans and Australians, and was perhaps the early form of Semitic groups."[36] These "totem" groups, it was believed, represented a primitive stage of sociological development that modern societies had moved beyond.

The leading sociologists at the end of the nineteenth century and beginning of the twentieth century disagreed over the extent to which the hierarchy of races was biologically based, as opposed to environmental or learned. Nevertheless, they agreed that these savage groups had survived into the modern world, and that they provided a rare window into the earlier phases of Western culture. They freely and repeatedly employed the hierarchical language of savagery-barbarianism-civilization throughout their work, and this language was racially coded against the standard of Western civilization.

PSYCHOLOGY

The new psychology referred to the study of the mind using empirical and experimental data, as opposed to rationalistic speculation. The new psychology was also based upon the depiction of non-White hunter-gather societies as sociologically deficient previous steps toward civilization because it was founded on the methodology of the comparative method, which depicted non-White social groups as the psychological equivalent of children. As Wilhelm Wundt, one of the founders of the new psychology, explained in *Outlines of Psychology* in 1896, "it is only the results of observations of children and savages which have been subjected to a similar psychological analysis, which furnish any proper basis for conclusions in regard to the nature of mental development in general."[37] Likewise, as G. Stanley Hall outlined in his explanation of the influence of anthropology on psychology, "the origin of language, character temperament, will probably never have any solution unless they are found in the study of infancy, the growth of which epitomizes under our eyes the history of the race, each day sometimes representing perhaps the race-development of centuries."[38] Such savage-child analogies were common in the literature on human development during the turn of the twentieth century.

William Torrey Harris was founding editor of the *Journal of Speculative Philosophy*, superintendent of public schools in St. Louis between 1868 and 1880, U.S. commissioner of education between 1889 and 1906, a member of the NEA's Committee of Ten, and editor of a series of educational monographs for Appleton Press. Harris was the leading American educator between Horace Mann and John Dewey. In the mid-1890s, Harris attempted to reconcile his Hegelian approach to pedagogy with the emerging new psychology in his book *Psychologic Foundations of Education*. Hegel himself once wrote, "The individual must traverse the stages of culture already traversed by the universal spirit."[39] Drawing on Hegel, Harris declared that the "greatest assistance to teacher comes from a knowledge of the three stages of thought and the three different views of the world that arise from them." Failure to appreciate the coordination of these stages fully, Harris admonished, could lead to "arrested development of the mind in the lower stages of its activities." Specifically, according to Harris, individual growth involved movement from the "atomistic" stage to the "pantheistic" stage to the "self-activity" stage. These psychological stages corresponded with the three sociological stages in the development of science and art. Drawing upon Hegel, Harris identified the first sociological stage of science as "the observation of things," the second as "interrelations of things," and the third as "Nature as part of a process which it studies in the history of its development." Harris continued, "There are three great historical epochs of art and poetry corresponding to the three great stages of advancement of the nations of the world." Harris identified the "lowest stage" of art as that which is "buried beneath a mass of customs and usages, . . . a condition a little above a condition of slavery," and he identified "the great nations of Egypt, East India, Persia and western Asia" as having inhabited this lowest sociological stage. The highest form of art, that which demonstrated "gracefulness," was that of the classic nations of Greece and Rome. Thus, Harris approached Western culture as the fulfillment of the highest stage of both psychological and sociological growth. Like his contemporaries, he also identified similarities between the undeveloped child and the savage adult. "The shallowest mind, the child or the savage, delight in monotonous repetition," he explained, ". . . The infant and savage do not and cannot see social relations." Harris concluded that the movement from the second to the third stage of psychological-sociological development "takes place at a well-defined epoch in the life of the child in modern civilization," but "[i]n savage life is never reached."[40] Thus, Harris confirmed the belief that the uncivilized savage was stuck in a state of arrested development equal to that of a child.

William James, the most respected psychologist of the 1890s, wrote little about race and recapitulation. As a pragmatist, James rejected the inherent and/or essential worth of individuals and racial groups, just as Dewey did. For James, humans began with the same general inherited instincts and impulses regardless of race, but these instincts were shaped and guided by the will of the individual and the social context in which the individual was housed. An early mentor and influence on James was Ralph Waldo Emerson. Like James, Emerson emphasized the dignity of the individual and dynamics of self-authorship, but nevertheless subscribed to the theory of recapitulation. Emerson wrote extensively on the inferior mental and moral traits of African Americans and conjectured that "the Negro must be very old & belongs, one would say, to the fossil formations." Accordingly, Emerson placed Whites at the top of a historical racial hierarchy created through "gradual composition, subsidence and refining,—from the Negro, from the ape, progressive from the animalcule savages of the waterdrop, . . . up to the wise man of the nineteenth century."[41] In contrast, James, as a teacher and supporter of W.E.B. Du Bois, the first Black scholar at Harvard University, held more egalitarian views toward African Americans. In addition, James's famous essay on "Great Men and their Environment" emphasized the significance of interaction of great men with their community, thus emphasizing the contingent, rather than essential, nature of greatness.[42] In other words, as a pragmatist James was skeptical of the static essence of all things, including racial categories. However, a close reading of some of James's work reveals a more complicated view.

In his *Principles of Psychology*, James explains how the inherited instincts of modesty and shame can be confirmed by the "The utter shamelessness of infancy and of many savage tribes," suggesting that the infant and the savage were to some degree psychologically equivalent, although later in the passage James also entertained the idea that modesty was contingent upon the social context in which it was embedded. In a footnote to this passage, James identified savage tribes as "Indian women in Brazil," "women on Timor," and "Australians"—all non-White.[43] From this, we can conclude that James concurred with the leading view of the period that these non-White hunter-gatherer societies represented an earlier stage of sociological development.

Despite his pragmatic and egalitarian views on race, James nevertheless believed that different White races had different characteristics that were linked to their biologically inherited instincts, and that, among these White races, there was a racial hierarchy of prevailing traits. In 1868, James commented on the difficulty of dealing with the "inferior races that live with us."[44] In a bizarre section of his *Principles of Psychology*, James surveyed the "human races" and concluded that the initial instincts of Germans and Italians led them toward different paths. "An untutored Italian," James explained, "has instinctive perceptions, tendencies to behave, reactions, in a word, upon his environment that a German lacks." However, this lack of inherited instincts for the German was ultimately a benefit because he could more easily be acculturated to civilization than the Italian, who held an initial advantage. James saw a similar process at work for males and females, because by age twenty, the female mind "is, in fact, finished in its essentials," while the male mind was "gelatinous" and "uncertain," a trait which in the long run turned out to be advantageous because his mind ultimately became more "efficient."[45] In other words, although all humans had the potential to achieve any sociological level via education and socialization, their status was somewhat limited by their heredity, sex, and national origin. Although James did not lend direct support to the theory of recapitulation, his work indirectly supported hierarchical models of human development.

Psychologist Charles Hubbard Judd served as director of the school of education at the University of Chicago after John Dewey departed, and later was a leading proponent of the scientific school survey movement. In 1909 he published *Genetic Psychology for Teachers*, an attempt to make the findings of the new psychology accessible to practitioners. Published as part of William Torrey Harris's International Education Series for Appleton Press, Judd's text was first presented to teachers in Green County, Ohio, in order to pass "the practical test." Harris wrote the preface to Judd's book, in which he outlined the influence of Darwin's theory of evolution on psychology. Accordingly, Judd made analogies between the savage and the young child throughout *Genetic Psychology for Teachers*, but unlike these previous authors, he explicitly identified Native Americans as inhabiting a savage degree of culture. "The most primitive writing was of the kind which all of you have seen represented in our histories," he explained, "where they describe the savage condition and early writing of the American Indian." In addition to linking the early childlike stage of writing to the writing of Native Americans, Judd also made a comparison to Chinese writing, suggested that China too was stuck in an earlier, child-like form of culture.[46] Throughout the text, Judd derived pedagogical strategies from the way primitive and savage ancestors had invented the discussed activity (e.g., writing, counting), thereby linking the sociological history of humankind to the developing stages of the child.

G. Stanley Hall was the earliest and most vocal proponent of the new education, founding advocate of the child study movement, and founding editor of the educational journal *Pedagogical Seminary* and the psychologically oriented *American Journal of Psychology*. In his classic text, *Adolescence*, Hall also echoed the view expressed by Wundt—under whom Hall had briefly studied—that pedagogy needed to be linked to the empirical research of the new psychology. "The animal, savage, and child-soul can never be studied by introspection," he explained, critiquing the methodology of the old psychology. Instead the child-savage needed to be understood in its evolutionary history by studying the growth of modern children and the ethnologies of primitive cultures, because both reflected a similar stage of cultural development. "The child and race are keys to each other," Hall explained, because, developmentally, "the child revels in savagery." To educate in accordance with latest psychological principles, Hall suggested that "The teaching art should so vivify all of the resources of literature, tradition, history . . . reinforced by psychonomic recapitulatory [sic] impulses." Hall argued for matching certain content and activities with the emerging "recapitulatory" instincts of the child. Hall suggested that the "Indian industries, basketry, pottery, bead leather, bows and arrows," be employed for their "educational value" by having students engage in these premodern activities like their savage ancestors did because Indian activity represented an earlier stage of development that aligned with the instincts of the child. Beyond providing insight into the development of the child, Hall was dismissive and even disdainful of the savage races. For Hall, the racial characteristics of the non-White races were considered biologically fixed. Nature, Hall explained, made the "savage hard to break to the harness of civilization." At different points in the text, Hall referred to the savage races as "rude," remarked on their unpleasant odor, and even compared them with animals.⁴⁷ Hall had never traveled to Africa, nor did he have any direct experience with American Indians and rural African American sharecroppers, so his impressions of the allegedly savage races were drawn purely from the work of contemporary anthropologists.

James Mark Baldwin was considered a major authority on child development in the 1890s, second only to Hall. Dewey cited Baldwin's work repeatedly in his course syllabi at the University of Chicago in the 1890s. Baldwin was also a leading recapitulationist. In his popular book, *Mental Development in the Race and Child*, Baldwin outlined what these psychological-sociological stages entailed:

> First, the epoch of rudimentary sense processes, the pleasure and pain process, and simpler motor adaptation, called for convenience the affective epoch; second, the epoch of sensation, memory, imitation, defensive action, . . . third, the epoch of complex presentation, complex motor coordination, of conquest, of offensive action, and rudimentary volition . . . and finally, the epoch of thought, reflection, self-assertion, social organization, union of forces, cooperation; the epoch of subjective references, which in human history merges import the social and ethical epoch.⁴⁸

As the title of Baldwin's book states, these stages were found in the history of both the individual and the race. In his 1909 book, *Darwin and the Humanities*, Baldwin reiterated that "social life, at any stage of racial evolution" corresponds with the "personal growth and capacity of the individuals of that group at that time." Echoing Hall, Baldwin found great promise in the fact that "genetic study . . . in psychology, has confirmed some of the most remarkable generalizations reached in . . . Anthropology."⁴⁹

Turn-of-the-century psychologists incorporated the findings of anthropologists into their cutting-edge work because the linear development of the White child and the premodern savage were considered to be parallel, if not identical. No one, not even James, questioned the basic logic behind this comparison. The existence of the parallel between sociological and psychological development was so taken for granted that it often did not even need to be stated outright. For example, James's colleague at Harvard, Hugo Münsterberg, wrote the following in his 1909 text, *Psychology and the Teacher*:

> The development of the consciousness of number is a slow and a late one in the child's mind. The child may learn the mere words of the numbers early, but the real consciousness of the relations which go beyond four or five are hardly developed before school age. It is well known that primitive peoples frequently cannot count beyond three.⁵⁰

This paragraph does not even make logical sense unless the reader supplies the necessary background knowledge, that the "child's mind" is the psychological equivalent of the mind of "primitive peoples." Without this implicit understanding—assumed to be shared by the generation of teachers to whom the book was directed—one simply cannot comprehend the passage fully.

ECONOMICS

The leading economist of the nineteenth century was John Stuart Mill. In his *Principles of Political Economy*, Mill outlined a deductive classical model of economics, in which rational individual entities competed in a theoretical marketplace based upon established rules such as production and distribution. In this classic work, he adopted and employed commonsense references to the savagery-barbarian-civilized hierarchy. "To civilize the savage," Mill explained, the savage "must be inspired with new wants and desires, if not of a very elevated kind," because savage tribes were inherently "averse to industry." Mill specifically identified the "Indians of Paraguay" as a "race of savages averse to consecutive exertion," and he had similar distain for the "savages of New Holland" because they "never help each other." In a chapter on wages, Mill explained how "as long as mankind remained in a semi-barbarous state, with the indolence and few wants of the savage," they would never develop the cooperative traits of "better workman and more civilized beings."[51] Thus, Mill connected contemporary state of savagery with non-White societies, and reinforced established notions of sociological hierarchy.

The most significant and well-known challenge to the formalism of Mill came in 1899 with the publication of Thorstein Veblen's *The Theory of the Leisure Class*. Veblen was a professor of economics at the University of Chicago. Rather than derive abstract economic principles from an ideal state of affairs as Mill has done, Veblen viewed economic history in more functional terms. Veblen considered economic classes to have derived from specific environmental and cultural interactions, not rationalistic principles. In his famous book, Veblen argued that the position and attitude of the upper class was a direct result of "the barbarian temperament" that had been genetically retained from an earlier time. Veblen's theory of cultural evolution was based upon a specific heredity theory that identified three basic European ethnic types: "The dolichocephalic-blond, the brachycephalic-brunette, and the Mediterranean"—classifications borrowed from Ripley's *Races of Europe* (discussed in Chapter 4). Each group could be further divided into the "peacable" and "predatory" variants, which were the result of self-selection and breeding during the savage stage of social evolution. The ethnic groups of the day, he argued, were variants of these primitive racial types. Specifically, the leisure class was a product of the predatory variant that had never fully progressed past barbarism. "The man of the hereditary present," Veblen explained, "is the barbarian variant, servile or aristocratic, of the ethnic elements that constitute him." In addition, Veblen informed readers that the "primitive savage takes his animism less seriously then the barbarian or the degenerate savage," demonstrating his acceptance of the savage-barbarian-civilized hierarchy.[52] Veblen's classification system divided each stage into good and bad variants, which actually gave the "ante-predatory" savage a degree of respect and appreciation, especially when compared to its "predatory" counterpart. However, it was the barbarian that occupied the core of Veblen's attention because, he argued, it was the predatory state of barbarians that made the biggest impact on the inequitable economic state of the civilized modern world.

The work of Mill and Veblen had little impact on the thinking of educators, but it was representative of a shift from formalistic to functional economic models that took place at the turn of the twentieth century. It was in this context that British scholar Benjamin Kidd first introduced the term *social efficiency* into the ideological discourse in his text *Social Evolution* in 1895.[53] Throughout the book, Kidd used the term *social efficiency* as a synonym for progress and civilization by referencing high and low stages of a group's efficiency. Kidd explained how "Maoris of New Zealand" are "slowly disappearing before the race of higher social efficiency with which they have come into contact."[54] *Social efficiency* would become a commonly used word during the early years of progressive education, employed to some degree by virtually every educational reformer from Harvard University president Charles Eliot, to educational psychologist William Bagley, to educational sociologist David Snedden, to John Dewey (see Chapter 3). The term meant different things to different people, but in every case it referred to being better acculturated to the modern civilized world.[55]

Kidd expressed his enthusiasm for the theory of recapitulation in his imperialist call-to-arms, *The Control of the Tropics*, published in 1898. In this work, Kidd argued that Westerners needed to develop principles to deal with the "natural inhabitants of the tropics" because "we are dealing with people who are at the same stage in the history of the development of the race that the child does in the history of the development of the individual." Kidd demonstrated how "primitive savagery" stretched around the entire globe in the area of the tropics, especially "Central Africa," "the West Indian Islands," and "Black Republic Hayti [sic]." He made it clear that these areas must be developed immediately and that "such a development can only take place under the influence of the white man." Kidd conjectured that the gap in sociological development between the Whites and the inhabitants of the tropics was perhaps "thousands of years of development." Rejecting the kind of "small minded" multiple White race theory espoused by Ripley, Veblen, and others, Kidd called for unity among all the "civilized people and races" of the United States and Europe in their quest to develop the savage races.[56] Referring to non-White societies as "lower" and "inferior races" throughout the text, Kidd linked the quest for progress and social efficiency directly to a hierarchical view of sociological development.

Mill, Veblen, and Kidd all associated civilization within the most advanced and highest form of economic development. Whether they were establishing positivistic economic laws as Mill did, tracing the barbarian roots of social inequity as

Veblen did, or charting the future of the civilized world through the cultivation of social efficiency as Kidd did, these scholars linked their economic vision to a hierarchical model of sociological development that traced groups through the stages of savagery, barbarianism, and civilization; Kidd even explicitly linked his vision to the theory of recapitulation.

HISTORY

The leading theory of historical development during the second half of the nineteenth century was the institutional germ theory—the idea that American democracy originated with the Teutonic-Anglo-Saxon race. In his famous 1882 article "The German Origin of New England Towns," Herbert Baxter Adams of Johns Hopkins University traced the idea of democracy to the "old English and Germanic ideas, brought over by Pilgrims and Puritans . . . ready to take root in the free soil of America."[57] This theory not only affirmed the exceptionality of the United States, but suggested that the nation represented the perfection of latent potentials and static essences carried over from Northern Europe. Similarly, political historian John W. Burgess of Columbia University argued that only those of Teutonic decent had the biological and ethical potential for stable democratic civilizations. "[E]ducation can only develop what already exists in seed and germ," Burgess argued, and so non-White races must "remain in a state of barbarism or semi-barbarism, unless political nations undertake the work of state organization for them."[58] For these scholars, democracy was not simply a way of life that could be learned; it was something inherent in the very biological makeup of the highest White races.

Although Adams and Burgess made passing references to the savagery of Native Americans in their work, they were far more concerned with the origins of American institutions than they were with biological origins of humankind and their racial competition. This focused their attention almost exclusively on tracing the history of White races. However, another nineteenth-century philosopher and historian, John Fiske, employed much more explicit evolutionary racial language in his veneration of the Northern European stock. Fiske was a leading figure in popularizing the theories of Darwin in the United States. In his 1879 work *Darwinism and Other Essays*, Fiske demonstrated his belief in Haeckel's version of the theory of recapitulation, when he insisted that Europeans shed their "structural peculiarities of the savage almost immediately after birth," just as all men shed the characteristics of fish before they are born. Citing Tylor's anthropological work on primitive culture, Fiske argued that the belief in inspiration had "grown out of more primitive belief in possession, which is found everywhere current among savage and barbarous tribes," and like Ward, Fiske insisted that some "savage races have degenerated in civilization."[59] Despite his views on racial hierarchy, Fiske was an abolitionist and opposed the mistreatment of Blacks in the South. So did Harvard historian Albert Bushnell Hart, who in his *School History of the United States* argued that slavery and the slave trade "were always mistakes" not only because they denied human rights to men, but also because they "brought into American a strange and then savage race."[60] Hart was silent on the issue of whether or not African Americans were still a savage race or whether they were capable of becoming civilized. Like all historians of the period, Hart consistently referred to Native Americans as savages throughout his work.

With the exception of Fiske, the leading historians of the late nineteenth century such as Burgess, Adams, and Hart considered themselves both historians and political scientists because they sought to explain how the United States inherited and perfected political ideas that were inherited from Europe. However, leading progressive historian Frederick Jackson Turner challenged this very idea directly in 1893 in his famous essay "The Significance of the Frontier in American History." In the context of the World's Columbia Expedition, Turner delivered a speech that would capture the imagination of subsequent generations. He offered a new national narrative based on his frontier thesis—that American democratic foundations could be attributed to the availability of free land, which throughout American history had served as a safety valve for immigrant and marginalized groups.[61] Through interaction with this savage wilderness, the unique American character was formed. As Jackson argued:

> The wilderness . . . strips off the garments of civilization and arrays [the settler] in the hunting shirt and the moccasin. It puts him in the log cabin of the Cherokee and Iroquois and runs an Indian palisade around him. Little by little [the settler] transforms the wilderness, but the outcome is not the old Europe. . . . The fact is that here is a new product that is American.[62]

There were many social and educational implications of Turner's thesis. First, Turner's thesis offered an interactionist instead of a biological-institutional explanation for American exceptionalism—thus contradicting the Teutonic germ theory because it cast American character as a contingent outcome of a particular time and place, instead of a manifestation of a latent potential carried over from Europe. Turner's theory suggested that non-Teutonic men could potentially become American, because such a status was based in a shared national experience, not necessarily the inheritance of specific institutional-biological germ. Second, Turner's thesis suggested that American progress was grounded more in process than the transmission of a specific body of content. The pedagogical implication was that no specific body of cultural content and/or product was any more significant than any other. The manner of individual-environment interaction was more significant than exposure to a specific body of cultural products. Third, because the frontier had recently closed, Turner's thesis suggested that national intervention was necessary to ensure America's continued progress. This challenged the *laissez-faire* approach of Spencer and Giddings and reinforced the social welfare agendas of Ward and Small. Overall, Turner's theory suggested the pragmatic notion that America was neither exempt from history, nor in the final stage of it. Rather, it was the continual process of history itself that gave American its defining features.

Despite the epistemological innovations of Turner's thesis, he nevertheless adopted many of the racial ideas of his nineteenth-century predecessors. In fact, the savagery of the frontier was a crucial component of Turner's thesis. He stressed the "savage conditions" of the "Indian frontier as a consolidating agent," which helped form the American identity. He spoke of "savage lords" who stood as adversaries between settlers and important natural resources and "a fierce race of savages" that "all had to be met and defeated" for the American experiment to succeed.[63] Turner did not clarify whether he considered American Indians the psychological equivalent of children.

James Harvey Robinson, another leading progressive historian and a leading advocate for the new history, did clarify his thoughts on recapitulation. Robinson clearly believed that savage societies still roamed the Earth, were culturally equivalent to children, and could provide insight into the development of Western civilization. Robinson, who served on the NEA's 1916 Committee on Social Studies, was one of the most respected historians in the United States, and his textbooks on European and world history were widely used. In his book *The New History*, which was quoted repeatedly in the 1916 Committee on Social Studies report, Robinson argued that much could be learned about the evolution of civilized society by studying "the savage that exists on the earth at the present time." Also like most of his contemporaries, Robinson argued that "inferences that may be made [between] the reasoning of the savage and the progressive unfolding of the infant's mind."[64] In his popular textbook, *Medieval and Modern Times*, in which Robinson employed his "new" historical approach of tracing the social and cultural—instead of merely the political and military—history of Western Europe, he referenced the encounters between the European explorers and the "savage natives" and "savage red men."[65] Robinson believed that these interactions were not merely clashes of cultures, but rather clashes between a civilized culture and a socially backward one.

*****

The basic beliefs of the theory of recapitulation remained largely unaltered as the younger generation of progressives challenged the *laissez-faire* and materialist-idealist schemes of their nineteenth-century predecessors. Twentieth-century scholars replaced the all-compassing theories of Spencer and Mill with discipline-specific theories that reflected the development and growth of the professional organizations. These new social theories depicted world history, not as a manifestation of inherent racial worth or actualization of static essences carried through time, but rather as contingent outcomes of numerous social and environmental interactions. The new psychological theories depicted the mind not as a series of mental faculties (e.g., imagination, memory, will, and so on) representing latent potentials waiting to be activated and strengthened, but rather as a series of inherited instincts that found satisfaction through environmental interaction. Yet, despite this epistemological shift, the progressives uncritically adopted the ethnocentric, hierarchical language of savagery-barbarianism-civilization, and accepted the psychological-sociological correspondence of children and non-White adults. For example, the idea of the "barbarian temperament" was central to Veblen's economic thesis, and the savage frontier was a driving factor in Turner's influential thesis on the formation of American identity. Furthermore, the correspondence of the sociological and psychological stages of humankind was central to the emergence of the new psychology as espoused by Haeckel, Wundt, Hall, and Judd.

Individually, turn-of-the-century scholars were often vague about exactly who these barbarians and savages were. But collectively in the work cited earlier, they named the inhabitants of Kamchatka, Tierra del Fuego, Dahome, Hawaii, Central Africa, New Holland, West Indian Islands, Figi Islands, Zulu-Land, and the Black Republic of Hayti [sic]. They named the Blackfellows of Australia, the northern Eskimos of Greenland, the Amazon Indians of Brazil, the North American Indians, Innuits, Tahitians, the Indian women of Brazil, the women of Timor, the Indians of Paraguay, and the Maoris of New Zealand. All of these groups were non-White, and all of these groups were assumed to be stuck in a child-like, culturally deficient stage of social development. The ethnocentric recapitulation approach to cultural development was such a matter of common sense that no one bothered to question it. For example, in the 1890s Dewey published lengthy book reviews of Harris's *Psychologic Foundations of Education*, Kidd's *Social Evolution*, Baldwin's *The Mental and Ethical Development of the Child and Race*, and Ward's *The Psychic Foundations of Civilization*. In each case, Dewey criticized the philosophical and psychological assumptions made by each author. However, he failed to comment a single time about the authors' overt use of the theory of recapitulation. Even for Dewey, the theory of recapitulation was a given.[66]

These progressive scholars were all Protestant, and often had direct links to religious leadership. For example, Small was an ordained Baptist minister, Harris's Hegelian philosophy equated the universal spirit with God, and Hall's psychology was underscored with Christian themes, Hall writing in 1894 that "the Bible is being re-revealed as man's great text-book in psychology."[67] Likewise, Dewey ended his famous proclamation "My Pedagogic Creed" with the uncharacteristic assertion: "I believe that . . . the teacher always is the prophet of the true God and the usherer in of the true kingdom of God."[68] In this context, the term *savage* not only meant culturally backward and sociologically deficient, but it also meant non-Christian. Civilization was synonymous with acculturation to Christian values.

By the turn of the twentieth century, recapitulations dominated the production and dissemination of professional knowledge in the social sciences and education. The U.S. commissioner of education (Harris) was a recapitulationist. The head of the Bureau of American Ethnology (McGee) was a recapitulationist. The editors of *The Journal of Speculative Philosophy* (Harris), *Pedagogical Seminary* (Hall), and *The American Journal of Psychology* (Hall) were recapitulationists. The leaders of the new psychology (Wundt), the new history (Robinson), and the child study movement (Hall, Judd) were recapitulationists. Leading social theorists (Baldwin, Kidd, Ward) and anthropologists (Morgan, Tylor) were recapitulationists. This generation of scholars was also unique in its intense interest in public education, and virtually every scholar listed above had some direct or indirect link to the reforms of the new education. James, Munsterberg, Hall, and Judd authored textbooks specifically for teachers. Hart, Turner, Adams, and Robinson authored high school history textbooks. Hart and Robinson served on the NEA's Committee of Ten, whose report on "History, Civil Government, and Political Economy" established the scope and sequence of courses for most American high schools prior to World War I. Hart and Adams served on the AHA's Committee of Seven, which further refined the influential recommendations of the Committee of Ten. In 1896, Small authored a widely read essay, "The Demands of Sociology upon Pedagogy," in which he critiqued the recommendations of the NEA's Committee of Ten and suggested a more holistic and interactive approach to the mind of the student. Small's essay was republished in pamphlet form with Dewey's "My Pedagogic Creed" and distributed to thousands of educators throughout the nation. These leading social scientists and educators shaped the intellectual context from which the new education was created. As we shall see in the next chapter, this intellectual context—permeated with the assumptions of the theory of recapitulation—made an immediate impact on the emerging ideas and materials of early progressive educators.

CHAPTER 2

Recapitulation

In 1916 a U.S. Bureau of Education bulletin outlined the three major "aspects of the education process" reflected in new science of learning. These aspects were "the significant psychophysical characteristics which mark stages of [the child's] growth, the demand of the social group into which the child is born and in which he must live, and the teaching method." In other words, the new science of learning entailed knowing the stages of psychological growth of the child, the stages of sociological growth toward civilization, and how to align the two in such a way that enabled learning to take place in an efficient manner. That is, the new education was largely based upon the pedagogical assumptions of the theory of recapitulation. Regarding the stages of child development, the bulletin identified "G. Stanley Hall and his school of child-study investigators" as the leading researchers. Regarding the stages of sociological growth, it identified "Ward, Giddings, . . . and others."[1] Thus, by 1916 mainstream educational theorists had accepted the recapitulation theories of Hall, Ward, and Giddings and employed them toward pedagogical reform. As early as 1895, Dewey had stated that "The ultimate problem of all education is to coordinate the psychological and social factors"—that is, to coordinate the emerging instinct-stages of the child, as revealed by the findings of the new psychology, with the historical modes of occupation that best represented them.[2] Likewise, progressive educators Harriet Maria Scott and Gertrude Buck argued that the curriculum ought to be based upon the correspondence of the instincts of children with the "representative phases or stages in world civilization."[3] Leaders in child study concurred. In *Essays in Child Psychology*, Paola Lombroso confirmed: "The child is a little compressed, synthetic picture of all the stages of man's evolution."[4] The coordination of the child and the development of the race was a central focus of the new education in the United States.

In addition to creating a framework for the education of White children, the theory of recapitulation addressed and solved a uniquely American problem—the education of American Indians, African Americans, and non-White students in territories acquired by the United States (Hawaii, Cuba, Puerto Rico, and the Philippines). Previous historical studies on the education of American Indians, Southern Blacks, and foreign children often mention the theory of recapitulation in passing. However, these studies fail to link the theory of recapitulation to the broader intellectual currents of the new education.[5] In this chapter, I demonstrate how the theory of recapitulation justified a differentiated curriculum for all students—White and non-White—under U.S. control based upon their perceived psychological-sociological stage. For Whites, who were believed to pass through the psychological-sociological stage of savagery and barbarianism as children, the curriculum was based upon matching their emerging instincts with premodern activities such as building a hut or spear, or with materials addressing premodern life such as the novel *Robinson Crusoe* and the poem "Song of Hiawatha." This approach appeared repeatedly in teaching materials of the new education. For non-Whites, who were believed to have been in an extended stage of savagery and barbarianism and who never fully reached the psychological-sociological stage of civilization, the curriculum was based upon industrial activities, physical training, and moral indoctrination.

Early progressive educators believed that people of color did not have the instinctual predisposition for civilized, democratic life that White students had. Christian ideals such as morality, industriousness, and cleanliness needed to be taught explicitly to non-White students at an older age largely through promoting physical restraint and engaging in manual activity. Therefore, the theory of recapitulation was used to justify racially segregated schools and to rationalize a differentiated curriculum aligned with the perceived instincts of each racial group. Many of the ideas that appeared in early progressive schools in the United States were also employed to teach people of color under U.S. control.

In this chapter, I demonstrate how the theory of recapitulation informed the education of American Indians and Southern Blacks, the teaching of foreign non-Whites under U.S. control, the pedagogical ideas of John Dewey, and many of the early experiments in progressive education. Of course, there were tremendous financial and social benefits to be gained by Whites relegating non-Whites to a lower socioeconomic status, such as cheap labor, international prestige, an expanded market for U.S. goods, and enhanced racial status. I am not suggesting that the theory of recapitulation was the only or even the primary rationale for economically exploiting people of color and casting them as second-class citizens domestically and abroad. Yet, the theory provided an ideological framework that reinforced White supremacy in explicit and implicit ways, while paradoxically justifying a more humane, child-centered approach to education. Thus, early child-centered education, U.S. imperialism, and U.S. policy on American Indians and African Americans were all cut from the same cloth.

RECAPITULATION FOR PROTO-PROGRESSIVES

In *Schools of To-morrow*, published in 1915, Dewey and his daughter Evelyn identified Jean-Jacques Rousseau, Friedrich Froebel, Johann Heinrich Pestalozzi, and Marie Montessori as progenitors of the new education.[6] Each of these European educators subscribed to general contours of the theory of recapitulation. Rousseau had outlined specific stages of child development and sociological development and, to some degree, coordinated them to one another. However, unlike most of the scholars of the eighteenth and nineteenth centuries, Rousseau did not consider the latest, civilized stage to be the greatest. In fact, he awarded his highest esteem to the savage stage, because the savage had developed above the brutish ape, but had not given himself over to what Rousseau considered to be the corrupting forces of civilization. As Rousseau explained, "nothing can be more gentle than [man] in his primitive state, when placed by nature at an equal distance from the stupidity of the brutes and the pernicious good sense of civilized man."[7] Regarding education, Rousseau emphasized the inherent goodness of the instincts of children, which roughly approximated the state of savagery, and suggested that education ought to capitalize on these benevolent impulses. In this sense, Rousseau was the godfather of child-centered education, something that Dewey recognized in the first chapter of his 1915 coauthored book, *Schools of To-morrow*. However, subsequent European pedagogues made a more immediate impact on the rhetoric and practice of early childhood education, and they subscribed more fully to the theory of recapitulation.

Friedrich Froebel, the German inventor of the kindergarten, wrote that through "the development of the inner life of the individual man ... the history of the mental development of the race is repeated." In reference to the theory of recapitulation, Froebel continued more specifically, "Inasmuch as he would understand the past and present, [the individual] must pass through all preceding phases of human development and culture."[8] Similarly, German pedagogue and proponent of the object method Johann Heinrich Pestalozzi wrote: "The child masters the principles of cultivated speech in exactly the same slow order as Nature has followed with the race."[9] The most famous pedagogical proponent of the application of the theory of recapitulation—although not the originator of the idea—was Johann Herbart, who wrote that "the educator shall see in the progress of his pupil a recapitulation of the great progress of mankind."[10] His German followers such as Tuiskon Ziller and Wilhelm Rein espoused Herbart's ideas throughout the nineteenth century, and even drew upon his theories to design and implement a recapitulation-based curriculum for the German primary schools.

Italian doctor Maria Montessori is perhaps the most enduring educator from the nineteenth century; interest in the Montessori method continued to grow long after the ideas of Rousseau, Frobel, Pestalozzi, and Herbart had faded. She, too, based her method in part on the coordination of the emerging instincts of the child with activities from correct sociological stage. In her book *The Montessori Method*, which was translated into English in 1912, she related the story of her mentor, Itard, who had rescued and educated a "savage" White boy whose parents had been killed and was abandoned in a forest. "The savage of Aveyron was a child who had grown up in a natural state," she explained. But Itard quickly realized that the boy's inferiority was not because "he was a degraded organism but for want of education." By employing innovative and experimental methods, Itard gradually and successfully led "the savage to civilization," by developing the boy "from natural life to social life." Based on Itard's experience, Montessori concluded, "we must prepare man, who is one among the living creatures and therefore belongs to nature, for social life, because social life being its own peculiar work, must also correspond to manifestation of his natural activity."[11] Thus, like Rousseau and Dewey, Montessori also proposed that education be based upon the correspondence of natural instincts with the appropriate modes of social life.

In her book *Pedagogical Anthropology*, translated into English in 1913, Montessori argued that the anthropological study of the history of humankind had much to teach the educator about the development of the White child. She related how the races of world differed in the size of their cephalic index, with non-White children at the bottom of the scale. Montessori explained, "the *cephalic index* and the *cranial volume* are the two anthropological data on which the criterion of normality of children's heads must be based." She continued, "the dark-skinned children . . . belonging to African races and the tribes of American Indians," belonged to the dolichocephalic racial group with the smallest cephalic index.[12] Drawing upon contemporaneous research in physical anthropology, Montessori confirmed that people of color were not only sociologically inferior, but anatomically inferior as well.

Cornel Francis W. Parker, leading proto-progressive educator in the United States, also subscribed the basic beliefs of the theory of recapitulation. Dewey had famously identified Parker as the father of progressive education.[13] Parker established an innovative child-centered curriculum in Quincy, Massachusetts, in the 1870s. He later served as principal of the Cook County Normal School in Chicago, where he continued his experiments with a less rigid, more humane, and democratic style of teaching young children than the approach used in most public schools. In his 1894 book, *Talks on Pedagogics*, Parker offered the following as a sample question and activity for students: "Show that the same characteristic area of surface has entirely different effects upon the different stages of savagery, barbarism, and civilization. What was the Valley of the Mississippi to savages? What to a civilized people?" Here, Parker confirms the beliefs of his contemporaries that all of the world's societies pass through the same psychological-sociological stages of savagery, barbarism, and civilization, and that American Indians represented a savage form of living that failed to develop the natural resources at their disposal due to their cultural inferiority. Earlier in the book, Parker wrote, "Many savages today will not allow themselves to be painted or photographed," confirming that Parker believed that non-White savages still roamed the Earth in the present.[14] Parker looked to the "development of the race in civilization" as a guide for many of his ideas. "The lower the grade of development in the human race," Parker reasoned, "the less there is known of number." However, regarding the theory of recapitulation Parker only provided a lukewarm endorsement of the theory, writing:

> It may not be a valid hypothesis to say that in the mind of each child numbers are developed precisely in the order that they have been in the development of the race; still it is something of a guide in attempting to answer the question in what direction should number be developed in the child. The line of development is apparent.[15]

Rousseau, Froebel, Pestalozzi, Montessori, and Parker laid the philosophical foundation for engaging and celebrating the emerging instincts of young child and designing the curriculum to align with them. Thus, the long tradition of child-centeredness that laid the foundation for the new education was grounded in the theory of recapitulation by pedagogues who subscribed to the general principles of the theory. All made commonsense references to the sociological deficiency of savages at a time when the word was racially coded to mean "non-White." All promoted the alignment of curriculum with the natural instincts of young children, which scholars believed to be instinctual deposits from the evolutionary history of the race. Beyond these precedents, the pedagogues of the progressive era drew upon of the emerging scholarship of the science of learning, which empirically affirmed many of the insights of these famous teachers. Concern for the humane treatment of the young child went hand in hand with a respect for children's inherited instincts, which originated from their recapitulated past.

TEACHING NATIVE AMERICANS AND SOUTHERN BLACKS

The first systematic application of the theory of recapitulation to education in the United States was directed toward Native Americans and Southern Blacks. The formal policy of educating Native Americans was launched and funded by the Dawes Act in 1887. Under this initiative, thousands of Native Americans were persuaded or forced to send their children to publicly funded schools specifically designed to strip them of their alleged savage tendencies and assimilate them to the civilized world. To do this, the children needed to be removed as much as possible from the sociologically deficient native stage of their parents. By 1902, the Bureau of Indian Affairs had established more than 300 boarding and day schools for Native Americans, mostly in the West, to teach native children how to be civilized. Commissioner Morgan endorsed a curriculum that surrounded Native Americans "with an atmosphere of civilization, maturing them in all that is good, and developing them into men and women, instead of allowing them to grow up as barbarians and savages."[16] Because day schools only had a limited effect on the alleged savage tendencies of the Indians, reformers preferred that children be completely removed from their reservations and placed in boarding schools.

The primary advocates for Indian child removal in the United States were Estelle Reel and Alice Fletcher.[17] Reel was the superintendent of Indian education from 1898 to 1910. Reel believed the Native Americans she sought to help were both biologically and sociologically deficient. Her experience teaching young natives confirmed that "the Indian instincts and nerves and muscles and bones are adjusted one to another, and all to the habits of the race for uncounted generations, and his offspring cannot be taught like the children of the white man until they are taught to do so." Reel justified the removal of Indian children from their parents and homes and their placement with Whites because doing so "places him [the Indian child] in the midst of the stir of civilized life, where he must compete with wide-awake boys and girls of the white race." She referred to the "inherited weaknesses and tendencies" of the Native Americans, suggesting that their inferiority was as much biological as it was sociological. As a recapitulationist, Reel confirmed that "the Indian mind is as the child's mind, or the minds of an era when science was in its infancy." She also viewed savagery as being synonymous with non-Christian, writing, "The Indian child must be placed in school before the habits of barbarous life have become fixed, and there he must be kept until contact with our life has taught him to abandon his savage ways and walk in the path of Christian civilization."[18]

Likewise, Fletcher drew upon hierarchical language of psychological-sociological development to rationalize the policies of forced assimilation for Native Americans. Fletcher wrote that the White race, as possessors "of the best portions of the Earth's surface," were destined to "redeem [the Indian] from the monotony and sleepiness of uncivilized ideas and methods." The references to "development" and "sleepiness" suggested that, as members of the human race, the Indians had a latent, untapped potential to be socialized to the civilized world, especially if they were exposed early. However, this process could be inhibited by their biology and their extended exposure to the savage-barbarian lifestyle. Accordingly, the theory of recapitulation not only rationalized a policy of taking children from their allegedly savage and barbarous parents, but it also informed the curriculum, which focused on manual and vocational learning because these activities were believed to be appropriate for the Indians' psychological-sociological stage. As Reel explained, "Industrial training will make the Indian boy a useful, practical, self-supporting citizen. It will make the Indian girls more motherly."[19] The purpose was to give the native children concrete skills that would be of use in the industrial economy, an approach suggested by Booker T. Washington, the former slave and leading authority on the industrial education of Blacks.

Washington was the most famous graduate of Samuel Chapman Armstrong's Hampton Normal and Agricultural Institute in Virginia, which was founded in 1868. Washington would go on to found his own school, the Tuskegee Normal and Industrial Institute, in 1881. Together, these schools formed the "Hampton-Tuskegee Idea," which prioritized economic development and the self-reliance of Blacks and American Indians over intellectual nourishment and political enfranchisement. Funded by Northern philanthropists, the primary objective of Hampton and Tuskegee was to train Black teachers for the racially segregated schools of the South. Manual labor was the central part of the curriculum, which was intended to teach students work habits, humility, and Christian morals. The curriculum was informed by the theory of recapitulation. Reflecting on the missionary work of his father in Hawaii, Armstrong reflected that the "civilization of the dark-skinned Polynesian people [was] in many respects like the Negro race" because both groups were "savages." Furthermore, drawing upon neo-Lamarckian notions of transmission of acquired characteristics, Armstrong continued that Negros lacked the "right instincts" for self-governance because "the Negro had three centuries of experience in general demoralization and behind that, paganism."[20] Armstrong argued that, due to biological and cultural restraints, African

Americans did not possess the intellectual and moral capacities for civilization. Therefore, their curriculum must be centered on a basic elementary academic curriculum, manual labor, and moral discipline.

The social studies curriculum at Hampton, which constituted much of the nonvocational part of the curriculum, was authored by Thomas Jesse Jones. As a sociologist and graduate of Columbia University, Jones brought a high degree of respectability to his work. Jones is generally credited with coining the term *social studies*, which he used to describe the teaching of history and social sciences at Hampton. Like Armstrong, Jones agreed that all races could eventually be sociologically equal, but educators had to respect the biological and social restraints they inherited. According to Jones, in his overview of the social studies program at the Hampton Institute, African Americans and Native Americans were sociologically backward races; they were unfortunate but innocent victims of history. Through no fault of their own, they had been left behind early in human development, while White society continued to progress beyond them. Reformers needed to be patient because American Indians and African Americans had "suddenly been transferred from an earlier form of society into a later one without the necessary time of preparation." As Jones explained, "Natural evolution from one social stage to another requires time."[21] As a result, exposing these "primitive" students to an academic curriculum would be futile and wasteful because they had not sociologically evolved far enough to make use of such knowledge and responsibility.

Jones's view of the political limitations of Southern Blacks, which constituted the majority of students at Hampton, must be considered in light of the Dunning historiographical school of Reconstruction, which dominated the study of that topic in the early part of the twentieth century. William Dunning, a history professor at Columbia University who was considered the foremost authority on the subject, argued that Southern Blacks were innocent victims and pawns in the Northern Radicals' game of political revenge upon Southern Whites. Reconstruction had failed, he argued, because immediately after the Civil War, illiterate and backward Southern Blacks were given political power for which they were not ready. As a result, the South quickly unraveled into chaos and disarray. Having squandered any chance of a peaceful transition to postwar society, the Northerners virtually forced Southern Whites to implement Black codes and later Jim Crow laws to reestablish order.[22] Thus, Dunning's historical narrative not only reinforced perceived racial hierarchies, but it depicted Southern Blacks as victims of history and confirmed the perception that they were unable to engage in the kind of thinking and action necessary for informed citizenship. This narrative made an enormous impact on the sociological view of African Americans and on race relations. According to Dunning, Armstrong, and Jones, the Black race had simply not arrived at the intellectual level necessary for self-governance, a point that the history of Reconstruction had allegedly proven empirically.

Nevertheless, Jones specifically positioned himself as a moderate between Southerners who thought that African Americans could never catch up, and radicals who asserted that "his race is the equal of any race." Jones also demonstrated his belief in the biological restraints of African and Native Americans. "The White youth grows to manhood without feeling any of the limitations which the colored youth feels," he explained, but, on the other hand, Blacks had to cope with the natural inherited impulses that made socialization difficult. However, the limitations of Blacks and American Indians were not solely a result of their inherited impulses. Jones also believed that it was due to the inadequacies of their sociological environment. Employing Giddings's "law of sympathy," Jones argued that social groups would emulate one another in proportion to the quantity and intensity of a particular trait found in the group. "An appreciation of this law of sympathy," Jones insisted, "contributes greatly to a knowledge of all race divisions."[23]

According to Jones, imitation via the law of sympathy explained why the limitations of Southern Blacks were greater than those of the Northern Blacks. The law of sympathy acted more intensely upon them because there was a greater concentration of Blacks in the South and a greater intensity of historical persecution. Likewise, the law of sympathy explained why American Indians who left the reservations achieved a higher level of civilization than those who had remained. Only complete immersion in civilized society, it was believed, could undo hundreds of years of savagery. Consequently, Jones concluded that racial progress occurred only when certain members of the race were isolated from the rest, so they would not regress back to their earlier forms. The law of sympathy explained why progress was such a slow, incremental process.

Jones's historical narrative of differentiated racial development not only informed the policy of what to teach the American Indian and African American students, but also constituted the substance of the curriculum. As Jones explained:

> The study of [the] stages in the development of the social mind and character is of great value to the pupil in that it gives him confidence that the present condition of his people is merely a stage and not a permanent condition; in that it enables him to recognize the weaknesses of his people more readily, especially those faults, usually overloaded in eagerness to develop the economic side; and in that it calls his attention to the highest stage towards which he must strive to educate his people, by correcting their faults and encouraging their virtues.[24]

Thus, Jones used history both to inform his Hampton students how and why they had arrived at a certain level of inequality, but also to inspire them to achieve to higher levels. Inequality was not simply the result of the purely biological inheritance of the race—a theory that Jones believed would hopelessly demoralize his non-White students. Instead, the sociological inferiority of Southern Blacks and American Indians could be explained by their historical circumstances. Social and cultural growth would require sustained access to the moral and cultural milieu of White, civilized society. Only the passage of time could remedy sociological inequalities, not necessarily individual initiative. The most efficient way to accomplish this progress was to prepare his Hampton students for the inferior roles they would likely take in the integrated society.

The textbooks adopted at Hampton, such as William Swinton's *Introductory Geography*, reflected the racially hierarchical ideology of the period. As Swinton wrote, "The races who, in their way of living, are the least civilized are called the savage races.... When we find people who are not so enlightened, but who still are not savages, and seem to be on the way to becoming civilized people, we call them semi-civilized, which means half-civilized." The students at Hampton learned these lessons well. In one example published in the *Southern Workman*, the flagship journal of the school, a student recited the "five large classes belonging to the human race," which included "the white peoples ... The Mongolians or yellows ... The Ethiopians or blacks ... [and] the Americans or reds." In another example, a student wrote in an essay: "The white people they are civilized.... The yellow people they half civilized ... the red people they big savages; they don't know anything [sic]." Another student wrote how "The Indian people some are good those remember the Church but some are bad those did not remember the Church and did not like to go to school and did not like to be try good man and not work [sic]."[25] The material used at the Hampton Institute reinforced the racial hierarchy embedded in the theory of recapitulation. However, it is important to note that these materials were not specifically designed for Black and Indian students. Swinton's textbook was written for White classrooms. In this sense, the social studies curriculum was not differentiated; the students at Hampton used the same materials and learned the same geography and world history as the White students. However, the lesson for each racial group would have been different based upon where they were placed on the racial hierarchy.

As early as the 1890s, Native Americans expressed resistance to their depiction as uncivilized savages representing an earlier step in the universal stages of cultural development. One of the most popular means of communicating cultural hierarchies to the American public beyond textbooks was the World's Columbian Exposition in Chicago in 1893—the location where Frederick Jackson Turner delivered his famous speech on the significance of frontier to American history (see Chapter 1). The exposition was meant to demonstrate the self-confidence, optimism, and progress of the United States. Accordingly, the Chicago exhibit included models of savage villages designed by American anthropologists, which were contrasted with the "The White City" displaying the latest achievements in technology and civilization. Enthusiastic White attendees reported on the educative experience of seeing "within the compass of a day's stroll ... the civilized, the half-civilized and savage worlds," and the exhibit garnered positive reviews from popular periodicals such as *Cosmopolitan* and *The Nation*.[26] Yet, one Native American opposed the message of the exhibit and expressed her frustration in a letter to the *New York Times* in October 1893:

> Every effort has been put forth to make the Indian exhibit mislead the American people. It has been used to work up sentiment against the Indian by showing that he [sic] is either savage or can be educated only by government agencies.... The Indian agent and their backers knew well that if civilized Indians got a representation in the Fair, the

public would wake up to the capabilities of the Indian for self-government and realize that all they all needed was to be left alone.[27]

The Indian author of this letter was not arguing on behalf of respecting and maintaining the premodern ways of Native Americans, nor was she celebrating their cultural achievements. Instead, she was arguing that the image of "civilized Indians" had been deliberately excluded because it would have disrupted the popular image of Indians as backward and incapable of self-government. Similarly, Richard Henry Pratt, headmaster of the Carlisle School for American Indians, criticized the depiction of Native Americans for focusing on their "valueless past," instead of their rapid progress toward civilization.[28] Former slave and African American leader Frederick Douglass also expressed dismay at the Columbian exhibition for its depiction of American Blacks as "African savages brought here to act the monkey" by engaging in "barbaric rites," instead of focusing on the great advances made by the race since emancipation. Protesting their exclusion from contributing to the exhibit, African American newspapers dubbed the exposition "the great American white elephant" and the "the white American's world fair."[29]

Despite the consistent depiction of Blacks and American Indians as backward and premodern, by the end of the 1890s some White educators were also beginning to challenge the Indian removal policy of forced assimilation that denigrated the Native American lifestyle. In 1899, Mary Collins, a Congregationalist missionary who had spent twenty-five years among the Lakota Sioux, protested that "Whenever children are taught to despise their home and parents it is a great mistake. I cannot too strongly protest against that." Collins attacked some of the stereotypes of Indian parents' alleged backwardness, cruelty, and cultural deprivation. "The Indian mother teaches her little child in the home. She takes care to teach what she thinks is right," Collins explained, "as much case as you do what you think is right. You would be surprised to go into the Indian home and see how careful they are the training of the children." In fact, by the 1920s, the tide had turned against Indian removal policy. A 1928 study commissioned by the Brookings Institute concluded that removing children from their parents and community "is at variance with modern views of education and social work, which regard home and family as essential institutions." In this instance, the progressive educators' focus on breaking down the artificial barriers between school and community was used as evidence to stop the removal of Indian children from their parents, whereas in the 1890s proponents of the new education justified Indian removal based on the idea that American Indians were driven by savage instincts, in accordance with the theory of recapitulation. The Brookings report concluded: "Indian parents nearly everywhere ask to have their children during the early years, and they are right."[30] Indian child removal was not phased out until the 1930s when Native American children began to be educated locally in their communities.

Despite these dissenting voices, most policymakers continued to pursue policies aimed at civilizing the savage. In fact, White educators applied the lessons they learned by teaching American Indians and Southern Blacks to other non-White populations in the newly acquired territories under U.S. control. For example, David Prescott Barrows was specifically selected to inform the educational policies in the Philippines when the United States won autonomy over the territory at the turn of the twentieth century because of his study of the education of American Indians in the West. As Barrows wrote upon his arrival in the Philippines in 1902, "The work with which I am charged is to investigate the actual condition for these wild tribes . . . with the hope of getting light on our Philippine problem from what has been achieved for the Indian."[31] Similarly, G. Stanley Hall identified a direct parallel between how "we teach Indians and Filipinos," reinforcing the view that people of color at home and abroad needed to be approached in a similar manner—as sociologically deficient in need of development under the tutelage of the Anglo-Saxon race.[32] A Southern U.S. legislator agreed that "the experience of the South for the past thirty years with the negro race" offered "lessons of wisdom for our guidance in the Philippines." Fred Akinson, who headed the effort to establish U.S. schools in the Philippines, also made the connection to the Hampton-Tuskegee model explicit. "We should heed the lesson taught us in our reconstruction period when we started to educate the negro," Akinson explained. "The education of the masses here must be agricultural and industrial one, after the pattern of our Tuskegee Institute at home."[33] William Torrey Harris concurred, arguing in 1904 that the Hampton-Tuskegee model was "so universal in character that it applies to the down-trodden of all races, without reference to color."[34] Informed by the theory of recapitulation, U.S. educators approached the non-White populations of the Philippines, Hawaii, Puerto Rico, and Cuba with assurance. Because they had extensive experience educating the savage at home, U.S. imperialists were confident that they could partially civilize the savage abroad.

IMPERIALISM AND THE NEW EDUCATION

In January 1899, the satirical magazine *Puck* published a political cartoon of Uncle Sam in a one-room schoolhouse standing over his new students, four frowning brown-faced children with sashes that read Philippines, Hawaii, Puerto Rico, and Cuba. "Now, children, you've got to learn these lessons whether you want to or not!" Uncle Sam insists in the cartoon while holding a threatening rod over the heads of the students. "But just take a look at the class ahead of you, and remember that, in a little while, you will feel as glad to be here as they are!"[35] Behind Uncle Sam's left shoulder, an African American custodian looks on while washing the window. Just inside the door to the school an American Indian student holds a book upside-down, while a Chinese American student gazes into the school from the outside. The rest of the room is filled with mostly White students engrossed in their studies, holding books with the names of the U.S. states on them. The cartoonist depicted the students from the new American territories as infantile, apelike savages indistinguishable from one another and in need of tutelage by White professionals. Around the room posters and lecture notes outlined the American policy of forced assimilation in the name of freedom and self-rule, including the North's reconstruction of the South and its establishment of schools like Hampton and Tuskegee.

The 1890s represented the high-water mark of what historian Eric Hobsbawm called "The Age of Empire" during which Western nations conquered and exploited much of the non-Western world; even the United States took its share of the spoils.[36] As a result of the Spanish-American War, the United States won autonomy over the Philippines, Cuba, and Puerto Rico, and annexed Hawaii as well. The United States reformed the education systems of these newly acquired territories in line with the theory of recapitulation.[37] Professional educators gave their unequivocal support for such policies. For example, in 1898 the NEA, of which William Torrey Harris was the elected chairman, issued a resolution pledging support for the Spanish-American War and for "the solidarity of both the American people and the Anglo Saxon races." As Harris explained in a separate essay, "The new burden of preparing our united people for the responsibilities of closer union with Europe and in a share of the dominion over the islands and continents of the Orient will fall on the school systems of the separate states."[38] In other words, according to Harris, the new education not only needed to inform the imperialistic policies abroad, but also needed to be directed toward preparing the "Anglo Saxon races" for their new imperialist position of "dominion over the islands and continents of the Orient" at home. The curriculum implemented at the schools established by the United States in its new territories followed the contours of the Hampton-Tuskegee model of industrial education. In another address, Harris proudly explained, "Instead of leaving the savage to work out his salvation from the abstract formula of Christianity, . . . [we] teach him to read, and give him literature that will fill his mind with the thoughts and observations and feelings that our civilized white people harbor in their minds."[39] Whether educators believed that non-Whites could eventually be brought up to speed in the civilized world was largely irrelevant because there was a consensus that the education of people of color at home and abroad needed to be vocational and industrial in nature.

At the annual meeting of NEA in Denver, Charles Bartlett Dyke, in an address entitled "Essential Features in the Education of the Child Races," reflected upon his experiences teaching in Hawaii. Dyke concluded that he "became firmly convinced that the psychical race differences are not eliminated in any appreciable number of generations be the education what it may . . . [therefore] primitive man must be trained for vocations that fit him for life in the white man's world." Dyke praised the industrial education established by Armstrong for African Americans and by Pratt for American Indians. Yet, he questioned whether Whites were really in the best position to teach the non-White students. He asserted, "No white man can *fully* understand the American Indian, or the negro," two groups he had identified as child races because the latest research in racial characteristics confirmed that these groups represented an earlier psychological-sociological stage largely dictated by their heredity. "Arrested development is a real problem in the education of all races," Dyke explained. "All men reach their intellectual growth, some early, some relatively late in life." In accordance with the theory of recapitulation, he related how "the primitive races attain their mental growth at a much earlier age."[40] Based on his experiences with the Hawaiians, as well as his readings in the latest scientific research, Dyke reached a pessimistic conclusion on the overall intellectual potential of non-White races:

> The races of men think, feel, and act differently not only because of environment, but also because of hereditary impulses. The Indian differs from the negro, the negro differs from the Hawaiian, the Hawaiian differs from the Filipino, and the white man, *their teacher*, differs from all of them. Education does not eliminate these differences. . . . The mass of children of primitive races are not well developed in the power of abstract reason and of personal initiative.[41]

Dykes's own personal experiences with the "child races" confirmed his belief in the appropriateness of the Hampton-Tuskegee model. However, he suggested that teachers must be recruited from the "child races" themselves, because only teachers from the same race as the children could truly understand their condition.

A similar approach was implemented in Puerto Rico. Frank H. Ball was the first supervising principal of industrial schools in Puerto Rico. He authored several annual reports for Congress, and he also presented his education work on the island to professional organizations such as the Eastern Manual Training Association. Like most progressives, Ball shared Harris's enthusiasm for the transformative power of education to improve the lives of the uncivilized. Ball believed that teachers of non-White children should be "missionaries" who "spread the light and the truth of educational gospel to their darkened minds." He agreed with Dyke that the Puerto Ricans were racially inferior, a result of "climatic and hereditary influences." Accordingly, Ball's industrial schools taught his Puerto Rican students "cooking and household training" in an effort to make them cleaner and more self-sufficient.[42] Prior to his appointment in Puerto Rico, Ball was in charge of manual training at John Dewey's University of Chicago Laboratory School. Thus, Ball had been promoted from perhaps the most progressive school in the history of the United States to the "darkened" world of Puerto Rico, where he implemented many of the ideas he had learned with young White children. This demonstrates the direct link between some of the progressive experiments on White students in the United States with many of the imperialist experiments abroad. In fact, teachers of non-White students were often recruited from the most progressive White schools. Many of the teachers at the Hampton Institute had graduated from the normal school of Quincy, Massachusetts, headed by the famous proto-progressive educator Colonel Francis W. Parker (see Chapter 2).[43]

Overall, early progressive educators had mixed views on the imperialist ambitions abroad. Harris was an unequivocal supporter of these policies and used his influence with the NEA to endorse the education of the foreign savages. In an 1899 address to the NEA titled "An Educational Policy for our New Possessions,"

Harris argued that the United States ought to "emancipate them from their tribal forms and usages and train them into productive industry and the individual ownership of land."[44] William James, on the other hand, was a harsh critic of the imperialist ambitions of the United States. He wrote an angry editorial for the *Boston Transcript* the same year called "The Philippine Tangle" in which he exclaimed that "Civilization is . . . the big, hollow, resounding, corrupting, sophisticating, confusing torrent of mere brutal momentum. . . . We are cold-bloodedly, wantonly and abominably destroying the soul of a people who never did us an atom of harm in their lives."[45] His personal correspondence from the time revealed that James was less concerned with the racial equality and civil rights of Filipinos than he was with his opposition to arrogance and the idea of greatness itself. As an advocate for pluralism and individualism, James viewed imperialism as a homogenizing force that stamped out diversity at home and abroad. G. Stanley Hall also questioned the mistreatment of native groups under imperialism, writing in an editorial entitled "The Point of View Toward Primitive Races" that "primitives have certain inalienable rights to life, liberty, and the pursuit of happiness, [and so] the ruthless interference with customs that have worked well for indigenous races should cease."[46] Hall never questioned that people of color were at present inferior; he merely questioned whether they needed to be forcibly developed for reasons that clearly benefitted the imperialists (see Chapter 4).

Almost all educators of people of color made some kind of reference to the innate or biological limitations of their students, which reflected a neo-Lamarckian approach to racial differentiation because, presumably, the racial characteristics of each race were acquired over centuries. However, these educators clearly believed in the power of education to overcome their inherited limitations to some degree, and that once these new traits were set non-Whites should pass them on to their offspring. Over generations, the races could be uplifted, if their exposure to civilization was sustained. In this sense, these educators believed that the sociological evolution of the non-White races could be sped up by education. However, they largely avoided anthropological and biological discussions of the exact mechanism for how this sociological evolution would take place. Were the child-like races supposed to mature phylogenetically over time as their collective biological makeup developed, or was a proper education supposed to mature each individual ontologically? This issue was never really addressed. However, the educator who engaged these issues most directly was John Dewey. Because he is generally considered to be the single most significant figure in the new education, an in-depth discussion of his racial views and how they related to the theory of recapitulation is warranted.

PRE-1916 DEWEY

Prior to 1916, Dewey shared four basic beliefs with the leading social scientists described in the last chapter—first, that all the societies of the world could be placed along a single, linear path leading through the sociological stages of savagery, barbarianism, and civilization; second, that all the individuals of the world could be placed along a single, linear path scale leading through what he called the "physical," "social," and "intellectual" psychological stages; third, that these sociological stages more or less corresponded with these psychological stages; and fourth, that non-White populations such as Africans, African Americans, Native Americans, East Asians, and Aboriginal Australians were stuck in an earlier sociological-psychological stage of development. However, as described in the introduction, Dewey made some important distinctions and divergences from the ideas of his contemporaries, while working within the basic framework of the theory of recapitulation.

Like his intellectual contemporaries, Dewey believed that all of the societies of the world, past and present, could be placed along a single continuum of sociological progress. As demonstrated in the last chapter, virtually every influential social scientist during the second half of the nineteenth century made commonsense references to the idea of society moving along a linear path of progress through some kind of sociological laws. Although Dewey did not believe in the existence of these laws on a positivistic or metaphysical level, as many of these thinkers did, he nevertheless adopted the language of linear progress throughout his early and middle years.[47] For example, in *Democracy and Education*, Dewey explained that students should understand "the entire advance of humanity from savagery to civilization has been dependent upon intellectual discoveries and inventions."[48] In his 1900 essay, "Some Stages of Logical Thought," Dewey outlined the stages of sociological growth more specifically as the static belief stage, discussion and argumentation stage, the modern experimentation stage, and the contingency stage.[49] All societies that progressed to civilization, Dewey argued, had passed through this sequence.

Dewey also believed that individuals progressed psychologically along a single, linear path. He shared this belief with leading genetic psychologists of the period. In his course syllabi and essays at the University of Chicago, Dewey made repeated references to the stages of child development. He also outlined these stages in his books *School and Society, How We Think,* and *Democracy and Education*.[50] For example, in *How We Think*, Dewey described three incorporative levels of curiosity: the physical, the social, and the intellectual stages. The first stage (physical) was represented by "an expression of an abundant organic energy." The second stage (social) included "the influence of social stimuli," in which children asked questions of others. In the third stage (intellectual), "Curiosity rises above the organic and the social planes and becomes intellectual in the degree in which it is transformed into interest in problems provoked by observation of things."[51] In *Democracy and Education*, Dewey again made repeated references to psychological growth. Dewey specifically outlined the "three fairly typical stages of growth" and how they related to subject matter. At the first stage, "knowledge exists as the content of intelligent ability-power to do." At the second stage, this knowledge is then "surcharged and deepened through communicated knowledge or information." At the third stage, "it is enlarged or worked over into rationally or logically organized material—that of one who relatively speaking is expert in the subject."⁵² Although Dewey continuously changed the descriptions and terminology for the psychological stages, he made repeated references to them in his pre-1916 writings.

Dewey not only believed the young child and savage to be psychologically-sociologically equivalent, but he believed that these child-like savage communities were still present on the Earth. For example, in a letter he wrote to Clara Mitchell in 1895 outlining his plan for his Laboratory School, Dewey explained how "child's interest in present forms of living" should "lead him back to social groups organized in that way [for example]—hunting and fishing to the Indians." Dewey continued, "This is geography as well as history because practically all stages of civilization are now presented somewhere on earth's surface [underline in original]."⁵³ Again in *School and Society*, Dewey argued that geography "presents the earth as the enduring home of the occupations of man."⁵⁴ In other words, like most of his contemporaries, Dewey suggested that native, primitive, and aboriginal societies did not merely represent different or alternative lifestyles, but instead they represented earlier forms of living that modern, civilized society had moved beyond in a linear scale of progress. As James Tufts explained in the 1908 *Ethics* textbook he coauthored with Dewey, "It is beyond question that the ancestors of modern civilized races lived under the general types of group life which will be outlined, and these types of their survivals are found among the great mass of peoples today."⁵⁵ That is, to Dewey and Tufts, the world was like a living museum of previous and current stages of sociological development, which could be arranged hierarchically along a single continuum from the primitive to the civilized. In the introduction to *Ethics*, the authors confirmed that the collaboration of the chapters were "in sufficient degree to make the book throughout a joint work"—confirming that Dewey shared the ethnocentric cultural beliefs expressed by Tufts.⁵⁶ These primitive groups, it was believed, had survived into the modern world and, thereby, provided a rare window into the earlier phases of Western civilization.⁵⁷

Dewey translated his ideas on cultural development into practical suggestions for dealing with racial diversity in classrooms and schools. Specifically, in 1903 he suggested that schools should encourage "the mixing people up with each other . . . by doing away with the barriers of caste, or class, or race, or type of experience that keep people from real communion with each other." For Dewey, schools helped students assimilate to democratic, scientific American life, which represented the highest form of sociological development. Accordingly, Dewey praised "The power of public schools to assimilate different races to our own institutions, through education given to younger generations." To address the concern of immigrant parents who may resent the acculturative function of U.S. schools because it denigrated their cultural heritage, Dewey proposed that schools could recognize the cultural elements of students' countries of origin by celebrating the "historic meaning in the industrial habits of the older generations—modes of spinning, weaving, metal working, etc. . . . [that were] disregarded in this country because there was no place for them in our industrial system."⁵⁸ When these abandoned occupations were appreciated in their own context as "historic," Dewey argued, family life would be enriched. Thus, we can see how Dewey considered the lifestyles of immigrant families as psychically equivalent, but sociologically deficient. That is, the immigrant societies were to be appreciated as prior steps toward the more advanced modern, scientific, democratic society of the United States, but not as culturally unique perspectives to be celebrated, valued, and maintained. Because Dewey equated culture with social occupations, all the societies of the world could be arranged hierarchically based upon the degree to which they had subordinated their environment.

In a 1903 essay, Dewey cited Jane Addams as a major influence on his thinking. Addams had worked closely with White immigrants in her famous settlement house Hull House in Chicago. In cooperation with several teachers from the Dewey School, Hull House had established a labor museum in 1900. The purpose of the museum mirrored the curriculum approach at the Dewey School because it focused on "old crafts," "primitive activities," "inherited resources," and "daily occupations" from the old world that had been abandoned and surpassed in the new world.[59] The objective of the museum was to build pride among the White immigrants by recognizing the historic contributions of everyday laborers, but also to demonstrate the seamless connection between the past and present. Consequently, immigrants who still engaged in these historical occupations such as weaving by hand would realize that their skills were no longer needed in the modern industrializing economy in their "historic" form. The message was that immigrants needed to modernize or be left behind. Addams believed that the recent immigrants with whom she worked represented an earlier, more primitive lifestyle. In *Democracy and Social Ethics*, she suggested that "[p]rimitive people, such as the South Italian peasants, are still in this stage . . . [w]e can all remember," in which "children long to be good with an intensity which they give to no other ambition." In accordance with the theory of recapitulation, Addams not only argued that Southern Italians represented an earlier sociological stage, but it was a stage that her fully developed civilized readers would recall from their own childhoods. Thus, the Southern Italian was the psychological-sociological equivalent of a civilized child. As Addams continued, "Their experiences in Italy have been those of simple outdoor activity, and their ideas have come directly to them from their struggle with Nature." In other words, Southern Italian adults were not only childish, but they were also in a primitive, natural state of development. As Addams explained, education ought to be child-centered by starting "with the experiences the child already has and to use his spontaneous and social activity," but then reoriented to the modern urban world.[60]

Addams's social theories applied only to the White immigrants with whom she was working. She had little to do or say about people of color. In fact, Addams's Hull House did not extend its services to Black migrants from the South. This unjust policy did not escape the eye of one of Addams's contemporaries, who commented, "The settlement seemed unwilling to come to grips with the 'Negro problem' in its own environs, yet Hull House was willing to be concerned with the same problem elsewhere in the city." Yet, the exclusion of Blacks was consistent with the attitude of most settlement house workers, who considered White immigrants capable of being developed for civilization, but African Americans as mostly unassimilable due to their backward nature. As one settlement house worker explained, Southern Blacks had been "savages themselves, utterly ignorant of civilization" and "held in subjugation even more degraded than the savage state of their ancestors."[61]

Like Addams, Dewey believed that many immigrant and non-White populations were sociologically deficient. However, his pragmatic view of race distinguished him from many of his peers. In particular, Dewey denied the philosophical notion—associated with Herbert Spencer and the social scientists of the nineteenth century—of latent biological potentials. That is, like William James, Dewey rejected the idea that certain individuals or societies had a latent potential to achieve or not achieve a certain level of intelligence or sociological development based on their biological makeup.[62] Pragmatism was the belief that knowledge was open-ended; it was constantly being refined and refashioned to meet the needs of newly discovered facts and new circumstances. Accordingly, Dewey's pre-1916 pragmatism was color-blind in the sense that one's level of development was not linked to skin color and biological background, because Dewey rejected the idea of unchanging essential types. Sociological level was a contingent outcome of people's interaction with a mediating social environment. Yet, for Dewey, these mediating social environments could be placed along a single sociological continuum leading from savagery to civilization, as outlined by leading nineteenth century anthropologists. For Dewey, White, Euro-American society just *happened to be* at the forefront of progress, but it did not necessarily need to be. History had just turned out that way.

Dewey used this contingent view of sociological progress to challenge some of the leading scholars and theories of his day. In particular, he offered three significant critiques of Spencer's philosophical notion of latent potentials, which was implicitly or explicitly present in many of pedagogical and sociological theories of the period. First, in his 1896 essay "Interpretation of Culture Epoch Theory," Dewey rejected the biological recapitulation theory—ontogeny recapitulates phylogeny—of Spencer, Ernst Haeckel, and G. Stanley Hall. He believed that the theory had been taken too literally as the unraveling of a biological potential inherent in the (presumably White) child. In its place, Dewey argued for an interactional recapitulation of the occupations and activities of the human race, not a retracing of its biological-anatomical instincts. Because all humans were psychically the same, Dewey insisted, all students had the potential to achieve civilization as long as they engaged in the linear reenactment of the processes underlying the sociological stages of the human race. Despite this significant divergence from the biological theory of recapitulation, Dewey stated clearly that he did "not question the fact of correspondence in a general way" between the psychological and sociological stages of development; rather, he questioned human development as the unraveling of a latent biological potential.[63] So, once again, Dewey's approach aligned the savage lifestyle with the young child, a view that reinforced the notion that adult savages were sociologically deficient.

Second, in his 1902 essay "Interpretation of the Savage Mind," Dewey attacked Spencer's notion of the savage as inchoate, lacking, and unformed. This important essay was specifically praised by William James and was cited by sociologists Albion Small, William I. Thomas, and Charles Ellwood as a justification for the psychic equivalence of the civilized and savage mind.[64] The traits of the savage, Dewey argued, "are outgrowths which have been entered decisively into further evolution, and as such form an integral part of the framework of present mental organization."[65] That is, the innovations of the savage were organically present in the occupations of contemporary civilization, not as steps that were discarded, but as stages of growth that were incorporated into the present civilized world. Dewey agreed with Addams that the savage had the potential to reach the sociological level of civilization, but did not reach this level because he was sociologically disadvantaged. Although the savage had made his *historic* contribution—much like the immigrant communities Dewey addressed in his 1903 essay—he no longer had anything to offer the civilized world. One has to assume that Dewey was speaking of savages past and present; that is, like his coauthor James Tufts, Dewey was referring to contemporaneous hunter-gatherer societies that had survived into the twentieth century. Despite Dewey's humanistic awarding of the savage with the potential to achieve the highest form of sociological progress, he nevertheless confirmed the view of savages as sociologically deficient when compared with the contemporaneous standards of the civilized world.

Finally, Dewey denied the significance of the transmission of acquired characteristics (neo-Lamarckianism) as a rationale for evolutionary racialism. He shared this view at the National Negro Conference in 1909. "It was for a long time the assumption . . . that acquired characteristics of heredity, in other words capacities which the individual acquired through his home life and training, modified the stock that was handed down," Dewey explained, "[but now] it is reasonably certain that the characteristics which the individual acquired are not transmissible."[66] Dewey's rejection of neo-Lamarckianism was supported by the empirical work of biologist August Weismann and the rediscovery of Mendelian genetics in 1900 (see Chapter 4). Both studies demonstrated that genes did not gradually blend or strengthen over time through acquired habits and traits.[67] As a result of this research, the doctrine of the transmission of acquired characteristics, which was a prerequisite for pre-Mendelian biological racism and the literal theory of anatomical recapitulation, had been empirically disproven. Drawing upon this research, Dewey concluded, "there is no inferior race, and the members of a race so-called should each have the same opportunities of social environment and personality as those of the more favored race." Dewey reasoned that the slight differences among the races were much smaller than the differences among the individuals within each race. Consequently, Dewey argued that the idea of dismissing individuals because of their race was an "injustice," and he insisted that all humans should have "a full, fair and free social opportunity."[68] However, Dewey's rejection of neo-Lamarckianism did not challenge the notion of the sociological deficiency of non-White racial groups.

In summary, Dewey rejected the idea that one's skin color and/or biological makeup reflected a latent potential to achieve or not achieve a certain level of sociological growth. All humans had the potential to achieve the level of civilization, if given the opportunity. This position was consistent with his definition of culture, which he defined specifically for an entry in the *Cyclopedia of Education* in 1911. He defined culture as "the habit of mind which perceives and estimates all matters with reference to their bearing on social values and aims." Dewey suggested that culture was a way of approaching the world thoughtfully and reflectively by creating products and ideas that were valued by the entire society, not merely the elites. However, these products and ideas also had to contribute to the growth of the social environment. "In other words," Dewey asserted, "manual and industrial activities at once acquire a cultural value in education when they are appreciated in light of their social context, in their bearing upon social order and progress."[69] That is, culture was something one acted upon and with, not something one mentally acquired. It was generic, shared, and accessible to all; it was an evolving, but organic, holistic social activity. Above all, for Dewey, culture did not venerate the old; it had to contribute to the progress of "the new." Dewey insisted that his definition of culture appreciated the contingent nature of knowledge and denied that culture was the unraveling of a latent potential. He criticized Spencer's philosophical system because it "discounted . . . all individual contingencies, all accidents of time and place, personal surroundings and personal intercourse, new ideas from new contacts and new expansions of life."[70] Dewey's linear historicism, in contrast, recognized that there was no predetermined path toward an idealized sociological stage; instead, all useful knowledge was the result of contingent new ideas that furthered the social occupations of the race.

Although Dewey's definition of culture recognized the open-ended nature of emerging knowledge, it was entirely based upon the interaction of "new contacts," and "new expansions of life." As a result, allegedly old, historic, aboriginal, primitive, savage, and barbarian forms of life had nothing to contribute to progress, other than being studied as prior steps toward the present. For Dewey, culture was not a variety of all contingent outcomes, but only those outcomes on the vanguard that contributed to the progress of the entire human race. So, at this point he subscribed to the basic principle of unilinear development as inherent in the theory of recapitulation.

RECAPITULATION AND THE NEW EDUCATION

In 1900 anthropologist Alexander Francis Chamberlain eloquently expressed the romantic viewpoint of the early progressive educator. "Adults emphasize too much the gap between the wisdom of childhood and their own knowledge," he protested, "and exterminate the genius of the young by the school-machinery of the own invention." Such a vision could have come from the pen of Dewey or Parker because like these innovators, Chamberlain proposed a more child-centered curriculum and more humane school environment, one that allowed the children to "grow naturally" instead of being "swamped by the mass of adults around him." Chamberlain published his plea in a book called *Child: A Study in the Evolution of Man*. Written with the cooperation of G. Stanley Hall and "the authorities of the Bureau of American Ethnology," Chamberlain's study presented the most comprehensive treatment of similarities between the development of the child and the lifestyle of the savage to date.[71] Chamberlain's book further demonstrates the intimate relationship between the anthropological study of non-White societies, the child study movement, the theory of recapitulation, and the innovations of the new education.

Drawing upon the broad evolutionary schemes of Spencer, Darwin, Fiske, and Hall, Chamberlain presented a "study of the child in light of the literature on evolution, an attempt to record and, if possible, interpret some of the most interesting phenomena of human beings in the beginning in the individual and in the race." He dedicated an entire chapter to the "Periods of Childhood," in which he generated an exhaustive list of philosophers, biologists, zoologists, sociologists, and anthropologists who suggested development schemes for the individual and race. Chamberlain also noted objections and critiques to various schemes, but the overall message of the book was that there was some clear coordination between the psychological and sociological development of the White child and the non-White races of humankind, thus confirming the theory of recapitulation. Another chapter, entitled "The Child as Revealer of the Past," cited several studies pointing to the continuity between apes, savages, and Whites. For example, one study by Louis Robinson conducted on four-day-old babies had them grasp a stick and suspend themselves for ten-second intervals, which Robinson then used to prove that our ancestors must have been tree dwellers. Another study based on observations of Navaho children by R. W. Shufeldt concluded: "The native instincts of these American Indians are exhibited in their young at a wonderfully tender age; and in this particular they differ vastly from our own children at a corresponding time of life, and reared as they have been for ages, in a civilized environment."[72] In his chapter on "The Child and the Savage," Chamberlain catalogued numerous studies demonstrating the similarities in religious belief, psychical development, morals, cognitive development, memory, emotional response, language, and imagination between the White child and the non-White savage adult. Therefore, Chamberlain's opus demonstrated that, despite several issues that were open to interpretation and dispute, the theory of recapitulation had the backing of longstanding European philosophical traditions as well as the latest studies by the scientific community. Thus, constructing a curriculum based upon the coordination of the emerging instincts of the child and the stages of sociological development was not only pedagogically sound, but also scientifically necessary.

Leading progressive educators aimed their theories at educators eager for applications of the new psychology to teaching. Consequently, the instructional materials, textbooks, and curricula created at the turn of the twentieth century reflected the ethnocentric assumptions inherent in the theory of recapitulation.

These educational materials offered practical advice on how to coordinate the psychological stages of the child with the sociological stages of Western society. The American Herbartians were perhaps the biggest proponents of a recapitulation approach to curriculum, which they called the culture-epoch theory. As Charles McMurry stated clearly in *Elements of General Method*:

> The idea of culture epochs, as typical of the steps of progress of the race and also of the periods of growth in the child, offers a deep perspective into educational problems. In the progress of mankind from a primitive state of barbarism to the present state of culture in Europe and in the United States, there has been a succession of not very clearly defined stages.... A child's life up to the age of twenty is a sort of epitome of the world's history. Our present state of culture is a result of growth, and if a child is to appreciate society as it now is, he must grow into it out of the past by having travelled through the same stages it has traced.

McMurry gave an example of how the fictional text *Robinson Crusoe* best captured the interest of an eight-year-old because the book addressed "man's early struggle with the forces of nature."[73] Young children were believed to have an instinctual interest in Crusoe's story, because they too were at an age in which they were struggling to overcome nature. Dewey objected to the matching of literacy products such as *Robinson Crusoe* or the poem "Hiawatha" with certain historical epochs as practiced by the Herbartians. Instead, Dewey argued that young students should be engaging with the processes of the struggles with nature themselves, not just reading about these struggles in a book. Dewey was explicit in his divergence from Hall and the Herbartians on this point: "whatever may be the worth of study of savage life in general, and of the North American Indians in particular, why should that be approached circuitously through the medium of 'Hiawatha' instead of first hand?"[74] However, the difference between the Deweyan and Herbartian approaches was subtle. Dewey's suggested curriculum focused on the recapitulated "firsthand" processes of the past, while the Herbartians focused on the literary texts that best captured the spirit of each cultural epoch. Dewey and the Herbartians, however, had a lot more in common because they both sought to align the stages of psychological growth with the stages of sociological progress.

In science education, the nature-study movement, which endorsed students' firsthand interaction with the natural environment, was justified in part by the theory of recapitulation because educators believed that children learned in a hands-on manner much like savages. As Wilbur Samuel Jackman explained in his textbook on nature study for common schools, children "must repeat, in a measure, the experience of the race ... [because their] primitive notions are not less genuine to the children than they were to early man."[75] Similarly in art, the Great Chain of Being served as a framework for the entire curriculum. "With each geological or racial stage has been found the appropriate and progressive proofs of his perfecting of his arts, his language, and his religious culture," leading art educator John Ward Stimson explained. "Through Black, Brown, Copper,

Yellow and then Aryan (White) branches... [humankind] ever approaches more or more some self-perfecting ideal."[76] Through beautiful hand-drawn images, Stimson demonstrated numerous examples of primitive and contemporaneous premodern art to demonstrate the linear development of the White artistic sensibility through the ages.

Ms. Emily Rice, who later taught at the Dewey School, proposed several revised elementary curricula throughout the 1890s based upon "both the child's experiences and the related experiences of the race." One version published in 1903 started with "Making and furnishing playhouses; comparison with the life of primitive man" in first grade and "Weaving and cooking; comparisons with primitive life in the hunter and shepherd stages" in second grade. In another example, the curriculum at the Horace Mann School of Teachers College in New York also dedicated the first two years of study to primitive life, according to a write-up by Charles McMurry in 1903. The curriculum included "Occupations; the eskimos as one phase of primitive life" in second grade, and "Primitive life; ... the Indian of Canada, Algonquins and Iroquois, Cliff Dwellers and Pueblos, Robinson Crusoe" in third grade.[77] Furthermore, the National Society for the Study of Education dedicated its twenty-seventh yearbook to the latest developments in the social studies. It featured a sample elementary curriculum co-created by University of Chicago psychologist Charles Judd that also placed Neanderthal man, Neolithic man, Iroquois Indians, and Whites along a hierarchical continuum. "Neolithic man (as illustrated by the Iroquois) had far better shelter than Neanderthal man," the authors explained, "... with all their many good qualities, the Indians were not a very cleanly lot. ... Our modern houses and modern skyscrapers are ... as far superior to long houses of the Iroquois as these long houses were superior to the damp, dirty, smelly case of Neanderthal man."[78] Thus, Judd explicitly identified Iroquois life as the sociological equivalent of White prehistoric men and women.

In *Organic Education*, Harriet Maria Scott and Gertrude Buck described the experimental approach they implemented in Detroit, Michigan. The curriculum they enacted with their young children was based explicitly upon "typical periods of civilization." As Scott and Buck explained: "These periods have been chosen as satisfying the natural instinct and interests of children at certain stages in their development and seen to be consecutive in the lives of most children, as well as in the history of civilization." They diverged from the exact scheme of the Herbartian culture-epoch approach, but they still believed that the basis of the curriculum should be the coordination of children's instincts and the history of the human race. In particular, they thought that the German origin of the Herbartian approach was problematic because of its overtly Christian outlook and its focus on only the history of "one or two chosen peoples." In place of the race-specific narrative of the Herbartians, Scott and Buck suggested a more anthropologically informed history of the race tracing all of humankind through the stages of development. For second grade, they focused specifically on "Primitive Man: savagery and barbarianism, showing development of satisfaction of fundamental needs of food, clothing, shelter."[79] Like Dewey, they were careful to incorporate the arts and other key components of civilization throughout their curriculum, so they were far less dependent upon the strict sequence of the culture epochs than the Herbartians.

Others, however, adopted the Herbartian approach wholeheartedly. "The theory of Culture Epochs is suggestive," Catherine Isabel Dodd explained in her textbook for teachers, "and in a general way guides many teachers . . . in their selection of suitable subject matter for children." Dodd suggested that during the first two years of school, "the child is in the myth-making age, and its tastes must be gratified by fairy tales and stories of the struggles of primitive man."[80] Likewise, Katherine Elizabeth Dopp developed and published a Dewey-inspired series of textbooks based on recapitulation approach, including *The Place of Industries in Elementary Education*, *The Tree-Dwellers*, *The Early Cavemen*, *The Later Cavemen*, and *The Early Sea People*. As Dopp explained, "Since the experience of the race in industrial and social processes embodies better than any other experiences of mankind, those things which at the same time appeal to the whole nature of the child and furnish him the means of interpreting the complex processes about him, this experience has been made the groundwork of the present series."[81]

In 1903 article for journal *The Elementary School Teacher*, the official journal affiliated with the Dewey School, Dopp explained the importance of recognizing the "differences as well as the likeness in the attitudes of primitive man and the child." The savage had many weaknesses that would not be appropriate for the modern world such as his violent and antisocial tendencies, so certain qualitative revisions needed to be made to the historically arranged curriculum for it to be effective. As Dopp reminded her readers, "The real attitude of the savage, fortunately, is not a normal one in child-life today [sic]."[82] The focus of the teacher was to prevent arrested development in the child by using the sociological stages of development as a guide. However, Dopp admonished that one should not follow the historical sequence too strictly.

Other studies drawing upon child study and the new psychology made additional child-savage analogies. In an 1899 article on the value of play in the development of the child, educator Walter Schell explained, "The truth of evolution is illustrated in the growth of every individual, and the child reproduces the social history of the race in his play." In this self-proclaimed "progressive" journal, Schell pointed out how "Savage and inferior races have little capacity for play."[83] Furthermore, as Edwin Ashbury Kirkpatrick explained in his text *Genetic Psychology*, "The child and the savage resemble each other chiefly because they are both to a considerable extent undeveloped intellectually."[84] Similarly, as James Sully explained in his popular book, *Studies in Childhood*, "In the presence of a new object a savage behaves very much a child, he shapes a new name out of a familiar one," demonstrating that primitives and children shared the same instinctual responses to stimuli.[85] Such savage-child analogies were common in the literature on human development and child study in the 1890s and 1900s. "What we call the superstitious fear of the savage race thus finds its parallel in the fears of the child in its earliest years . . ." insisted Herbartian pedagogue, C. C. Van Liew. "Fetishism and idolatry are products of this epoch in the race"—activities in which "totem" groups, African Americans, and Native Americans were believed to engage.[86]

The striking thing about the pervasiveness of the theory of recapitulation in the education literature is how men and women, theorists and practitioners, Europeans and Americans, idealists and pragmatists all saw such promise in the scheme. Even those like Parker and Dewey who expressed hesitation about applying the theory too literally, never directly questioned its general principles. No one pointed to the inherent ethnocentrism in a pedagogical scheme that depicted non-White adults as the equivalent of White children.

****

For about two decades around the turn of the twentieth century, the theory of recapitulation represented a point of general consensus among educational reformers because it provided guidance for how to educate all students based on their race. Whether the racial characteristics of individuals were inherent or learned was largely irrelevant to those implementing the ideas of the new education at the ground level. However, over this period there was a gradual movement away from the strict biological and Germanic interpretations of the theory toward a looser, more anthropologically informed version. University of Chicago sociologist George Vincent stated one example of the loosening of the theory of recapitulation in his 1897 dissertation, *The Social Mind and Education*. In this work, Vincent expressed what was essentially Dewey's approach to the theory:

> The parallel between the development of the individual and that of the race . . . has been subjected to criticism. . . . Educationally the theory of parallel development is fruitful in suggestions, but it may easily be made the basis of artificial schemes, such as certain *doctrinaire* forms of the "Culture Epoch theory [italics in original]." . . . The real parallel is in the process, the progress from analysis to synthesis, and in the gradual development of fully self-conscious effort out of vaguely conscious effort.[87]

Vincent defended this position throughout the text, by pointing to the excesses of educators who interpret the theory of recapitulation too literally, instead of using the theory as a general basis for the curriculum. He argued that the historical processes themselves were more important than the content corresponding with each epoch. Despite this subtle refashioning of the theory, Vincent never doubted that savage groups represented an earlier psychological-sociological stage of development. It would be another two decades before leading scholars fully abandoned this belief.

CHAPTER 3

Reform

The theory of recapitulation went largely unchallenged in the years leading up to World War I; the theory was the leading lens through which scholars examined and explained racial difference. However, there was a subtle shift in emphasis between 1900 and 1916 from a belief in the biological-anatomical version of the theory toward the sociocultural version of the theory. That is, scholars began to shift emphasis from a belief in the innate and instinctual basis for the sociological deficiency of people of color and immigrants toward a belief in the learned or environmental basis of their sociological deficiency, even while maintaining the savage-barbarian-civilization hierarchy. This shift was underscored by concern for the social nature of the individual. Anxious about the closing of the American frontier expressed in Frederick Jackson Turner's famous 1893 address and the clustering of new immigrant groups in urban areas, scholars emphasized the social nature of existence. As professor of education Charles DeGarmo explained in 1907, "The growth of cities and the disappearance of the frontier have made non-social individualism detrimental to our further progress."[1] The American frontier could no longer serve as a place for immigrant groups to forge their American identity; immigrants were now moving to the very cities in which leading intellectuals also lived. As a result, the civilized and the allegedly barbarian and primitive immigrant groups would need to learn to live together. The progress of the nation demanded a reformed educational system that addressed the new social nature of learning and existence.

Accordingly, leading educators of the 1900s and 1910s were obsessed with the social nature of education. Between 1895 and 1916, educators published dozens of books incorporating the latest findings of child study, the new psychology, and the new social sciences with the term *social* in the title. This shift from the individual to the collective nature of learning reflected the philosophical shift from static essences to contingent interaction described in Chapter 1. The language of the period captured this turn. For example, John Dewey based his innovative curriculum at the University of Chicago Laboratory School (1896–1904) on the idea of *social* occupations. After the publication of the influential 1916 NEA report, most schools began referring to history and social sciences as the *social* studies. And virtually every educator of the time agreed that the major function of public education was to maximize *social* efficiency, although scholars used this term in a variety of ways. As the new education gained momentum and popularity, it reinforced the messages of racial hierarchy inherent in its ideological origins. This chapter focuses on how the theory of recapitulation impacted the teaching practices and materials of the American classroom, while simultaneously reflecting the subtle shift from the anatomical-biological version of the theory expressed by G. Stanley Hall toward the sociological-cultural version espoused by Dewey.

EXPERIMENTS IN THE NEW EDUCATION

Perhaps no period captures the imagination of educational historians and theorists more than the burgeoning days of John Dewey's Laboratory School at the University of Chicago. At this experimental school, Dewey and his teachers implemented an iconoclastic, progressive curriculum based on student interest, experiential learning, and an embryonic democratic community. The successes of the Dewey School have been examined and praised by numerous historians. Sidney Hook even called the Dewey School "the most important experimental venture in the whole history of American education."[2] In *School and Society*, Dewey explained the pedagogical significance of the modified recapitulation approach to curriculum that he enacted at the school. "We can trace and follow the progress of mankind in history, getting an insight also into the materials used and the mechanical principles involved," Dewey reasoned. "In connection with these occupations the historic development of man is recapitulated." Dewey argued that his approach aligned with the latest psychological and anthropological research on primitive societies. Dewey related how students "go on through imagination through the hunting to the semi-agricultural stage, through the nomadic to the settled agricultural stage."[3] Similarly, in *Ethical Principles Underlying Education*, Dewey insisted that "a study of still simpler forms of hunting, nomadic and agricultural life in the beginnings of civilization; a study of the effects of the introduction of iron, iron tools, and so forth, serves to reduce the existing complexity to its simple forms."[4] This approach was based upon the premise that historical content taught to students should be presented as immediate problems, which also happened to have historical and scientific significance. Dewey based his curriculum on what he dubbed *social occupations*, which were historically significant activities that aligned the emerging instincts of the child with sociological knowledge that fit each stage.

Dewey coordinated the psychological and sociological stages of man with one another, because he viewed the development of the human race as taking place in a similar manner as the development of the individual. As Dewey explained in his essay "Some Stages of Logical Thought," the stages he outlined represented "modes of thinking easily recognizable in the progress of both the race and individual."[5] In practice, at Dewey's University of Chicago laboratory school, this meant coordinating the earliest stages of psychological development with the savage stage of sociological development. The Dewey School curriculum was based in part upon the historical reenactment of the social progress of the human race leading from savagery to barbarism to civilization. Accordingly, the early years were based on primitive life. In fact, one of the first visitors to the Dewey School was initially struck by the savage-child analogy, complaining in racially overt language: "Their purpose for why we should inflame the minds of our little civilized Aryans with the ideal of a savage Indian life, I can't see."[6] As another early observer of the Dewey School described:

> [A teacher] directed me to a class in primitive life where children had spent some weeks in working out, with the aid of the teacher, what the earliest people must have done when they had no clothing, or food, or shelter, or means of defense. She told me how they had thought of a spear by fastening a stick between the split ends of a club; how they had made bowls out of clay, and discussed caves as the first homes, and skins as the first clothing. How they had moulded [sic] in clay their ideas of man and animals in those days, and had become so interested that they had begged to write a report on their work for a school paper.[7]

Two teachers at the Dewey School, writing about the industrial curriculum at the school, reported how they approached a topic as both historical and problem-based:

> The study of the hammer is a good example of what may be done in this line. It can be traced back from the tool in the boy's hand through various stages to the rock in the hand of the savage. Through such study the child unconsciously learns much of the history of the race.[8]

Yet another visitor to the Dewey School reported the significance of savage life for young students:

> The study of history is preceded by that of primitive culture. The children are told of the savages who dwelt in cave, hut, or wigwam. They are shown pictures and models in illustration, and questioned as to the natural resources upon which savages must depend. . . . In natural sequence there follows the industrial life of primitive Greece, of Rome, and of the United States.[9]

After students were introduced to the social occupation for each psychological and sociological stage, they eventually arrived at the modernist stage of civilization, which included the introduction of the techniques of the professional and/or expert. However, this content was to be taught sequentially in the same order that the human race had originally discovered it. As a result, the societies of non-White "primitive" societies (i.e., semi-agricultural, agricultural, nomadic) were approached as prior steps toward the sociological stage of the industrialized West. The "primitive peoples" to whom Dewey referred all happened to be represented by non-European, non-White societies.

In fact, students at the Dewey School were specifically led to reach these ethnocentric conclusions. As Dewey School teacher Lauren Runyon taught her students: "In getting land from the Indians the same methods were used that have prevailed through the ages when a people with a superior weapons and brains, in sufficient number, meet an inferior people." That is, according to Runyon, who was implementing Dewey's educational vision, members of more technologically advanced societies were not merely different, but comparatively superior to less advanced societies. In another sample activity from the Dewey School—reflecting the modified recapitulation scheme underlying the entire curriculum—students were instructed to "compare the American rivers with those of Africa, the Indians with the Negroes, and the degree of civilization of tribes in America with that of other peoples he has studied."[10] Through such comparisons, the Dewey School students were to arrive at the conclusion that modern, civilized society had surpassed the primitive Indian and African ones in a process of linear cultural development.

Furthermore, in *Schools of To-morrow*, published in 1915, Dewey and his daughter Evelyn depicted the curriculum of several innovation schools around the United States that implemented a similar recapitulation approach to that used by the Dewey School. For example, the Deweys wrote that at the Elementary School of the University of Missouri, "pupils study the history of shelter from the first beginnings with a cave or a brush thicket, through the tents of the wandering tribes and the Greek and Roman house, to the steel skyscraper of today." That is, they traced the industrial history of the Western world. In Chicago schools, the Deweys speculated, "The children are perhaps studying primitive methods of building houses, and on their sand table they build a brush house, a cave dwelling, a tree house, or an eskimo snow hut"—explicitly coordinating Native American "eskimos" with "primitive" child-like behavior. Likewise, as the Deweys explained, in Gary, Indiana, the student "learns to handle materials which lie at the foundations of civilization in much the same way that primitive people used them, because this way is suited to the degree of skill and understanding he has reached." Thus, in accordance with Dewey's educational approach, these schools had set up their curriculum to coordinate the psychological stages of child development with the sociological stages of the civilized world. In fact, in the conclusion, the Deweys reiterated, "When a child learns by doing he is reliving both physically and mentally some experience which had proved important to the human race; he goes through the same mental processes as those who originally did these things."[11] This was the subtle, common link that ran through all the schools the Deweys had studied.

One of the schools evaluated and praised in *Schools of To-morrow* was P.S. No. 26 in Indianapolis, Indiana, which was located in the "poor, crowded colored districts of the city and has only colored pupils." Appearing in a chapter on social settlements, the Deweys insisted that P.S. 26 was not an attempt to solve the race question. However, they later proclaimed that "the success of the experiment would mean a real step forward in solving the 'race question' and peculiar problems of any immigrant district as well." The grouping of newly arrived immigrants with African American students reaffirmed Dewey's conviction that racial disparity was a result of sociological, not biological, deficiency. This grouping also implied that, like recent immigrants, U.S. Blacks were not yet fully assimilated into modern society. Full acculturation required time because, like recent immigrants, African Americans were allegedly stuck in an earlier form of sociological development. The Deweys highlighted how the principal of P.S. 26 had done much to improve the sociological, intellectual, and physical environment of the students. Nevertheless, the Deweys recognized that "changes in social conditions must take place before" the "colored" inner-city inhabitants of Indianapolis could be "independent and prosperous."[12] They did not specify exactly what this meant.

The students at P.S. 26 were mostly being taught vocational content, in accordance with the Hampton-Tuskegee model. This knowledge would potentially allow them to transform their immediate environment and improve their economic condition, and move along the scale of sociological development, but the curriculum did not necessarily equip them to challenge and transform the broader political and social system that segregated and oppressed them. In fact, *Schools of To-morrow* received an enthusiastic review in the *Southern Workman*, the periodical of the Hampton Institute, in which the reviewer interpreted the Deweys' study of P.S. 26 as an endorsement for their own approach to educating Blacks.[13] This semi-endorsement has led some historians to be highly critical of Dewey's praise for P.S. 26 in light of his professed democratic vision.[14] However, if viewed in the broader content of his prewar pragmatism, Dewey's praise for P.S. 26 was consistent with his modified approach to the theory of recapitulation. For Dewey, education had to take place in a particular linear sequence that allowed students to best subordinate their social environment. If their social environment was deficient, they could only go so far because the students required a more advanced sociological stage to stimulate further development. In other words, the students of P.S. 26 could only be developed up to the present time, but if their present time was sociologically deficient—as a prior step in linear sociological-psychological development—and could not be mediated by a more advanced sociological stage, then the students could go no further. As a social center, the Deweys implied, the school needed to reflect the specific sociological stage of its community with all its deficiencies.

The curricula described in John and Evelyn Deweys' book, *Schools of To-morrow*, demonstrated that innovative schools in Indiana, Missouri, and Illinois had also, to some extent, set up their curricula as historical reenactments of the human race that traced sociological development from the primitive stage to the civilized stage.[15] This demonstrates that the theory of recapitulation had not only made a substantial impact on the rhetoric of the new education, but it also, to some degree, influenced classroom practice. *Schools of To-morrow* marked a key turning point in the transition from the new education to progressive education. The new education was characterized by high-profile local experiments such as the Dewey School and those schools documented in *Schools of To-morrow*. However, progressive education was a national movement aimed at transforming every school in the nation. To determine the extent to which the ethnocentrism inherent in the theory of recapitulation found its way into educational materials at the national level, we turn to three sources: the 1916 NEA Committee on Social

Studies report, which established and spread the idea of the social studies; the rise of the idea of *social efficiency*, which had a wide-ranging impact on the rhetoric of educational reform; and the content of children's literature and social studies textbooks. All of these efforts were specifically designed to bring the innovations of the new education to a national audience.

ORIGINS OF THE SOCIAL STUDIES

In the autumn of 1916, a team of educational surveyors visited a high school in Elyria, Ohio, described as "a fairly typical American community."[16] The school survey was one of dozens of studies conducted during the early part of the twentieth century by teams of educational experts. Local districts invited these researchers to collect and analyze quantitative and qualitative data on their curriculum and administration, after which they issued a series of recommendations on how to increase educational efficiency in their schools. During the visit to Elyria High School, one surveyor, Arthur Dunn, participated in an exchange with students that demonstrated to him everything that was wrong with the current state of history and civic education in America.

Dunn, who was the U.S. Bureau of Education specialist in civic education, entered a general history course of mostly high school freshmen. The course was the most popular social studies elective at Elyria High School; 95 percent of students took the course before they graduated. The class covered the entire history of the world in only one year. "Owing to the immediate amount of material to be covered," the teacher complained, "we give very inadequate treatment to the period from 1815 to the present. The plan followed is essentially that of the textbook."[17] The textbook to which the teacher referred was Philip Van Ness Myers's *A Short History of Medieval and Modern Times*. With the exception of few maps and several small portrait etchings of historical figures, Myers's book consisted of 422 pages of small-print text.

This particular day, the class was covering the barbarian invasion of Europe. Race and the savage-barbarian-civilization hierarchy were at the center of the discussion. Dunn dismissively described the scene as "entirely a memory lesson, and the pupils experienced great difficulty in remembering the names of the different invaders; and they did not seem to care." Unable to contain himself anymore, Dunn interjected and asked the class, "Why are you studying these barbarians?" After some reflection, a student responded, "Statesmen need to know because history repeats itself." Dunn replied, "But you are not a statesman. Why do *you* need to know [italics in original]?" After further reflection, another student responded, "To learn about the origin of our language; to learn about the development of civilization."[18] Dunn was not satisfied with this answer, either, and so he probed further. "How many of you read the newspapers?" he asked. "How many of you have seen the word Hun in the newspapers in connection with the great war in Europe?" There was no response. "Are any of you descended from the Huns, or

Saracens, or the Iberians, or Teutons, or other barbarians mentioned?" The students were silent and perplexed. Finally, one boy responded that he was "probably from the Teutons," but he was not sure.

Based on this exchange, Dunn concluded that "the work these pupils were doing in general history is a matter of uninteresting routine, with no direct value in the present processes of growth." Instead, in his report he suggested that Elyria adopt the recommendations of the NEA Committee on Social Studies report, which had recently been published. Dunn had served as the committee's secretary. Specifically, in accordance with the recommendations of the committee, Dunn insisted that "in the ninth year the course in general history should be dropped" and be replaced by a new Community Civics course that focused on "observation of the occupational activities of the community, the vocations of the children's parents, and those in which the children show conspicuous interest."[19] Dunn complained that the history curriculum he observed in Elyria High School had "no direct value in the present processes of growth." Dunn lifted the phrase "needs of present growth" directly from Dewey; the phrase appeared in one form or another nearly two dozen times in the social studies report. Dunn served as the secretary for the Commission on Social Studies, and had earlier served as a consultant for the schools of Indianapolis, Indiana. Many of the ideas he had helped implement in Indianapolis schools made their way into the 1916 social studies report.

Dunn wrote little about race, but the reader can infer some of his views from how and why he cited Dewey and the specific pedagogical recommendations he made. In his 1907 text *The Community and the Citizen*, Dunn declared that "no better preparation can be made" for the reading of his text than "a careful reading of Professor Dewey's 'Ethical Principles Underlying Education,' quoted in the preface, and 'The School and Society' by the same author."[20] In both of these texts, which drew upon his experimental curriculum at his Laboratory School, Dewey outlined his rationale for setting up the curriculum as a historical reenactment of the history of the human race. That is, Dewey outlined how and why children should retrace the history of the race from savagery to barbarianism to civilization.[21]

Drawing upon the ideas Dewey presented in these two works, Dunn expressed a similar linear view of sociological development. For example, in the *Community and the Citizen*, Dunn made reference to shortcomings of the "savage tribes" who put to death their sick. But "As men become civilized," Dunn assured his readers, civilized man learned to be more compassionate for the weak and helpless.[22] Dunn implemented these ideas into his recommendations for the Indianapolis public schools. He argued that the Indianapolis schools had not been doing an adequate job of making the content for civic education relevant to students, especially in the elementary grades. To reform the curriculum in light of Dewey's psychology and his revised theory of recapitulation, Dunn suggested the use of the book *Robinson Crusoe*, so students could identify with the "story of a single-handed struggle with nature, emphasizing by contrast our dependence upon community life." To underscore the contrast between the primitive and civilized sociological stages, Dunn suggested that the students should study the superiority of the social nature of "their own home life." After reading *Robinson Crusoe*, Dunn explained, students should study "Hiawatha's childhood . . . giving opportunity for a study of Indian family life and a comparison of it with their own home life and the life of Robinson Crusoe." Students should follow these activities by engaging "in clay work and basketry, making objects suggested by the story of Robinson Crusoe and Hiawatha"—not to learn from these primitive examples on their own terms, but rather to appreciate their *historic* significance and to understand how modern White society had advanced far beyond savagery by engaging in social and cooperative work.[23] Dunn believed that by comparing primitive and modern life, students would grow to see the advantages of industrialization and socialization. Therefore, the study of the sociological history of the entire human race, which Dewey advocated, served as the organizational scheme for the entire elementary curriculum Dunn recommended. The curriculum was meant to justify and idealize the industrializing modern economy and the students' place at the forefront of this process.

In 1913, the NEA appointed the Committee on Social Studies to update the history and social science curriculum in light of the expanding enrollments in U.S. public schools and the development of the new education. The social studies subcommittee was part of the larger reform project, the Commission on the Reorganization of Secondary Education, whose 1918 report would be known as the *Cardinal Principles*. The majority of the Committee on Social Studies was made up of educators, including school principals and education professors. However, the four most influential members of the report were Dewey, Dunn, Thomas Jesse Jones, and James Harvey Robinson. Dewey did not have any direct role in the committee, but his influence was crucial because his ideas allowed the views of the other three to align. These men were trained in the social sciences, not schools of education. Their perspectives were grounded in the latest research in their respective disciplines.

As explained in the previous chapter, Jones was a sociologist who had trained at Columbia University under Franklin Giddings. Jones's work with American Indians and African Americans at the Hampton Institute in Virginia provided him with firsthand experience at acculturating minority youth to modern society through a curriculum he dubbed "social studies." Dunn was also a sociologist who had studied under Albion Small and George Vincent at the University of Chicago, both disciples of Lester Frank Ward and colleagues of Dewey. James Harvey Robinson was an established historian who had served on the NEA's Committee of Ten. Early in his career, Robinson shared the humanist views outlined by historians in the Committee of Ten and Committee of Seven reports, which both suggested a four-year sequence of chronological history courses. However, his views about the utility of history evolved in the decades that followed. In a 1910 address to the NEA on the role of history in industrial education, Robinson introduced that idea that history teachers should not only present a disinterested account of the past, but they should also cultivate "enthusiasm for progress which always must come with a perception of the relation of the present to the past."[24] In *The New History*,

Robinson developed these ideas further, arguing that, if the subject were to be vital and relevant to a changing society, history would have to address economic and social issues and be tied more directly to present concerns. He shared these views with other "new" historians such as Frederick Jackson Turner, Carl Becker, and Charles Beard.

As demonstrated in the previous chapters, Robinson, Jones, Dewey, and Dunn were all recapitulationists, who believed that the lifestyles of people of color and certain White immigrants from Eastern and Central Europe represented earlier sociological steps toward Euro-American civilization. In addition, Robinson, Dunn, and Jones agreed on four major principles. First, they agreed that the present treatment of history and the social sciences did not reflect the emerging research base of the new psychology and new education. For the social scientists of the group, Dunn and Jones, this research base was positivist in nature and pointed toward a more efficient, rational society. Social problems were to be identified by experts and then corrected through scientifically implemented solutions. Such a curriculum was meant to instill confidence in students about the ability of experts, especially in municipalities, to conduct orderly rational change. Dunn and Jones believed that systematic reform was necessary to offset the erosion of social values brought on by industrialization and the immigration of Southern and Central Europeans. Robinson, on the other hand, held more pragmatic views of society. Along with his friend Dewey, Robinson viewed research as contingent, flexible, and responsive to the emerging demands of society. In *The New History*, Robinson depicted historical conclusions as relative and provisional. He believed in the power of historical knowledge to improve, not just control, the lives of all Americans.

Second, these men agreed that history and social science content should be made more relevant to adolescents. This impulse was inspired by the influx of immigrants and non-college-bound students into the high schools. This idea was also driven by the onset of World War I, which highlighted the need for knowledge about world events.

Third, they agreed that stronger connections needed to be made between the social sciences and history both to accommodate the growing interest in social sciences in schools, and also to make the curriculum more scientific and efficient.

Finally, like most progressive intellectuals, they recognized that the schools needed to reflect an ontological shift from the nineteenth-century emphasis on the autonomous individual to a concern for the collective, systemic web of social existence. All these ideas came together in the work of Dewey.[25]

Dewey believed that education was the evolutionary process by which civilization is preserved and carried forward. It provided the means by which society transmitted its accumulated, but constantly reassessed, experience to achieve "a more socialized value through the medium of increased individual efficiency." The continuous interplay between the individual, society, and disciplined knowledge is central to Dewey's philosophy. He sought to introduce factual content into children's lives in a manner that would have immediate significance and meaning to their social lives. In *The School and Society*, Dewey demanded that history be approached as an "indirect sociology." Its goal should not be to amass information, but instead "to use information in constructing a vivid picture of how and why men did thus and so achieved their successes and came to their failures." Although the early years should be directed toward reliving the race experience, Dewey argued, historical knowledge must ultimately arrive at "a more thorough and accurate knowledge of both the principles and facts of social life [providing] . . . preparation for later more specialized historical studies."[26]

Dewey's writings were quoted at crucial points in the Committee on Social Studies report. Dewey's call "to meet the needs of present growth" appeared as the ultimate goal of social studies education throughout the text; the term was employed in one form or another more than twenty times. For example, the goals of civics, the report explained, were designed "with reference to the pupil's immediate needs." Accordingly, the committee reported that historical topics should be selected "chiefly upon the degree to which such topic can be related to the present life interests of the pupil, or can be used by him in his present processes of growth."[27]

To address this issue of balancing preparation for college versus preparation for life, the committee again quoted Dewey directly, stating that "the needs of present growth . . . would also provide the best possible guarantee of the learning needed in the future [in college or elsewhere]."[28] The words within the brackets were added by the committee. Here, the committee used Dewey's words to argue that college preparation and life preparation were the same, because they both required intellectual growth, only they took place in different contexts. In a passage that the committee quoted from Dewey's *Ethical Principles Underlying Education*, Dewey argued that "history is vital or dead to the child according as it is, or is not, presented from the sociological standpoint." The Committee on Social Studies considered its recommended Community Civics course the embodiment of the "sociological standpoint," or the window through which historical content should be filtered. As the committee explained, "Community civics affords opportunity to use history to illuminate topics of immediate interest."[29] Dewey's concepts of "present needs of growth" and "indirect sociology" enabled the committee to reach a compromise between the precollegiate academic content of the Committees of Ten and Seven and the more utilitarian suggestions of the new educators.

The phrase "needs of present growth" was taken from the first chapter of Dewey's *Schools of To-morrow*, which was published only a year before the Committee on Social Studies issued its recommendations. The phrase was essentially a synonym for matching the content from the correct sociological stage with the accompanying psychological stage of the student. In other words, it was a way to draw upon the theory of recapitulation to determine the appropriate curriculum for all students based upon the characteristics of their race and developmental stage. Just a few years before Dunn had specifically suggested a curriculum based upon the theory of recapitulation for the immigrant students of Indianapolis, Jones had used the theory of recapitulation as the basis for his curriculum at the Hampton Institute, and Robinson had affirmed his belief in the validity of the theory in his book *The New History*. The impact of the Committee on Social Studies report was slow but substantial; by the 1930s, about a third of all schools had implemented its recommendations.[30] For the early and middle grades of the social studies curriculum, the theory of recapitulation dictated the specific content to use such as "Hiawatha" and *Robinson Crusoe*. However, for the older grades the theory had less immediate utility. Consequently, a new term was employed in reference to adolescent education, *social efficiency*. This term, which had heterogeneous meanings, was used with great frequency as a major objective of public schooling in the United States between 1895 and 1920.

SOCIAL EFFICIENCY

Curriculum historians have repeatedly suggested that *social efficiency* was the reigning ideology of the new, or progressive education, after the 1910s. There is some evidence for this. In fact, in addition to "needs of present growth," the Committee on Social Studies identified social efficiency as a major objective, writing, "the keynote of modern education is social efficiency and instruction in all subjects should contribute to this end."[31] However, historians have incorrectly traced the origins of the idea of *social efficiency* to scientific curriculum making and the business administrative techniques of Frederick Winslow Taylor, when, in fact, the term originated with the theory of recapitulation.[32] As discussed in Chapter 1, the first scholar to employ the term *social efficiency* in a substantial way was recapitulationist Benjamin Kidd in his book *Social Evolution*. For Kidd, the term was essentially a synonym for the civilized individual or society, although given Kidd's outspoken enthusiasm for imperialism, the term had racial overtones as well. As demonstrated earlier, Dewey employed the term *efficiency* as an educational goal in *School and Society*.

Many of those who first employed the term used it in a racial and developmental manner. For example, U.S. Senator Henry Cabot Lodge argued in 1896 that "there is a limit to the capacity of any race for assimilating and elevating an inferior race . . . of less social efficiency and less moral force." Similarly, in 1903 Frank Lester Ward applied the term *social efficiency* to his egalitarian view of race, writing that "the principle differences between races, peoples and nations are differences in the degree of social efficiency." In a 1902 book on imperialism, John A. Hobson criticized Kidd's racialized version of social efficiency, arguing that Kidd's phrase "signifies nothing more or less than capacity to beat other races, who, for their failure, are spoken of as 'lower.'"[33] One scholar, Ira W. Howerth, even linked the phrase specifically to the stages of sociological development, writing, "Social efficiency demands conformity of individual capacities and powers to a state of imperfection, to a division of labour determined by the stage of civilization." As Howerth further explained, "The social aim in education is the constant increase of social efficiency at such a rate as will produce the maximum development possible to the school period."[34] As demonstrated by these examples, the term *social efficiency* had multiple meanings from the start, although all agreed that White Euro-Americans were the most socially efficient race, and that social efficiency was a highly desirable trait that needed to be taught to all students. Social efficiency, at this point, essentially meant maximizing the rate of passage through the stages of development toward civilization.

The first scholar to use the term *social efficiency* in relation to education in a major way was William Bagley, educational psychologist at the University of Illinois, who introduced the term in the context of a nuanced discussion of the new psychology in his 1905 book *The Educative Process*. In the book, Bagley made several references to the social equivalence of children and savages. Bagley explained how both "children and savages possess" a "great abundance of energy," and how "children and savages are laymen" in making sound judgments. Throughout the text, Bagley used the term *primitive* to connote both the base instincts of the young child and the instincts of the premodern adult. For example, he explained how the "primitive art of hunting and warfare" of hunter-gatherer societies evolved into differentiated trades in "civilization." Elsewhere, citing G. Stanley Hall, Bagley explained how "primitive interests of early childhood" need to be reshaped for the higher purposes of civilization. Overall, Bagley's book included an extensive discussion of the findings of child study in which he concluded, "in no uncertain terms" that the "child at different levels of his growth has different needs and capacities that must be catered to in different ways."[35] Students would develop more efficiently if teachers approached the content of the curriculum in a way that matched the content with the inclinations of each psychological stage.

In *The Educative Process*, Bagley introduced the term *social efficiency* as "the standard by which the forces of education must select the experiences that are to be impressed upon the individual." He defined the term further to include three aspects. First, socially efficient individuals must not be "a drag upon society." Second, they must "interfere as little as possible with the efforts of others." Third, the socially efficient individual must lend "his energy consciously and persistently to that further differentiation and integration of social forces which is everywhere synonymous with progress."[36] When formulating his definition, Bagley cited Dewey's *School and Society*, Samuel Train Dutton's *Social Phases of Education in the School and the Home*, and the work of Michael Vincent O'Shea as major influences. All three scholars were to some degree recapitulationists, who drew heavily upon child study and the sociological history of the human race in their respective formulations.

Dutton's *Social Phases of Education* was a collection of essays and lectures, in which he addressed a wide range of educational topics. Although Dutton did not specifically use the term *social efficiency* in his book, he used the term *efficiency* eight times as a basic synonym for self-motivated and effective. He discussed how boys would "take pride in their own efficiency" and students should feel an obligation to "contribute to their own efficiency." At one point, Dutton specifically praised the work being done through the Hampton-Tuskegee model with "negroes and Indians," and suggested that scholars had much to learn from these endeavors. He confirmed the prevailing view of the time that "the only hope of elevating the Indian and African lies in a sort of industrial reformation." If this physical work had been so effective with "the heathen and the savage," Dutton pondered, then shouldn't such work be applied to the education of White children in public schools? Dutton concluded: "All this experience with criminals and with the savage races shows us that what science has taught concerning evolution and the development of species must be applied in education, before the evil nature will shake off the rudiments of barbarism which still cling to it."[37] Thus, Dutton's introduction of the term *efficiency* was at least tangentially related to racial hierarchy, the stages of sociological development, and the theory of recapitulation.

Michael O'Shea, however, stated his endorsement of the theory of recapitulation clearly. O'Shea was a professor of education at the University of Wisconsin. In his 1903 book *Education as Adjustment*, he drew upon the work of Dewey, Herbart, William Torrey Harris, James Mark Baldwin, and James Sully to conclude, "All evidence indicates that the individual's development is a kind of recapitulation of this racial course," because "analytic activity appears relatively late in the child and as it has appeared late in the race."[38] Again citing Dewey in *Dynamic Factors in Education*, published the next year, O'Shea reiterated the theory that "the child in his individual development recapitulates in his interest the industrial history of the race."[39] In both works, O'Shea pointed to "efficiency" as a major goal of schooling.

President of Harvard University Charles Eliot published *Education for Efficiency* in 1909, one of the earliest uses of the term by a major academic figure. For Eliot, education for efficiency meant "effective power for work and service during a healthy active life," and included three elements:, "improving the body ... imparting the habit of quick and concentrated attention [and] ... the motive power for some enthusiasm or devotion." Although he made passing reference to "national efficiency," Eliot's main concern was with the development of the individual; he even warned against efficiency that was too "materialistic" or "utilitarian." Significantly, Eliot confirmed his belief in the theory of recapitulation, writing, "For the savage or semi-civilized man, and for some children who pass through barbaric stages of development, authority is needed to restrain them from injuring themselves."[40] Thus, Eliot confirmed that savage and semi-civilized men and children were psychological-sociological equivalents.

By the 1900s, the term *social efficiency* was becoming more common in the educational discourse, and it was slowly losing its affiliation with the stages of child development. This can be seen in the work of Irving King, professor of education at Iowa State University. King was a former student of Dewey, and his first book, *The Psychology of Child Development*, included a robust introduction by his mentor. Dewey fully endorsed King's approach, which Dewey dubbed the "functional-genetic standpoint" to child psychology. In this study, King confirmed Dewey's pragmatic approach to the theory of recapitulation, that the psychological-sociological stages of man were contingent outcomes of history, not the unraveling of a latent potential. "That the individual passes through certain biologic stages should be regarded, not as proof of an evolution from a lower form," King insisted, "but rather as evidence as to what course of evolution has been, once granted that it is a fact." Like Dewey, King suggested that teachers should focus only on those stages of psychological-sociological development that had meaning in the present, and not necessarily lead students through each particular stage. As King explained, "We do not mean to say that the study of the backward reference in the child's life is not necessary, but that the value of such study for the teacher consists solely in applying it to the elucidation of its significance in the child's present experience." Nevertheless, King confirmed the underlying belief inherent in the theory of recapitulation that the child was the psychological-sociological equivalent of the savage adult and vice versa. The child's "mythmaking stage is not a result of his savage ancestry, but of the fact that he has an underdeveloped mind, and undeveloped minds have pretty definitive ways of reacting the world over, whether their possessors be children or savages."[41] In other words, even though the savage adult was not biologically or anatomically limited to that stage of development, nor was the child biologically determined to pass through the savage stage; the two were still equivalent because they were both "undeveloped," and they shared the same social deficiencies. Throughout the text, King depicted the maturation of children's abilities as an increase in their "efficiency," although he did not specifically use the term *social efficiency*.

In 1912 King published *Social Aspects of Education*, in which he used the term *social efficiency* several times. King described his study as a depiction of how schools "became more efficient as agencies of instruction as well as more effective promoters of social progress." For evidence, he drew upon "modern savage and barbarous societies" such as "southeast Australians" because "The efforts of present-day savage and barbarous peoples to instruct their children throw interesting light upon the social nature and social relations of educational agencies." King portrayed the lack of efficiency of people of color through the example of the "Pueblo boy" whose "lingering savage ideas and phlegmatic nature . . . go entirely unrebuked by their parents."[42] The very next year, Irving King published *Education for Social Efficiency* in which he again drew liberally upon the major assumptions of the theory of recapitulation. "Man to-day is not markedly different in intelligence from the man of ancient times," King explained, "nor even from the savage of the present day. He simply knows more." King again confirmed Dewey's view that all men are psychically equivalent; they differ only in their education and sociological level. "Savage peoples show astonishing degrees of kindliness, hospitality, truthfulness, and justice along with much that is unlovely if not abhorrent . . . [yet] the same traits appear in the most civilized races." However, King also spoke of "lower, less-developed races," confirming that non-White races tended to be, if not biologically, then at least sociologically deficient. Just as the Committee on Social Studies had done, King endorsed a history curriculum that focused less on "national and race prejudices" and more on material that was relevant to the daily lives of students.[43]

To Bagley, Dutton, O'Shea, and King (and perhaps Eliot) social efficiency was achieved through the application of the theory of recapitulation, because basing a curriculum upon the theory led to a more efficient and effective classroom. Instead of working *against* the instincts of children, the theory of recapitulation guaranteed that teachers were working *in accordance* with the instincts of children. In this way, more information and skills could be covered in less time. For example, Laura Runyon, who published an essay praising the Dewey School, began her description by declaring that "Dr. Dewey had discovered a way to abbreviate the amount of knowledge a child must have to be respectable, so that it could be learned in elementary grades."[44] In other words, Dewey had found a way to teach students in a more socially efficient way by aligning the stages of psychological development with the stages of sociological development. As a result, more content was covered. Furthermore, the history of the human race demonstrated that increased social efficiency of the individual and the race was achieved by making better use of education as a means of social progress. A teacher who applied the findings of the new psychology in an effective manner not only made the curriculum more humane and enjoyable for children, but also made it more efficient by covering more content in a shorter amount of time; socially efficient teaching also hastened the overall progress of the race.

The term *social efficiency* was not racially coded in the same way that the term *savage* was. However, the term was quickly absorbed into the racial discourse and a consensus was reached that differences in racial accomplishments could be attributed to differences in social efficiency. All these scholars agreed, and their examples demonstrated, that non-White societies did not merely have different social efficiencies appropriate for their own needs and contexts; rather, they had quantitatively and qualitatively inferior social efficiency when compared to the civilized White sociological stage. A society could be placed on a linear scale of development based upon its social efficiency. In this sense, the rise of the social efficiency idea was intimately related to the theory of recapitulation, although over time this connection became less significant.

Some scholars were not sure what to do about the theory. In *Methods of Teaching*, W. W. Charters, professor at the University of Missouri, made no textual references to the sociological and psychological stages of development, and he introduced the recapitulation approach to education only to dismiss it; his rejection of theory was unequivocal:

> The chief trouble with the culture epoch theory is while it is a pretty theory it will not work. It is impossible to find a class of children and find these stages standing out in any definite way. In a general way there may be some parallelism between the development of the race and the development of the child, but it is not sufficiently definite for the educator to use in building a course of study upon.[45]

However, the very next year in *Teaching the Common Branches*, W. W. Charters gave a lukewarm endorsement for the theory of recapitulation, writing, "as a source of suggestion for simplifying schoolwork and letting the children do primitive things, it has been illuminating and useful." In particular, Charters demonstrated how "primitive implements—stone hammers, skins, spears, bows and arrows, shells, spades, etc.", as implemented at the Dewey School and other experiments of the new education, "are of great use in the grades."[46] Charters thought that idea was useful for the early grades, but was less effective for older students. In 1923, Charters radically switched gears and published the book *Curriculum Construction*. The book consisted of overviews of the findings of 57 recently published empirical studies in a variety of subjects. Abandoning developmental psychology altogether, Charters declared that the content of the curriculum must be stated in terms both "of ideals and of activities." In order to determine the ideal activities for students, Charters suggested that various jobs needed to be analyzed in order to determine "the duties and information upon which special emphasis must be laid in the curriculum."[47] Thus, Charters framed his method in purely technocratic terms aligned with a narrow conception of social efficiency as utilitarian and vocational.

Because of their connections with intelligence testing and eugenics (see Chapters 4 and 6), the new proponents of the social efficiency approach to curriculum, such as Charters, are often depicted as racial determinists. However, these scholars rejected many of the ethnocentric first principles of their predecessors such as the sociological-psychological stages of humankind. Instead of viewing differences between Whites and people of color as degrees of sociological development, these new curriculum theorists considered racial differentiation the result of scientifically determined differences in intelligence. This new view was both a rejection of the inherent superiority of the White Euro-American sociological stages, while at the same time a return to the nineteenth-century idea of latent anatomical potentials. Paradoxically, the introduction of behavioral psychology and psychometrics into the education discourse both challenged the ethnocentrism inherent in the theory of recapitulation while at the same time reinforcing the scientific basis for racial inequality. Changes in the uses of the term *social efficiency* reflected this shift in emphasis from child development to social control. Although King and Bagley first used the term in relation to the stages of child development, by 1912 King and others were using it in relation to using the school as a sorting mechanism to engineer social progress (see Chapter 6). Either way, the term *social efficiency* endorsed using a curriculum differentiated by race.

RACE IN TEXTBOOKS

Although much of the discussion about the innovations of the Dewey School, social studies, and maximizing the social efficiency of the curriculum drew upon the latest developments in social and pedagogical theory, the textbooks from the period lagged far behind. Many textbooks absorbed the rhetorical and findings of the new social sciences, while others continued to convey the theories from the nineteenth century. Either way, textbooks unequivocally communicated messages about racial hierarchy to students, and many drew directly upon the theory of recapitulation to do so. In addition, popular children's literature of the day conveyed the same messages of social hierarchy and White supremacy as the work of leading educators and social scientists. For example, *Peter Pan* by James M. Barrie depicted the story of a boy who never grew up, essentially remaining in the barbarian stage forever. Peter Pan lived on the premodern Neverland island, inhabited by a group of young White male protagonists called the Lost Boys, barbarous pirates, and a tribe of Native American "redskin" antagonists—groups perceived to be at the same sociological-psychological level as children. "By all the unwritten laws of the savage warfare it is always the redskin who attacks, and with the wiliness of his race," Barrie explained in *Peter Pan*, conveying the racial stereotypes of his day; "he does so just before the dawn, at which time he knows the courage of the whites to be at its lowest ebb."[48] Similarly, Johann David Wyss's *The Swiss Family Robinson* related the story of a shipwrecked family having to remake their life on an island inhabited by savages. The book went through several revisions and editions; one 1885 edition edited specifically for schoolchildren conveyed an egalitarian view of the savage mind. "[A]mongst human beings, even those we call wild or savage are clever by nature, and possess minds which can be improved by instruction" the Swiss father explains to his son Fritz, "as plants are by cultivation and grafting."[49] Earlier versions of the story had no interaction with natives, so this aspect was added by subsequent editors to make the book relevant to a Western world obsessed with the mind of the savage.

As demonstrated above, educators such as Dunn repeatedly recommended that teachers specifically *Robinson Crusoe* by Daniel Defoe and "The Song of Hiawatha" with young students. These popular texts not only had literary value, but they were meant to convey to students what premodern life was like so they could compare and contrast it with the civilized world. Defoe's *Robinson Crusoe*, first published in 1719, related the adventures of a shipwrecked British sailor who confronts cannibalistic "Savages" on a Caribbean island. Stripped of civilization, Crusoe must work with what he has to rebuild his life in the wilderness. The protagonist eventually befriends one of the "Savages," names him Friday, teaches him English, and coverts him to Christianity.[50] Defoe's story reinforced the importance of Christianity as a counterweight to moral relativity, and it depicted the natives as non-White cannibals, who could only be redeemed by Whites. Similarly, Longfellow's epic poem offered a sympathetic and romantic view of the American Indian Hiawatha, who ultimately introduces and endorses Christianity for his people. Suggesting that a longing for Christianity was innate, Longfellow wrote: "That even in savage bosoms/ There are longings, yearnings, strivings/ For the good they comprehend not."[51] The message of these popular works for children was the same: Native Americans were child-like and sociologically deficient, and their only hope for redemption lied in adopting the civilized, Christian sociological stage of the Whites.

Beyond children's literature, the discipline most directly charged with addressing and explaining the racial diversity of the world was geography. The geography textbooks of the period reinforced the racial stereotypes children read about in fictional texts such as *Peter Pan, Robinson Crusoe, The Swiss Family Robinson*, and "Hiawatha." As leading African American scholar W.E.B. Du Bois sardonically reflected in *Dusk of Dawn*, "In the elementary school it came only in the matter of geography when the races of the world were pictured, Indians, Negroes and Chinese, by their most uncivilized and bizarre representations; whites by some kindly and distinguished-looking philanthropist."[52] Such images were designed to demonstrate not only the diversity of the world's societies, but also how these societies were hierarchically arranged from savage to barbarian to civilized. For example, Francis Appleton's *Elementary Geography* conveyed Morgan's classification system to students, with brief descriptions: "According to their degree of civilization, different nations are classed as Civilized, Half-Civilized, Barbarous or Savage." Appleton described the savage stage as "poorly clothed.... They are fierce and cruel and take delight in war." Describing the inhabitants of Africa, Appleton's text related, "Few white men have gone there to live. The people back from the coast are negroes, mostly ignorant and savage."[53] Alexis Everett Frye's *Elements of Geography* conveyed a similar message about the inhabitants of New Guinea:. "There are fertile lands in the island, but its black people are savages, and do not make much use of the rich soil."[54] The *Elementary Geography* text of Charles F. King included racial stereotypes such as, "Nearly all Indians, like savage people in general, are fond of war" and "Africa is noted for its great desert, it intense heat, and the many savage tribes that live there."[55] Henry J. Roddy's *Elementary Geography* asserted, "The great islands southeast of Asia are occupied by a branch of the yellow race.... This includes many savage tribes and some half civilized peoples."[56] Because nearly all Americans attended common schools by the 1890s, and geography was a key part of the curriculum, it is safe to assume that nearly every student at the turn of the twentieth century had a working definition of a *savage* as an undeveloped, bellicose, culturally deprived, backward person of color.

After getting this foundation in geography in the early grades, students would study history in the later grades. We have already seen the dismissive use of the term *savage* by James Harvey Robinson in Chapter 1; his textbooks were some of the most widely used of the period. However, Robinson never stated his racial views as clearly as David Saville Muzzey did. In his textbook *An American History*, by far the most widely adopted text in the United States around the time of the founding of the social studies, Muzzey espoused similar ethnocentric and racist views. He insisted that Native Americans "had generally reached a stage of development called 'lower barbarianism,' a stage of pottery making and rude agricultural science ... like the Mississippi negro of today." That is, both American Indians and Southern Blacks were stuck in an earlier form of development. At the end of the book, Muzzey specifically reflected on the "growing problem of relations to inferior races." He lamented how "we" [i.e., White Americans], have a "race problem" greater than any other nation, because "negroes" are "perhaps a century behind whites in civilization."[57]

Depicting the savagery and barbarianism of non-White societies was uncontroversial and required little subtlety. However, describing the cultural worth of the multiple White social groups and nations required more nuance. In one example, a textbook on citizenship written by Milton Bennion, dean of the School of Education at the University of Utah, continued to employ the Teutonic germ-theory narrative of Herbart Baxter Adams. "The political inheritance of modern Europe and America is derived mainly from three sources," Bennion argued: "Hebrew law, Roman law, and Teutonic customs and ideal of political life." American society was the final depository of these ideas. This view was echoed in popular world history textbooks such as Philip Van Ness Myers's in which the author explained how Christianity "has been the most potent factor in modern civilization." This text was the one used by the students in Dunn's study of Elyria, Ohio, described above. Myers depicted his Eurocentric world history as a dramatic competition among races. At the beginning of the Middle Ages, the "Celts were in front of the Teutons," and "the Slavs were in the rear of the Teutonic tribes," while "the Arabians were hidden in the desert" and "the Mongols and Turks were buried in central Asia." However, despite their initial limitations, the Teutons "had personal worth ... because of their free independent spirit, of their unbounded capacity for growth, for culture, for accomplishment, the future time became theirs." According to Myers, the Teutons were the only race of modernity and progress. The superiority of Northern European lifestyle was the direct result of these long-term historical developments.[58]

Some authors conveyed pedagogical theories about how lower races ought to learn. Bennion explained how citizenship required giving oneself over to the broader goals of the civilized, social world—an approach aligned with the social efficiency standpoint to education. Citizenship required "a subjection of bodily appetites and passions to the well-being of the present and future generations, and, in general a consecration of individual ability and effort to the permanent welfare of mankind." These appeals to physical, not merely intellectual, restraint must be understood in light of the racialist idea that certain immigrant groups exhibited unwanted instincts and impulses that they had acquired either through some form of the sociological "law of sympathy" or through neo-Lamarckian biological inheritance. As one curriculum reported, "In the first place while retaining some of the follies and stupidities of the savage, the Italians appear to have kept not a little of his virtues."Another curriculum explained how "various people of non-Aryan origin—Hungarians and Roumanians [sic] ... show their nomadic, Asiatic origin in their individualism, their quickness to adapt themselves to outside civilization."[59] Although they were part of the single history of humanity, Bennion argued, certain immigrant groups did not have the proper social inheritance, and so they needed to be brought up to speed. The most efficient means of doing this was not through the "the teaching of superficial and largely unproductive French and German," Bennion asserted, but rather by teaching civic behavior directly. They needed to be taught how to conduct themselves with a sense of responsibility and social consciousness. David Snedden, professor of education at Teachers College and leading advocate for using schools for social control, endorsed Bennion's text as the "best working textbook [on citizenship] of its kind." Snedden appreciated how the text, which had been tried with high school seniors and college freshmen for several years, addressed "contemporary problems of citizenship in their functional aspects."[60] Citizenship was not an abstraction, but rather a role that demanded concrete responses to emerging local and national problems. In essence, Bennion was teaching his students how to think and act with the self-restraint of the Teutons, the most civilized of all the races.

As we have seen, many scholars at the turn of the twentieth century hedged their positions by pointing to both the hereditary and social origins of racial differences. Textbook authors did the same. For example, in 1897 normal school professor Ellwood Kemp wrote a textbook on teaching history, in which he outlined his complicated position on the social and biological evolution of races. Both factors, he insisted, played an equal role. "I do not mean by historic forces," he explained, "merely forces which act between man and man, directly, . . . but also forces which act upon man, indirectly, as climate, soil, natural production, and the circumstances of physical nature." These forces had "etched their way into the skins of men and made some black, others white, and others yellow; made some jaw bones one shape, and some another." Kemp positioned himself as a moderate between those who exaggerated the accomplishments of the Teutonic race (that progress was purely biological or spiritual) and those who proposed that progress is a universal human endowment (purely environmental and learned). No progress can result, he explained, "without both the physical and the mental forces acting upon and within the community." Because the interaction of the biological with the physical world had created such racial inequalities, it would require both of these forces to overcome them.[61]

Ultimately, Kemp agreed with Bennion that civilization was the process of overcoming the limitations and restraints imposed by biological impulse, a view that leading social scientists of the period confirmed. As time passed, the forces of these racial limitations weakened their hold as the mind was liberated from them. As humankind became less and less dependent upon the environment and more the master of it, the difference between the races narrowed and diminished. The more humans internalized the social forces surrounding him, Kemp argued, the more liberated he became from his physical limitations. "[A]s paradoxical as it may seem," he explained, "the more these forces have asserted their rule, and the more he has wielded to their guidance, *the freer he has become* [italics in original]."[62] Kemp suggested that, with the help of Whites, the other races could slowly but surely free themselves from the biological, spiritual, and cultural restraints that held them back. Freedom for Kemp came through the submission of the individual to the larger social forces of civilization—one of the guiding ideas of social efficiency and the new education.[63] Kemp's theories were not buried in unread books and scholarly periodicals. As a normal school professor, he taught these ideas directly to future teachers.

A decade and a half later, Royal Dixon presented an alternative view. In his text *Americanization*, Dixon demanded reform in state and national laws to make naturalization an easier process. Unlike other reformers, he directly recognized the poor working conditions of many immigrants and insisted on improvements.

Furthermore, unlike Bennion, he did not suggest that foreigners had to suppress their native instincts in order to become American. On the contrary, he believed that the unique racial characteristics of each group had something to offer the nation. It was precisely this multiethnic background that gave American its uniqueness. "The poem of the Swiss, the Bulgar, the Armenian, the poem of the Russian Jew, the Scandinavian," Dixon argued, "each of these epic inheritances must contribute to the sentiment, the historical justification of our country."[64] The new America, he continued, would only be united when it transcended the Teutonic germ theory and instead rewrote its own history as the cumulative experience of all immigrant groups. As Dixon explained:

> That which is needed most of all for the welding together of the aesthetic-spiritual interests, which are the common interest of all the races, and hence the one line of pursuit for native and alien minds, is some educational system in the teaching of history which will do away with he accumulated, confusing mass of mere annual events from ancient to recent times, and will cut through all ages, as it were, in cross sections to trace, discover the evolution of America.[65]

Although the frontier thesis of Frederick Jackson Turner included the absorption of frontier immigrants, Turner's influential narrative did not address the recently arrived immigrants, who did not necessarily appear in the frontier version of American history. In contrast, Dixon proposed that the histories of each (White) ethnic group be traced through time for the artistic and spiritual contributions each one made.

Dixon's history was still Eurocentric, but it differed in its emphasis. First, it stressed the blending of all Western societies, not the mere adoption of the "civilized" Teutonic one. Second, it suggested that the native and the recently arrived foreigner were products of the same historical narrative of aesthetic-spiritual interest—what Dixon called "the epic American consciousness." His emphasis on the artistic achievements of the races, instead of their institutional and intellectual developments, made it easier to construct such a "welded" historical view. Third, Dixon explicitly objected to the kind of the narrowly conceived utilitarianism of Snedden and Bennion, but he agreed that schools needed to address citizenship directly. "By nourishing the spiritual consciousness of the American in this patriotic method," he argued, "the way lies open to training the political consciousness of the young man in such a manner that civics as a study would be no fruitless instruction."[66] In Dixon's view, Adams's Teutonic germ-theory narrative did not serve the purpose of instilling patriotism, especially because it glorified the Germans, who were now American enemies. On the other hand, the new patriotic world history, Dixon believed, would lead to improved racial relations between aliens and immigrants.

Despite their differences, Dixon's and Bennion's texts both demonstrate that there was agreement on the need for history to address citizenship more explicitly and to inspire patriotism, an idea espoused by the Committee on Social Studies report. For Bennion, this meant addressing the skills of citizenship directly and tracing the development of uniquely American institutions through the Adams's "germ-theory" narrative. For Dixon, this meant recasting history to include the multiple (White) immigrant groups into a grand narrative of aesthetic-spiritual evolution. In both cases, the history espoused by nineteenth-century historians was considered outdated and, perhaps, even counterproductive to the goals of enhancing patriotism and training citizens.

In practice, this new history blended elements of both Dixon's and Bennion's approaches. For example, Kate Upson Clark's textbook, *Teaching the Child Patriotism*, reverted to the biographical and biblical approach to history instruction by focusing on the traits and deeds of heroic Americans. "Washington's Farewell Address should be read often in every American Family," Clark argued, "and portions of it should be known by heart to every American child." However, beyond this she addressed more explicit elements of citizenship aimed at immigrants, including chapters on personal responsibility in politics, sacrificing for patriotism, patriotism and health, a patriot's manner and morals, and work as a vital part of patriotism. As she explained, "laziness,—the inherent aversion to work,—has been a chief obstacle to progress in all ages." Hard work was at the core of what it meant to be American. Although such a position would seemingly be utilitarian and anti-intellectual, Clark viewed the spiritual and intellectual elements of Americanization as equally important. In fact, like Dixon's, her book concluded by addressing the aesthetic-spiritual element of Americanism. "Science, Education, Culture, Economic Reform," Clark argued, "these are good and necessary things, but they are, each and all, only parts of the greater Gospel, and that is what we must teach our children." This was a direct attack on the secular, scientific brand of the new history that had entered American schools since the turn of the century. Such a history informed, but it did not inspire. In its place, Clark offered an atavistic brand of romanticism. She included a catalogue of relevant American and biblical stories, each meant to impart important moral lessons.[67] Educational policymakers supported the push for formal patriotism in the years prior to World War I. Numerous local agencies opened up night schools for immigrants, and dozens of states organized committees on Americanization and passed Americanization laws. For example, in 1915, the state of Michigan mandated that all eighth-graders "write from memory the first verse of the Star Spangled Banner and all the words to America," and in 1918 a Texas law demanded that teachers devote at least ten minutes of each school day to developing "intelligent patriotism."[68]

The logical place for teachers to address the race problem in the United States was in the recommended senior capstone class, the Problems of Democracy. The Committee on Social Studies specifically designed the Problems of Democracy course to address relevant and enduring social problems with high school students who were about to enter civil society. Its purpose was for high school seniors to explore contemporary social problems through interdisciplinary study. However, it did not specifically list the inequality of American Indians and Blacks as an issue or relevant topic to be covered. In fact, the 1916 report was completely silent on issues of race and racial inequality. However, some authors of textbooks used in the class did address race. Sociologists who authored many of texts used in the Problems of Democracy course generally subscribed to the same assumptions about race and sociological stages outlined earlier, and these ideas found their way into the textbooks used in social studies classrooms, including the Problems of Democracy course.[69] Because it took nearly a decade for authors to publish books specifically for the class, most schools used civics textbooks such as Howard Copeland Hill's *Community Life and Civic Problems* and Ray Oswald Hughes's *Community Civics* and sociology textbooks such as Charles Ellwood's *Sociology and Modern Social Problems* and Henry Reed Burch and S. Howard Patterson's *American Social Problems*.[70]

The most popular textbooks of the period included references to the biological and sociological deficiency of people of color. For example, Hill's civics text referenced how one of the chief causes of the "lack of progress among backwards peoples of the earth," such as Indians and Blacks, was their failure to overcome their immediate bodily needs.[71] Hughes's civics text included a section on the "Melting Pot" in which the author listed the problems of assimilating "the Yellow Man," the "Black Man," and the "Red Man." He explained how "Some Indians, especially the tribes now living in Oklahoma, have shown great capacity for progress in civilization." Yet other Indians, Hughes lamented, such as those who refused to wear collars and who continued to "live as they did a thousand years ago," will never be assimilated. He concluded that Native Americans had progressed the furthest toward civilization because "no one thinks of the race difference between them and the whites as he does between the whites and the yellow or black men."[72] Thus, Hughes reinforced a racial hierarchy of progress extending from Black to red to yellow to White. In addition, these books related, either directly or indirectly, the assumptions of the Dunning historiographical school by explaining how during Reconstruction, Blacks had demonstrated that they were not prepared for the responsibility of full citizenship because they were sociologically backward.

Charles Ellwood's sociology text devoted an entire chapter to "The Negro Problem," in which he asserted his belief that heredity played a bigger role in racial differentiation than many other scholars had acknowledged. "It is obvious," he insisted, ". . . that the Negro may, on the side of his instinctive and hereditary equipment, be inferior to the white man in his natural adaptiveness to a complex civilization."[73] Ellwood traced many of the undesirable traits Blacks allegedly possessed to their historic African and enslaved lifestyles. Thus, he argued that Blacks were not inherently inferior; they were just not a good fit with modern society, because their instincts had been formed under such different sociological conditions. Burch and Patterson's sociology texts also devoted a chapter specifically to the race problem. They reiterated Ellwood's view that "The natural selection of a tropical environment . . . has produced in the Negro qualities which cannot be overcome by a few centuries of civilization." The authors explained how the African slave's "moral ideals were low and their conception of family undeveloped," and how slavery, "hindered the development of [Black men's] independent manhood." As a result, Negroes were "childish" and characterized by "an unconscious exaggeration and untruthfulness." Ultimately, the authors of the textbooks commonly assigned in the Problems of Democracy course reinforced the conception of American Indians and African Americans as underdeveloped, childlike races in need of sociological-psychological development. These races were, in the words of Burch and Ellwood, "a natural people," who might "lapse into barbarism."[74] Not only did these authors lament the unfortunate political power provided to Blacks during Reconstruction, but they consistently praised the work that was being done through the Hampton-Tuskegee model. They supported the education being provided for African Americans, but doubted that Blacks would culturally progress toward civilization any time in the near future.

******

The Committee on Social Studies 1916 report, the idea of social efficiency, and the contents of textbooks and children's literature were not specifically about race, and they rarely addressed race directly. Nevertheless, these texts reflected and conveyed the hidden ethnocentric assumptions of the period. Although it would be an exaggeration to say that these authors deliberately sought to perpetuate racial inequality, their ideas did reflect and reinforce a set of assumptions about the inferiority of non-White races. These assumptions, in turn, created a context in which the social oppression and political disenfranchisement of people of color in the United States and abroad could be maintained into the near future. Even though the members of the Committee on Social Studies and the authors of social studies textbooks endorsed a curricular vision based on critical thinking, social problems, and relevance, they did not identify racial inequality as a major issue to be critically analyzed. In fact, most social scientists of the time agreed that the race problem, as it was called, was overwhelming and unsolvable in the short term, and they openly endorsed the Hampton-Tuskegee model. Discussions of social efficiency intermingled with discourses on imperialism and, as we shall see in the next chapter, anxieties about the feeble-minded and the immigration of allegedly inferior White races.

CHAPTER 4

Racism

Racism, according to historian George M. Frederickson, "is not merely an attitude or set of beliefs; it also expresses itself in the practices, institutions, and structures that a sense of deep difference justifies or validates."[1] As the twentieth century progressed, segregation of Southern society gained momentum under Jim Crow laws, legalized by the "separate but equal" policy endorsed by the 1896 Supreme Court decision *Plessy v. Ferguson*. The gap in pay between Black and White teachers doubled between 1870 and 1915, causing W.E.B. Du Bois to declare in 1911 that African American schools were worse than they had been 20 years ago. Racial segregation laws in the South extended beyond schools to trains, buses, restaurants, and other public facilities.[2] White and Black children were consciously and unconsciously socialized into a hierarchical world, where, according to one historian, "adult white southerners tried . . . to teach both black and white children to 'forget' any possible alternative to white supremacy."[3] In addition, many communities in the North began to segregate their schools when thousands of African Americans migrated to Northern cities. The failed experiences of educators in the Philippines and Hawaii provided further evidence for the perception that non-Whites were incapable of being civilized along the lines of Whites. The racist attitudes expressed by scientists, psychologists, and educators both drew upon and reinforced the Jim Crow laws that peaked just as the new education began to expand into a national movement.

For the final decades of the nineteenth century and first decades of the twentieth century, the theory of recapitulation was the leading lens through which to view the races of the world, and as such, the theory served as a justification for subjugation of people of color by Whites. As described earlier, there was a virtual consensus among social scientists and educators that non-White races represented earlier, abandoned sociological stages that Whites had surpassed. However, in the decades before World War I, the theory of recapitulation began to lose its appeal, because anthropologist Franz Boas and his associates challenged the validity of the theory (see Chapter 5), and biologists made major advances in understanding the mechanism of heredity. Specifically, scholars challenged and eventually overturned the theory of the transmission of acquired traits, or neo-Lamarckianism. As a result, educational psychologists began to reject the theory of recapitulation as a pedagogical and explanatory tool, and scholars began to make fewer references to the psychological-sociological stages of humankind. This development potentially could have been a positive step toward an egalitarian view of people of color. Unfortunately, most scholars simply replaced the ethnocentric framework of the theory of recapitulation with an even more racist framework of static racial types, intelligence testing, and eugenics aligned with the quantitative study of heredity. This chapter depicts the shift from the theory of recapitulation to heredity and eugenics and its impact on the racial views of leading scholars of the new education.

FROM NEO-LAMARCKIANISM TO EUGENICS

Neo-Lamarckianism refers to a resurgence in the 1890s in the belief, first expressed by Jean-Baptiste Lamarck in the early nineteenth century, that the physiological and mental traits a species acquired in its lifetime were passed on to offspring. In other words, if a giraffe stretched his neck in search of food and lengthened its neck over the course of its life, then this adaptation of the elongated neck was passed on to its offspring. Over time, the necks of all giraffes were lengthened by this process of passing on the acquired trait of the stretched neck. Likewise, if a race of humans became smarter by exerting their brains, their strengthened intelligence was passed on to their offspring. Over time, the brains of certain races were enlarged and strengthened by passing on the acquired trait of the exercised brain. The evolutionary ideas of Herbert Spencer were entirely based upon the transmission of characteristics acquired through adaptation to the environment, and even Darwin accepted that some acquired traits were transmitted.[4] The belief in neo-Lamarckianism was so pervasive in the nineteenth century that Carl Kelsey commented in 1916, "men no more thought questioning it than did those of earlier times question the revolution of the sun around the earth."[5] However, Darwin's great contribution to evolutionary theory was that the primary engine of evolution was not acquired characteristics, but actually natural selection. That is, there was a natural variation in any species and the individuals that just *happened* to have traits that were a better fit for the environment survived and passed on their traits to their offspring, while those with less useful traits died off. Neo-Lamarckianism suggested that the universe had a sense of purpose and direction, that the adaptations, advances, and acquisitions of an individual or race during its lifetime made a difference to its offspring, and that the biology of races could be changed relatively quickly via the transmission of acquired traits. In contrast, Darwinism suggested that the universe had no sense of purpose or direction, that advances and acquisitions of an individual in its lifetime made no difference to its offspring, and that the traits of races were relatively fixed in the short term. As Lester F. Ward explained, neo-Lamarckianism allowed a "race to develop through its own exertions," while Darwinism put races "completely at the mercy of a little known process of 'natural inheritance.'"[6]

At the turn of the twentieth century, neo-Lamarckianism began to lose its backing by biologists, and most scientists began to accept Darwinism as a mechanism for evolution. August Wiesmann was the leading Darwinian of the 1890s, and he engaged in high-profile academic disputes with the leading neo-Lamarckian, Herbert Spencer. Wiesmann had conducted numerous laboratory experiments such as cutting off the tails of mice and observing that their offspring did not inherit the acquired trait of the cut tail. Wiesmann's endorsement of Darwin's natural selection received an enormous boost with the rediscovery of Mendelian genetics by Hugo DeVries, Carl Correns, and Eric von Tshermak-Seynegg in 1900. Gregor Mendel's study of peas suggested that genes passed on their traits in whole, unmodified form; they did not blend with other genes or modify over the life of the individual, as neo-Lamarckianism suggested. As biologists accepted Mendelian genetics as a more likely explanation for evolution, some anthropologists and sociologists began to question the linear stage theory of cultural development as well.

By 1909 University of Chicago sociologist William I. Thomas confirmed that the inheritance of acquired characteristics was no longer believed to be true. "It should be observed that Spencer constantly assumes that the mind of the child is modified by the experiences and practices of his parents, whereas the weight of opinion at present time inclines to the view that nothing of this kind happens," Thomas explained. "The characters of the body and mind acquired by the body after birth are probably not inherited by the child." Because the anatomical theory of recapitulation of Haeckel and Hall was based largely upon the transmission of acquired characteristics, Thomas expressed his skepticism for the theory, although he did not dismiss it outright. Thomas essentially restated the position that his University of Chicago colleagues Dewey and Vincent had worked out a decade earlier—that the mind of the child and the savage are psychically the same, but sociologically different. Differences in race and sociological level were socially acquired, not linked to biological inheritance or acquisitions by ancestors. "We have every reason to think that the mind of the savage and the mind of the civilized are fundamentally alike," Thomas explained. "The savage is not a modern child, but one whose consciousness is not influenced by copies set in civilization."[7] The reference to "copies" connotes the sociological idea of *imitation* that exerted a large influence on social theory at the turn of the twentieth century.

Psychologist James Mark Baldwin (see Chapter 1) and French sociologist Gabriel Tarde were the two scholars credited with inventing the subfield of social psychology. Both figures had made "imitation" a central component of their respective schemes. In 1901, leading sociologist Charles Ellwood proclaimed that, of all the psychological and sociological theories, Tarde's imitation theory was the most "widely accepted and most in the public eye."[8] In fact, sociologist Franklin Giddings's law of sympathy (see Chapter 3) was based in part on the idea of imitation suggestion. Thomas confirmed that much racial differentiation could be attributed to imitation, not heredity. In a rare instance of recognizing the racial bias inherent in the theory of recapitulation, Thomas concluded: "The white child is not a savage, but one whose mind is not yet fully dominated by the white type of culture." Nevertheless, Thomas still recognized the "rough parallelism between the mental development of the child and the course of civilization."[9] Thus, by 1912, the biological-anatomical theory of recapitulation had lost much of its scientific backing, although the sociological-psychological aspects of the theory continued to linger.

At the beginning of the twentieth century, the door was opened for a new approach to race, one based on Dewey's idea of psychic unity and learned sociological and environmental difference. In fact, this is how University of Pennsylvania sociologist Carl Kelsey interpreted the rejection of neo-Lamarckianism. "[T]o realize that, no matter how bad the environment of this generation, the next is not injured provided that it be given favorable conditions," he explained, "is surely to have an optimistic view."[10] However, many scholars interpreted Mendelian genetics not as an argument for the biological similarities of races, but instead as an argument for the primacy of heredity over environment. They argued that Mendel's work proved that specific traits were linked to specific and immutable germs that were inherited at birth. The first major studies to call attention to the determinism of heredity actually predated the rediscovery of Mendelian genetics. Sir Francis Galton's *Hereditary Genius: An Inquiry into Laws and Consequences* was published in 1869, and Richard Dungdale published *The Jukes: A Study in Crime, Pauperism, Disease, and Heredity* in 1879. This was followed by numerous studies outlining the alleged threat that inferior heredity posed to Euro-American civilization. Karl Pearson, the groundbreaking statistician, published *National Life from the Standpoint of Science* in 1905. Charles Davenport, director of the Station for Experimental Evolution in Cold Spring Harbor on Long Island, published *Heredity in Relation to Eugenics* in 1911. H. H. Goddard, director of the Vineland Training School for the Feeble-Minded Girls and Boys in New Jersey, published *The Kallikak Family: A Study in the Heredity of Feeble-Mindedness* in 1912. Edward Ross, professor of sociology at the University of Wisconsin, published *The Old World in the New: The Significance of Past and Present Immigration to the American People* in 1914. Edwin Grant Conklin published *Heredity and Environment in the Development of Man* in 1915. Madison Grant published *The Passing of the Great Race* in 1916. Lothrop Stoddard published *The Rising Tide of Color against White World Supremacy* in 1920. William McDougal published *Is America Safe for Democracy?* in 1921.

Collectively, these writers were eugenicists. Galton invented the term *eugenics*, which he defined as "the science that deals with all the influences that improve the inborn qualities of a race."[11] Positive eugenics focused on enhancing socially desirable traits in a particular race; negative eugenics focused on removing destructive or degenerative traits from the general population. Leading eugenicists believed the following: first, that individual intelligence, disposition, behavior, and morality were largely the products of specific, inherited units or germs; second, individuals with bad heredity could make an exponentially detrimental impact on society over generations through the proliferation of their offspring by passing along the unmodified inherited germ; third, certain races of bad heredity could water down the gene pool of the entire population with undesirable traits over time, especially if they procreated faster than the superior races; fourth, the recent immigrant races from Eastern and Southern Europe tended to have lower intelligence and a higher likelihood of undesirable traits; fifth, political leaders had a moral responsibility to take action against the onslaught of inferior traits brought on by recent immigrants from less desirable areas. In 1909, Stanford University professor of education Ellwood Cubberley stated the eugenicist position clearly and succinctly. "These southern and eastern Europeans are of a very different type from the north Europeans who preceded them," he explained in his widely used textbook *Changing Conceptions of Education*. "Illiterate, docile, lacking in self-reliance and initiative, and not possessing the Anglo-Teutonic conceptions of law, order, and government, their coming has served to dilute tremendously our national stock, and to corrupt our civic life."[12] Through organizations and meetings such as the Eugenics Record Office, The Galton Society, the International Congress on Eugenics, The American Eugenics Society, and the Race Betterment Conferences, eugenicists exerted substantial influence on policymakers and public discourse on immigration.

Although eugenicists' theories rested on shallow, inconsistent, and even contradictory empirical grounds, their ideas gained a high degree of respectability in the schools. By 1914, 44 universities and colleges in the United States offered classes on eugenics, and by 1928, 326 offered courses on the topic.[13] In addition, the vast majority of high school and college science textbooks in the 1920s and 1930s legitimized eugenics and passed along its racist message to students.[14] Despite the effort to spread their message of race betterment through breeding, eugenicists were not terribly concerned with education because by the time the children with undesirable traits had reached school age, it was too late; they were already in the country and on the road to procreation and social assimilation. In 1913, Charles Davenport classified eugenics into eight categories: racial anthropology, genealogy, heredity, differential selection of mates, differential fecundity, differential survival, migration, and "culture of the innate traits, relations to eugenics of education, religion, and work for individual and social welfare."[15] Thus, education was only a subcomponent of the eugenicists' overall program. The ultimate objective of the eugenicists was the removal of inferior germs from the hereditary pool altogether. The most effective policies to accomplish this were the sterilization of problematic, feeble-minded individuals, and the limitation (or elimination) of the immigration of peoples from less desirable countries. The eugenicists were ultimately successful at achieving both. With the blessing of the U.S. Supreme Court—"Three generations of imbeciles are enough," wrote Chief Justice Oliver Wendell Holmes—tens of thousands of allegedly feeble-minded young adults were sterilized in the United States between the 1910s and the 1970s, and with the passage of the National Origins Act of 1924, the immigration of people of Eastern and Southern Europe was sharply curtailed.[16]

The efforts of eugenicists were supported by the new focus on multiple White races outlined by William Z. Ripley in his popular book, *The Races of Europe*, published in 1899. Ripley drew upon the latest work of anthropologists to dismiss the "absurdity of the misnomer Caucasian, as applied to the blue-eyed and fair-headed Aryan race of Western Europe." In place of the single European origin theory, Ripley suggested that Europeans were composed of three major racial groups: Teutonics, Alpines, and Mediterraneans. Ripley's racial distinctions were based on their cephalic index (the shape of their head), a metric, Ripley argued, that was "one of the best available tests of race known." His conclusions, he insisted, were based upon "strictly scientific canons." Ripley generally ignored the theory of recapitulation in his book, and there was little discussion of psychological-sociological stages of humankind. Nevertheless, he still placed Europeans at the top of a racial hierarchy, and identified Mediterranean Europeans as an "intermediate between the extreme primary types of the Asiatic and negro races respectfully."[17] Ripley's distinction among European types provided a useful language for eugenicists worried about the influx of immigrants who did not originate from the Teutonic stock. For example, Madison Grant employed Ripley's three-race classification system in his eugenicist call-to-arms, *The Passing of the Great Race*, and Carl C. Brigham used Ripley's races in *A Study of American Intelligence* in 1923.

Ripley's study was challenged by Kelly Miller, an African American professor and later dean at Howard University. Miller was an outspoken critic of segregation and racism. He challenged the irrational racism of Southerners and attributed the sociological deficiencies of the Black race to its historical circumstances and economic deprivation. He provided statistical evidence for the economic and social advances of the race, and he implored Whites to look to the best of the Black race to see what could be accomplished for the rest. As Miller explained:

> when reference is made to the Negro we are prone to think of a composite savage, and banish from the mind the superior man who has emerged from this dark and forbidden background. And yet it would be easy to isolate hundreds of thousands, if not millions, of Southern whites who in intelligence, thrift, and general respectability, would not rank above a corresponding number of Negroes that might be chosen.[18]

Miller argued that variation within each race exceeded the variation across races, yet he nevertheless equated the less educated of his race with the savage, and maintained an elitist attitude toward them. Miller resented the suggestion that the emergence of African Americans was dependent upon the cooperation and support of Whites. "The Negro is building up his own society based upon character, culture and the nice amenities of life," he explained, "and can find amble social satisfaction within the limits of its own race." Miller requested political and legal equality for his race, so that Whites and Blacks could "mingle in business and in public life."[19]

In a 1917 essay on eugenics, Miller feared that "the fifty thousand negroes belonging to the professional class" were reproducing more slowly than "the great bulk of the race," because the elites were putting off marriage until after they had established their professional careers. As a result, they were barely managing to maintain their own numbers, potentially leading to "the extinction of the higher element of the negro race." Miller attributed this low reproductive rate to a "sort of social captivity," in which the "educated negro" was "submerged in a white environment," and to the fact that there was no Black middle class from which to draw new professionals. However, rather than try to curtail the reproduction of the great mass of Black laborers, Miller suggested a more egalitarian solution: recruit more African Americans into the professional class from "the mass below." He concluded by calling for further study of eugenics and the Black race.[20]

Miller's short but fascinating essay on eugenics reveals that leading Black intellectuals did not necessarily view the eugenics movement as an ideological tool for White supremacy. W.E.B. Du Bois never commented on eugenics, and Miller clearly did not view the movement with hostility. In fact, Miller's solution of recruiting professionals from the laboring class to offset the elite's demographic erosion was democratic and consistent with his views on racial uplift. Eugenics did not necessarily have to lead to sterilization laws, immigration reform, and demographic labeling. Miller embraced the latest scientific findings, including eugenics and other contemporaneous theories that were ultimately used to justify White supremacy. He employed nineteenth-century notions of racial competition and struggle, but inverted them by emphasizing the demographic resiliency of his own race.

For example, in his 1914 book *Out of the House of Bondage*, Miller dismissed American Indians as "hopelessly incapable of comprehending the White man's ways of doing things and the reason thereof" because Indians lacked "the negro aptitude of mind." Miller employed further eugenicist language when he praised the rapid rise of the Negro race compared with the state of American Indians. "If the red Indian does not live, he cannot become civilized," he averred. "On the other hand, if the negro continues to live and multiply he cannot escape the happy lot." Miller mocked the White scholars who predicted that the "Negro would steadily disappear under the stress of Aryan competition and arrogance," because African Americans had in fact "doubled their number, under the strain and stress of conditions that would have caused almost any other of the weaker breeds of men to pine away and die." He boasted how the "negro outstrides the European element of our population in the natural rate of increase," and as a result, is "destined to inherit all of the accumulated and transmitted culture of the ages."[21] Embracing the social Darwinian metaphor of survival of the fittest, Miller underscored the thriving of his own race at the expense of others.

The Bureau of Education reported that in 1916–1918, seven times more White students attended high school than Black students.[22] The reason for this discrepancy was easily explained by the fact that Black students were believed by most Whites to be cognitively inferior, an idea that was well established by the latest quantitative assessment techniques. Prior to this consensus, very few scholars questioned the innate inferiority of Blacks. One rare exception was a study published in 1913 by Marion J. Mayo, *The Mental Capacity of the American Negro*, which compared the mental efficiency of White and Black students in integrated high schools in New York City. Mayo introduced his study with a lengthy discussion of how previous studies of race (such as Ripley's *Races of Europe*) had based their findings on pseudo-scientific study of non-White societies by anthropologists and the measurements of anatomical differences among races. However, modern science no longer put much faith in the validity of these studies because they focused on external factors. Because all the students in his study resided in New York, Mayo insisted that he was measuring "the influence of race heredity rather than . . . physical or social environment."[23] Mayo employed the highly subjective criteria of scores awarded to students in both races by teachers. Nevertheless, aware of the Ripley's multiple European race theory, he was careful to select White students of English, Germans, Irish, Italian, and Jewish descent. Mayo supplemented his findings with available data from other cities such as St. Louis, Nashville, and Memphis, demonstrating that Blacks required more time to complete the course of study than White students, which served as a justification for segregated schools.

Despite his problematic data, Mayo reported that the "the negro as a race is somewhat less variable in hereditary endowments than is the white race," but overall he found that "white pupils rank higher in every subject of study; but the difference in standing, though present in every instance, is numerically not very big." Mayo speculated that many Black students might have performed worse in English because they came from homes where poor English was spoken because "the taste of the colored pupils is more primitive." He also pointed to the inferior sociological and educational conditions provided for Black students, especially in the South. Ultimately, based on his data, Mayo reached a radical conclusion. "The fact of superior culture may be due solely to a difference in opportunity, and not at all to superior endowment," Mayo averred. "It is possible that a people may pass from barbarism to culture without increasing in the least its hereditary mental aptitude."[24] Mayo still employed the savagery-barbarism-culture hierarchy in his conclusion, despite his attempt to move beyond the anthropological assumptions that engendered the sociological scale. He also contrasted "barbarism" with "culture," implying that those in the barbaric sociological stage had no culture at all. Nevertheless, Mayo's research represented a rare instance in which quantitative data were employed to counter claims of the racial superiority of Whites.

Mayo's conclusions challenged the presiding racism of the period. However, Mayo's study was quickly eclipsed by the publication of Lewis Terman's more widely read *Measurement of Intelligence* in 1916. In the preface to the book, Stanford professor Ellwood Cubberley wrote that he considered Terman's study "one of the most significant books, viewed from the standpoint of the future of our educational theory and practice, that has been issued in years." Directed at "rank-and-file" teachers and school administrators, Terman's study reported his data on the administration of the Binet-Simon intelligence test on thousands on school children, including African Americans and American Indians. Based on his data, Terman identified a general "dullness" among the "Spanish-Indian and Mexican families of the Southwest and also among negroes," whose average mental age was allegedly three years lower than that of the average White. The dullness of these groups was so frequent, Terman continued, "that the whole question of racial differences in mental traits will have to be taken up anew by experimental methods." Providing yet another endorsement for the Hampton-Tuskegee model and educational segregation, Terman asserted, "Children of this group should be segregated in special classes and be given instruction which is concrete and practical." In case study of one Black boy with an IQ of 80, Terman predicted that the boy's mental capacity would never exceed the twelve-year-old level.[25] Race permeated the interpretation of all of Terman's data. White students who were "feeble-minded," Terman explained, scored "far enough below the actual average of intelligence among races of western European descent that they cannot make ordinary school progress."[26]

In contrast to Mayo (whose work was not cited), Terman's intelligence tests allegedly assessed academic potential, not academic achievement. Nevertheless, his data confirmed that those students whose parents came from Western European descent and who held professional positions consistently scored higher in intelligence than those students whose parents were of non–Northern European descent and of working-class background. Thus, his data justified the existing social order, but traced social inequality to innate and hereditary differences. Through books such as *The Intelligence of School Children* and *Intelligence Tests and School Reorganization*, Terman encouraged wider use of his tests in public schools to identify retarded and feeble-minded students and endorsed a policy of segregating such students into special classes.[27] In the 1920s, scholars published a flood of studies based on comparative intelligence testing among races, including Chinese Americans and Mexican Americans, reinforcing the view that people of color were cognitively inferior.[28]

Miller's and Mayo's refutations of Ripley's book received another damaging counterpunch in 1923 with the publication of Carl Brigham's study of nearly two million army recruits during World War I. Headed by Harvard University professor Robert Yerkes, the study of army recruits used the Binet-Simon intelligence test. H. H. Goddard had first employed the Binet-Simon exam in the United States in his studies of the feeble-minded and immigrants. With the input and cooperation of Goddard and professor of educational psychology at Teachers College Edward Thorndike, Yerkes served his nation by using the intelligence test to sort soldiers for appropriate roles in the war. Based on his study of recruits, Yerkes later concluded, "the mental age of the American born soldier is between thirteen and fourteen years" and the "soldier of foreign birth serving is less than twelve." Yerkes used the data to endorse eugenics and admonished readers not to "ignore the menace of race deterioration" suggested by his study.[29]

In *A Study of American Intelligence*, Brigham aligned the intelligence testing data with the language of Ripley's text on European races. Brigham included charts of the average intelligence levels of recruits from different national origins, and even included a chart outlining "tentative estimates of the proportion of Nordic, Alpine and Mediterranean blood of the European countries." Predictably, English, Scotch, and Germans topped the scale of intelligence, and the Russians, Italians,

Polish, and Blacks filled the bottom rungs. Journalist Walter Lippman and leading educators Dewey and Bagley (see Chapters 5 and 6) directly challenged the use and implications of intelligence testing. Nevertheless, by World War I, eugenicists had successfully replaced the psychological-sociological language of savagery-barbarism-civilization with the quantitative, hereditary language of innate differences in intelligence and heredity. Leading progressive educators such as Charles Judd, Michael O'Shea, and W. W. Charters—who were all previously advocates of the theory of recapitulation (see Chapters 2 and 3)—supported eugenics and even served on the Central Committee on Race Betterment.[30]

With genetic psychology and the theory of recapitulation on the wane as a framework for explaining racial difference, heredity and intelligence became more popular explanations in educational scholarship. In fact, by 1912, Dewey's former student Irving King, who once expressed enthusiasm for the pedagogical implications of Dewey's modified theory of recapitulation (see Chapter 3), now endorsed eugenics. In a discussion of race betterment through educational progress, King announced the rejection of neo-Lamarckianism and the adoption of Darwinism by scientists. "Such useful variations in the parent may be transmitted by heredity to the offspring," he explained. "Useful adaptations made by an individual in its own lifetime are not so transmitted." That is, as King explained, while parents' naturally occurring variations were passed on to their children, traits acquired by adaptation (i.e., through education) were not. Based on the new science of genetics, King called for "human improvement through conscious and wise preservation of useful variations in children." Citing the work of Goddard, he confirmed the fears of eugenicists that "mentally deficient classes furnish a large percentage of delinquents, paupers, and criminals." He argued that teachers should focus on the selection, promotion, and development of superior children, and they should encourage these children to have "healthy offspring, the only avenue by which his native endowments may be preserved to the race."[31] King's discussion of race betterment and social progress was littered with numerous references to the savage stage of psychological-sociological development, demonstrating how the language of the theory of recapitulation continued even after scholars began to question its validity.

William Carl Ruediger in his 1910 book *The Principles of Education* explained all that was at stake for educators with the dismissal of the neo-Lamarckianism. "Will John and Mary be inherently better scholars because their parents spent much of their time over books?" he asked. "Would they be inherently poorer scholars if these same parents had had no opportunity for study and had spent their lives in manual labour?" In other words, did education offer the potential to transform and uplift the biologically and socially disadvantaged? Although scholars were still debating the issue, Ruediger concluded, "The evidence so far adduced seems to point to that conclusion that such traits are not transmitted." He followed his discussion of acquired traits with one on eugenics in which he insisted that teachers "need not despair," because education could still make a difference, even if that difference was limited by native capacity. In addition to a discussion of eugenics, Ruediger's text contained an extensive discussion that traced the "steps from barbarism to civilization" of the Teutons.[32] As King, Ruediger, and others recognized, the rejection of neo-Lamarckianism was a significant turning point in educational theory; it had major implications for the classification and education of people of color. As a result, it was addressed directly by the leading thinkers in the field. However, scholars disagreed about the implications of the discovery.

G. STANLEY HALL AND WILLIAM BAGLEY

G. Stanley Hall was a neo-Lamarckian until his death because his anatomical theory of recapitulation required him to be one. As late as 1914, Hall insisted, "The central nervous system differs from all others in that it is par excellence the organ of registration or of physiological memory. It is there that traces of ancestral experience are stored." In other words, the mind was different from the rest of the body in its physiology, because it could pass on its biologically acquired traits. Hall aimed his comments specifically at Weismann and Pearson, who were challenging the principles behind the genetic transmission of acquired characteristics.[33] As one contemporary wrote, Hall endorsed an "extreme form of the theory that the growth of the mind of the individual recapitulates the mental history of its ancestors, and by his assumption that acquired mental characteristics are inherited."[34] Hall believed that the differentiated races of humankind were determined by both sociological and biological means. Most important, Hall insisted that all races of the world could be placed on a linear scale of psychological-sociological development. Yet, in Adolescence he argued for the preservation of "primitive peoples," because "Without knowing them and their ways, we cannot understand children, religion, or education, our own earlier history or that of our institutions." He endorsed the psychological study of these "vanishing races."[35]

Throughout his writings, Hall maintained that non-White groups represented an earlier version of White civilization—which, he argued, was precisely why they ought to be preserved. "[T]he Ancient Romans, the Germans of the days of Tacitus were barbarians, as were the residents of England in the period of Roman occupation," Hall reasoned, and so he asked, "What would the world be had they been exterminated or permanently crushed and enfeebled?" Hall's argument was that these non-White groups were once the psychological-sociological equivalent of White ancestors, and as such they may one day develop to be civilized, or perhaps even surpass the civilization of the Western world. He continued, "And many races that now seem doomed to extinction have as much promise of future development as these races did."[36] When Hall turned his attention to Southern Blacks, he even suggested that "The Negro has some excellent traits which the whites lack," including his rich emotional life, his cheerfulness, more intense religious nature, and a "keener and more sympathetic appreciation of nature." These traits made African Americans seem shallow and child-like, and closer in evolutionary time to humans' natural state. Nevertheless, Hall was advocating that the Southern Black lifestyle should be preserved, not destroyed, and he even suggested that a museum should be dedicated to the celebration of Blacks' contributions. In this sense, Hall was a proto-pluralist, although his assertion that Southern Blacks reconnect with their African roots "for some great advance in the future under leaders of its own blood and color" suggested that the time was not yet right for their political enfranchisement in the United States.[37] With this assertion, Hall essentially reinforced the White supremacy of the period.

Furthermore, in 1908 Hall delivered an impassioned plea in an article called "How Far Are the Principles of Education along Indigenous Lines Applicable to American Indians?" on behalf of respecting the sociological attributes of the American Indian. Most progressive educators never addressed the education of American Indians, so Hall was unique in his interest in this group. Hall argued for teaching Indian children in their own language so that it may be preserved, and he suggested that, while still working within the Hampton-Tuskegee model, Indians should maintain their traditional arts and crafts: "I do not object to some of our industrial arts for him, but I plead for the pious conservation of all that is good and that can be kept or restored of the old tribal life—its traditions, folklore, arts, industries, and above all its free, manly spirit." Despite Hall's plea for compassion and cultural respect for the Indian, he never questioned whether American Indian societies represented an earlier, sociologically deficient stage. As Hall emphatically charged, "It is the slaughter of the soul of a people, in this case probably the most noble of races living in this stage of development."[38] In other words, for Hall the Indians were not objectively or essentially noble by contemporaneous standards, but merely the noblest example of those living in the savage stage of development.

Hall's views on race were fully consistent with the anatomical theory of recapitulation, which he continued to espouse until his death. At the same time, his views were forward-thinking in his appreciation for the necessity of preserving sociological differences. He even criticized the curriculum of the Hampton-Tuskegee model, writing, "Even at Hampton and Carlisle, the last thing taught the Indian youths . . . is to know or respect the best things in their own history, culture or industries."[39] Thus, we can see the futility of trying to place Hall into neat categories such as racist or pluralist; he was both. He still believed in the inherent inferiority of people of color, a status that was caused by a combination of biological and sociological factors. Yet, he thought that non-White social groups ought to be preserved as a representation of earlier sociological forms and because certain aspects of their lifestyle such as native art and industries could actually be perceived as superior to the civilized world.

William Bagley's career began more than a decade after Hall's, so Bagley's position on race was far more complex because he followed the developments in biological and racial theory with an open mind. Bagley had far less invested in neo-Lamarckianism than Hall did. As a consequence, he equivocated on important issues related to race and culture. In an address delivered in 1908, Bagley greeted the challenge to neo-Lamarckianism with enthusiasm because he thought that the abandonment of the theory would shift emphasis upon education as the primary means of race improvement. "The principle, now almost conclusively established, that the characteristics acquired by an organism during its lifetime are not transmitted by heredity to its offspring, must certainly stand as the basic principle of education." However, Bagley also confirmed his belief in the sociological-psychological equivalent of the child and savage, writing, "the child of today, left to his own devices and operated upon in no way by the products of civilization, would develop into a savage indistinguishable in all significant qualities from other savages," apparently missing the connection between the theory of recapitulation and the transmission of acquired characteristics. Despite this inconsistency, Bagley established his position clearly that education and environment trumped heredity and race. Drawing upon the successes of the Japanese and Chinese, Bagley argued that "as far as race is concerned . . . all that is racially significant depends upon the influences that surround the young of the race during the formative years."[40]

In the first pages of *The Educative Process*, Bagley again asserted that biologists had recently grown skeptical of the transmission of acquired traits, asserting, "characteristics that are acquired during the life on an organism . . . are not transmitted through the germ cell to the offspring." Bagley did not address the social worth of non-White societies in his book, but he did dismiss the innate differences among White groups. In reference to physical traits, Bagley concluded: "When we compare man with other animals, we find that his tendency to variation is not particularly marked. Indeed it is safe to say that man is one of the least variable of all animal forms." Bagley argued on behalf of the primacy of culture as a driving factor in teaching and learning. "Races and nations are distinguished from one another by their ideals far more than by their inherent physical and mental peculiarities," he explained. "The German, the Celtic, the Slavic and the Romance ingredients become indistinguishable after two generations because their distinctive race or national ideals have been dropped and an American ideal has been assimilated."[41]

A few years later, when Bagley published *Educational Values*, he shifted position in light of the work on the significance of heredity by Edward Thorndike and Karl Pearson. Between the publication of these books, Bagley submitted and withdrew a manuscript to *Popular Science Monthly* because "the conclusions of such men as Thorndike and Pearson have led me very radically to modify the views I expressed in the paper."[42] In *Educational Values*, he now asserted that, "in so far as human conduct is governed in part by heredity influences and in part by experiential influences—we can speak of heredity and environment as the two large rubrics of 'conduct-controls.'" To account for the new research on heredity cited above, Bagley included a chapter on the "Limitations of Educative Forces" in which he asserted, "differences in mental capacity follow the same laws with regard to their inheritance as do variations in physical characteristics." Nevertheless, he refused to discount the significance of education. "There seems to be little doubt that the differences in mental capacity shown by different individuals must be attributed very largely to hereditary influences," Bagley concluded, but it "is not to be inferred from this that educative forces have no significant function in modifying human conduct." Combining his enthusiasm for the rejection of neo-Lamarckianism with his insistence that education, environment, and culture can make a significant difference despite heredity, Bagley again used the example of the Japanese and Chinese to improve their race via education and the adoption of Western ideals as evidence for his case. Bagley wrote:

> Witness, for example, the change that two generations of Western culture have wrought in the character of the Japanese people, and even more remarkable transformation which Western culture is working in China today. If natural selection ever had an opportunity permanently to fix race-characteristics, it certainly had that opportunity in China. . . . The improvement of the human race through breeding is doubtless a possibility, but opportunities for its improvement through education are still far from realized.[43]

Through this passage we can determine Bagley's complicated and perhaps even inconsistent position on heredity and race. He retained his belief in the psychological-sociological stages of humankind affiliated with the theory of recapitulation, but he rejected the transmission of acquired traits. He accepted the significance of heredity, yet rejected the eugenicists' claim that the best path to racial betterment was selective breeding. He maintained his faith in education and environment as the most efficient means of race betterment, yet he reinforced the ethnocentric belief that the redemption of non-White societies could only be accomplished by adopting Western ideals.

After World War I, Bagley shifted his position yet again. He now dismissed much of the quantitative work done on behalf of determining the degree of environmental and hereditary influence, and he severely criticized the idea of using intelligence tests to predict student success. He linked intelligence testing to determinism and again insisted on the power of education to trump the limitations of heredity. He attacked educational determinists at both the physiological and sociological level. At the physiological level, he reasoned that the "essential elements of the nervous system are emphatically *not* the stable and unchangeable structure that iris pigment and bones of the nose just as emphatically are [italics in original]." That is, the mind is not a collection of immutable inherited traits, in the same way that inherited physical traits such as eye color are. The mind is formed slowly through interaction with the environment. At the sociological level, Bagley asserted, "The great mistake of the determinist has been to confine his thinking to organic evolution. He forgets that with the dawn of mind new forces were let loose which transformed the entire character and course of progress."[44] Making an argument very similar to Dewey's, Bagley insisted that interaction with the environment makes a significant impact on the development of mind because the brain does not develop in a vacuum. Instead, the mind develops through social interaction.

In 1925, William Bagley collected his published critiques of these intelligence tests in a book entitled *Determinism in Education*. Bagley was careful not to dismiss the idea of differences in "native endowment." Nor did he question the possibility that these differences were to some degree tied to race. However, he refused to accept the deterministic assumption that intelligence was innate and fixed. He argued that "education plays a positive and indispensable role in the development of intelligence" and "education is (or can be) in some measure a 'leveling-up' process." Drawing upon his background in functional psychology, Bagley questioned the very definition of intelligence as something one has as opposed to something one does, and he insisted that it was impossible to separate innate intelligence from the acquired traits, cultural level, and educational history of the individual. Bagley specifically targeted the "fatalistic" thinking of Galton, Brigham, and Terman throughout his text to argue that intelligence tests were actually "measures of one's educational opportunity," not one's biological or cognitive potential.[45] The ideas expressed in the book essentially brought Bagley back to the environmentalist position he first expressed in 1908. The figure most significantly affiliated with the hereditary position on race was Edward Thorndike.

EDWARD THORNDIKE

In the late 1890s, Thorndike developed an innovative psychology that rejected the major building blocks of his field, such as the inheritance of acquired characteristics, imitation suggestion, the psychological-sociological stages of humankind, and the theory of recapitulation. His psychology both built upon and challenged the innovations of functional psychology of Dewey and James. Because he overturned the major concepts affiliated with the theory of recapitulation, one might think that Thorndike would open the door to a color-blind or even a pluralistic outlook on race and culture. However, the opposite occurred. Thorndike applied the quantitative techniques and absorbed the inegalitarian conclusions of the eugenicists. As a result, he ultimately became the most notorious and consistent proponent for the determinism of innate differences associated with new education.

Thorndike was first hired at Teachers College, Columbia University, in 1899 as a genetic psychologist to meet the rising student demand for classes in genetic psychology and child study. He was highly skeptical of the research upon which these subfields were based, especially the theory of recapitulation. After a careful and reasoned analysis, Thorndike rejected the theory of recapitulation outright in the first volume of his three-volume book *Educational Psychology*:

> On the whole the recapitulation theory in the case of mental traits seems to be an attractive speculation with no more truth behind it than the fact that when a repetition of phylogeny, abbreviated and modified, is a useful way of producing an individual, he may be produced in that way. In intellectual capacities the child of two years has passed all the stages previous to man. It is difficult to prove even one instinct in ten that occupies in his ontogeny the same relative position in time that it occupied in his phylogeny.... Consequently one cannot help thinking that the influence which it has exerted upon students of human nature is due, not to rationale claims, but to its rhetorical attractiveness.[46]

Furthermore, Thorndike reasoned:

> The notion that maturity is the main factor in the differences found amongst school children, so that grading and methods of teaching should be filled closely to "stage of growth" is also false. It is by no means very hard to find seven-year-olds who can do intellectual work at which one in twenty seventeen-year olds would fail.[47]

In the place of the theory of recapitulation, Thorndike proposed an innovative psychology based on his laboratory experiments on animals. When he studied under William James at Harvard University, he experimented on chickens in the basement of his mentor's house. He later expanded his studies to cats and monkeys to determine the origins of intelligence for all species. Based on these studies, Thorndike proposed that all learning could be reduced to two laws: exercise and effect. The first law suggested that the more frequently a response occurred, the greater the tendency for it to repeat. The second law suggested that responses resulting in pleasurable outcomes would likely become habit, and inversely those that had negative outcomes would be more likely to be stamped out. Instead of viewing learning as a reliving of the race experience, Thorndike viewed learning as the accumulation of stimulus-response bonds in life of the individual.

Thorndike is often contrasted with Dewey, his Columbia University colleague and fellow progressive educator. One historian even famously declared that the twentieth century was a battle between the educational ideas of Dewey and Thorndike; Thorndike won and Dewey lost.[48] Because Thorndike was the godfather of standardized testing that came to dominate educational policy at the end of the twentieth century, this statement is valid. However, it obscures the similarities between the two men, especially before World War I. First, both Dewey and Thorndike had immense respect for William James and traced their own approaches to his pragmatic ideas. James had great respect for Thorndike and Dewey as well, and he publicly and privately praised their work. Second, like James, both Dewey and Thorndike were functional psychologists who rejected the faculty psychology of the nineteenth century, as well as Wundt's methodology of introspection (examination of one's own mental life). Instead, both emphasized the psychological significance of experience and interaction, and the methodology of laboratory experimentation. For Dewey, the laboratory was the holistic, qualitative study of children in the context of the school; for Thorndike, it was the quantitative study of animals and children in his laboratory, where variables could be controlled and isolated. Third, both Dewey and Thorndike considered mental and physiological responses to be coterminous; mental life was shaped by physical interaction and vice versa. As Thorndike wrote in his famous empirical study disproving the validity of mental faculties, "The mind is . . . a machine for making particular reactions to particular situations. It works in great detail, adapting itself to special data of which it has had experience."[49] Learning was focused, interactive, and context-bound. Fourth, both men were Darwinians who believed all psychology originated in the inherited instincts of the species' past. As Thorndike wrote in 1909, "Darwin showed psychologists that the mind not only is, but had grown . . . and that the mind's present can be fully understood only in the light of the total past."⁵⁰ Fifth, they agreed that all activity and learning originated with the inherited instincts of the species' past, but these instincts were shaped by interaction with the environment. "The bequest of heredity are invested and made productive by the environment," Thorndike explained in a passage that could have come right from Dewey. "Instincts and capacities are modified and transformed by experience."⁵¹

Thorndike's emphasis on instincts is significant because it distinguished him from the extreme behaviorism of psychologist John Watson, with whom Thorndike is often associated. Neither Dewey nor Thorndike would ever agree with Watson's radical statement: "there is nothing from within to develop. If you start with a healthy body, the right number of fingers and toes, eyes, and a few elementary movements that are present at birth, you do not need anything else in the way of raw materials to make a man."⁵² For Dewey and Thorndike, instincts were the origins of all learning; learning was about habit formation via the interaction of inherited instincts with immediate problems in the environment. Finally, both scholars rejected neo-Lamarckianism. As Thorndike stated clearly in 1913, "The burden of evidence is thus against the transmission of acquired mental traits."⁵³

Despite these major areas of overlap, Dewey differed on two major issues: the determinism of heredity and the significance of social psychology. Dewey rejected the significance of heredity and individual difference, believing that all people were essentially born equal. Rejecting the idea of latent potentials, Dewey believed that differences among students were largely the result of experience and opportunity, not innate, hereditary, or racial differences. Thorndike, on the other hand, believed that individual difference was the major problem of education. As Thorndike wrote in *Principles of Teaching*, "the responses of children to any stimulus will not be invariable like the responses of atoms to hydrogen . . . but will vary with their individual capacities, interests, and previous experience."⁵⁴ In his groundbreaking study on fifty pairs of twins (fraternal and nonfraternal) in New York City, Thorndike concluded provocatively that differences in mental traits among individuals owe "nine tenths of their amount to original nature."⁵⁵ Dewey basically believed the reverse to be true. "That anything which may properly be called mind or intelligence is not an original possession," Dewey insisted in 1917 address to the APA, "but is a consequence of the manifestation of instinct under the conditions supplied by associated life in the family, the school, the market place and the forum."⁵⁶ Dewey's psychology was more social and holistic than Thorndike's mechanistic approach, and Dewey believed that all humans more or less inherited the same instincts. For Dewey, inherited race, gender, and ethnicity were largely irrelevant to one's acquired sociological level.

The second area of disagreement between Thorndike and Dewey was the significance of social psychology. For Thorndike, learning was driven by individual difference and was determined by the stimuli and responses experienced by the individual learner. For Dewey, the mind was social, and its development was dictated by the forms of associated living in which it was embedded. Addressing Thorndike directly in 1915, Dewey concluded that the "behaviorist movement ... radically simplifies the whole problem by making it clear that social institutions and arrangement, including the whole apparatus of tradition and transmission, represent simply the acquired transformation of original human endowments."[57] In other words, Thorndike correctly focused on interactions. However, by focusing solely on the relationship between stimuli and responses and reinforcements and punishments, Thorndike's psychology reduced the social world to only these immediate factors, without accounting for how these factors were mediated by the individual and permeated with the social inheritance of the race. For Dewey, the most significant factor in explaining the development of the mind was the interaction among different social ideas. Learning for the individual occurred "in connection with interaction with new elements in [the person's] surroundings."[58] For Dewey, real-world learning did not take place in a vacuum or scientific laboratory, as Thorndike suggested; it took place in a sociocultural context.

Thorndike's emphasis on the significance of hereditary and difference impacted his views of race immensely. In his discussion of racial difference in the third volume of *Educational Psychology*, Thorndike did not reference or draw upon the theory of recapitulation at all. He also made only a few passing references to the savage-barbarian-civilization hierarchy of sociological stages. Instead, he expounded his ideas about the significance of heredity and individual difference and how these factors manifested themselves in the different races. Thorndike did not dismiss the significance and importance of education and environment, but he thought that racial, hereditary, and individual traits significantly limited the impact of these other factors. As he explained:

> We may even expect that education will be doubly effective, once society recognizes the advantages given to some and denied to others by heredity. That men have different amounts of capacity does not imply any the less advantage from or need of wise investment. If it be true, for example, that the negro is by nature unintellectual and joyous, this does not imply that he may not be made more intelligent by wiser training. ... It does mean that we should be stupid to expect the same results from him that we should from an especially intellectual race like the Jews.[59]

Thorndike's depiction of the racial traits of Jews and African Americans were fairly typical of the period, but, unlike his contemporaries, he did not align these groups with a specific level of sociological achievement. Rather, these traits could be explained by inherited, innate differences. Thorndike's evidence for racial differences included ethnographic data from explorers and anthropologists who visited non-White communities around the globe. However, somewhat skeptical of the unscientific nature of these observations, Thorndike reinforced his assertions with quantitative data on the divergences among races on the performance of physical and mental tasks.

Summarizing a study conducted by Robert Woodworth on the mental traits of different races, Thorndike reported, "only 9 1/2 percent of the Negritos were as quick as the median white.... The Negritos also made many more errors.... The reputed Pygmies were still less capable than the Negritos." Thorndike continued, noting that the Pygmies performed worse on Woodworth's test than the "so called 'feebleminded' and 'higher grade imbeciles'" in state asylums. Based on this evidence, Thorndike concluded that "The most notable fact of the races of men seems to be their great mental variety," both within and across races. He resisted the conclusion that all the races could be ranked hierarchically, and he reasoned that the mental differences between races are relatively small (he estimated a standard deviation of less than 10). Yet these small differences in intellectual capacity compounded over time when slightly superior individuals interacted with others in their race, allowing one race "to progress in civilization much more rapidly than the other."[60]

Ultimately, Thorndike considered heredity to be the single most important factor in learning and social worth, because, as he reasoned, "stupid parents have stupid children, hot-tempered parents have hot-tempered children, and musical parents, musical children."[61] For this reason, he supported the use of intelligence testing to sort students, and he supported eugenicist efforts to curtail the immigration and reproduction of undesirable individuals. Writing in 1914, he pledged to inventory the mental traits of "Mexican immigrants of the last four years," and to investigate what the United States "has got from Italy, from Russia, from Scotland and Ireland; and what they are doing for America."[62] He participated in Robert Yerkes's intelligence testing of U.S. soldiers during World War I and stood by the conclusions of his colleagues. Yet, Thorndike questioned the scientific basis of some of the work being done on eugenics. In a review of Davenport's book *The Feebly Inhibited*, he wrote that he welcomed "the studies of the Eugenics Laboratory and appreciates the devotion that inspires them." But he was "left unconverted by each one." In particular, he rejected Davenport's notion that mental traits could be linked to a single germ, and instead insisted that "human mental traits are due to a number of determiners."[63] Overall, Thorndike was a supporter of public education for all children, but his deterministic views on race prevented him from reaching the kind of optimistic visions and conclusions of Dewey.

*****

The evolving and inconsistent racial views of Miller, Hall, Bagley, and Thorndike—as well as their divergent views on neo-Lamarckianism—demonstrate that intellectual history does not progress in tidy or linear ways. Hall continued to espouse his belief in neo-Lamarckianism and the theory of recapitulation, yet counterintuitively he was the most vocal White advocate of his generation for the preservation on non-White cultures, and the only major progressive educator to show any concern for the education of American Indians. Bagley greeted the rejection of neo-Lamarckianism with enthusiasm because it confirmed his belief in the significance of education as the driving force in race betterment. Yet, persuaded by the evidence of eugenicists, Bagley temporarily changed his mind on the primacy of nature over nurture for a few years, then changed it back after World War I. Thorndike, on the other hand, consistently viewed the rejection of neo-Lamarckianism as justification for the primacy of heredity over education.

As King, Ruediger, Miller, and Thorndike recognized, the rejection of neo-Lamarckianism was a significant turning point in educational theory; it had major implications for the classification and education of non-White and feeble-minded students. King and Ruediger viewed eugenics as a topic that could be addressed in schools, which could be used as a means of social control. Miller embraced eugenics enthusiastically to underscore to the resilience of his own race, at the expense of American Indians. The rapid demographic and cultural rise of African Americans demonstrated that neo-Lamarckianism was wrong, and that races could be improved quickly through economic liberation and exposure to civilization. Miller argued that improved educational, economic, and social opportunity would allow his race to flourish even more.

Between 1915 and 1925, most educators slowly replaced the hierarchical language of savagery-barbarianism-civilization with the allegedly more scientific, quantitative language of innate intelligence and heredity. In theory, intelligence testing was a less racist approach than the anthropological approach of placing savages past and present on a single sociological scale, because, potentially, non-Whites could have performed well on the intelligence tests, which could have disrupted the basic assumptions of the racial hierarchy (see Chapter 6). In fact, the facilitators of the intelligence tests argued that their instruments were assessing cognitive potential and ability, not cultural acquisition. However, in reality the intelligence tests were permeated with cultural bias, and so it was no surprise when Brigham's scale of racial intelligence placed the English and other Northern Europeans at the top and Blacks at the very bottom. Likewise, Thorndike's research confirmed that African Pygmies had the lowest intelligence of all racial groups, underscoring the belief that the savage Africans represented an earlier sociological stage.

Instead of merely being dismissed as sociologically deficient savages, by 1916 non-Whites were considered intellectually and innately inferior, providing further support for Jim Crow segregation. Even Bagley, who was a leading proponent for the power of education to overcome heredity, asserted in 1925 that "no one can seriously doubt the general superiority of the whites over the negroes in native intelligence."[64] Once again, the hierarchy of races that underscored White supremacy remained intact as one generation of scholars passed the torch to the next. Just as the architects of early progressive education inherited the racial views of their nineteenth-century predecessors, even while challenging their epistemological assumptions, so too did the positivistic, quantitative-minded generation of post–World War I scholars inherit the racial hierarchy of their professional antecedents. The methodological and philosophical assumptions of leading educators about racial hierarchy changed, but their conclusions did not.

CHAPTER 5

Relativity

At Harvard in 1890s W.E.B. Du Bois related how he was taught that there were "vast differences in the development of the superior and the 'lower' races; that this could be seen in the physical development of the Negro." He recalled visiting a museum and viewing a "series of skeletons arranged from a little monkey to a tall well-developed white man with a Negro barely outranking a chimpanzee." Later in the decade, White scholarship on race shifted from the anatomical inferiority of Blacks to the alleged inferiority of "brain weight and brain capacity, and last to the 'cephalic index.'" In Germany and the United States, leading scholars taught Du Bois that "Africa was left without culture and without history," and after the First World War "the new technique of psychological tests . . . put black folk absolutely beyond the possibility of civilization." Du Bois was struck by how quickly the scientific justifications for White supremacy changed. The early academic career of Du Bois coincided with the three major shifts in scientific rationalization for the inferiority of Blacks described in the previous chapters: their alleged anatomical inferiority, their cognitive inferiority, and finally their sociological inferiority. Du Bois originally accepted the scientific nature of this research, but soon began to view it with skepticism. Like Kelly Miller, Du Bois accepted "evolution and survival of the fittest, provided the interval between advanced and backward races was not made too impossible." However, he "balked" at the assertion that the gap between races was unbridgeable in the short term. Du Bois "began to see that the cultural equipment attributed to any people depended largely on who estimated it." In protest to the perspective reflected by this research, Du Bois ultimately concluded: "The eternal walls between races did not seem so stern and exclusive. I began to emphasize the cultural aspects of race."[1]

The greatest figure in introducing the relativistic and perspectival aspects of culture and race in the United States was German-born anthropologist Franz Boas. Boas suggested that cultures were dynamic, contingent, and relative to their particular history and location. In 1904, Boas boldly suggested that studying foreign and primitive cultures could "impress us with the relative value of all forms of culture, and thus serve as a check to an exaggerated validation of the standpoint of our own period."[2] Boas and his associates attacked the anthropological validity of the theory of recapitulation, challenged the inherent inferiority of people of color, and introduced a relativistic view of culture and race. They also employed their research to challenge the conclusions of eugenicists and racists.

In the final two chapters, I explore how the radical ideas of anthropologist Franz Boas and his associates made a limited impact on some progressive educators, but were ultimately rejected by most educators in favor of the more moderate stance on the sociological deficiency of non-Whites and immigrants. In this chapter, I outline the critiques of scientific racism, eugenics, and theories of sociological hierarchy espoused by Boas and his associates. I contrast the Boasian position of cultural relativity with the cultural pluralism of W.E.B. Du Bois, Carter Woodson, Horace Kallen, and Randolph Bourne, who approached race through a dynamic, interactional lens, but nevertheless viewed cultural pluralism as an idealized, final stage of sociological development. Drawing upon the ideas of the cultural pluralists, John Dewey revisited and revised his own views on race and culture during and after World War I, to a position very close to the cultural relativity of the Boasians. This chapter provides important context for the next, in which I demonstrate how leading progressive educators in the 1920s rejected the cultural relativity position of Dewey and the Boasians and maintained their belief in the sociological deficiency of people of color.

CULTURAL RELATIVITY

Boas and his associates Clark Wissler, Alexander A. Goldenweiser, A. L. Kroeber, and Margaret Mead professed four beliefs that refuted the theory of recapitulation and directly challenged the research of eugenicists. First, the Boasians believed that social groups should be viewed independently and approached through their own unique histories. Rather than place primitive societies upon a preexisting social hierarchy of predefined stages, each society ought to be approached on its own terms. Consequently, primitive societies were not necessarily less developed, inchoate versions of White society, but in most cases they reflected characteristics and behaviors as complex and developed as civilized ones. As early as 1887, after his ethnographic study of the Bella Coola Indians of the Pacific Northwest, Boas confirmed "the fact that civilizations are not something absolute, but that is relative, and that our ideas and conceptions are true only so far as our civilization goes." Boas reasoned, "The physiological and psychological state of the organism at a certain moment is a function of its whole history."[3] Societies, he reasoned, were manifestations of their own unique historic interactions.

Drawing upon his ethnographic work in early 1890s, Boas targeted the methodological rigor of the comparative method, which assumed that cultures around the world developed along a single linear path. The comparative method was the methodological justification for the theory of recapitulation, and Boas approached the orientation with skepticism. Although societies at the same level of culture appeared to be similar, Boas argued, in reality they arrived at their level of culture through different paths and reflected many different traits. "We no longer believe that the slight similarities between the cultures of Central America and of eastern Asia are sufficient and satisfactory proof of a historical connection," Boas insisted, "... because the general laws, although implied in such a description, cannot be clearly formulated nor their relative value appreciated without a thorough comparison of the manner in which they assert themselves in different cultures." Boas believed that the individual processes of sociological development were far more important than the content and comparative achievements of each society. He proposed that anthropologists abandon "the misleading principle of assuming connections wherever similarities of culture were found" and instead focus on "processes of growth [that] can be discovered by means of studies of cultures in small geographic area."[4] That is, instead of viewing social groups as developing along the global, linear scale of social progress as outlined by Spencer, Tylor, and Morgan, social groups ought to be studied as unique historical contingencies of particular times and locations. Similarly, in 1912 Boas's associate, Clark Wissler, insisted that "Culture is of great variety, and hence must result from activities that tend toward divergent and accidental ends.... Culture is essentially a social product, an accumulation, systematized in some manner."[5] The next year, Boas's former student Alexander Goldenweiser concluded based on his dissertation research, "All cultures are historical complexes ... that have originated within its own borders ... largely independent of its environment."[6] Elsewhere, Goldenweiser confirmed that similarities among social groups emerged from a "variety of origins and processes," not a universal set of sociological structures.[7]

Second, Boas and his associates believed that good fortune, environment, education, health, and social and economic structures played a much larger role in cultural development than biology, heredity, and anatomy, thus directly challenging the conclusions of leading eugenicists and racists. In the introduction to the 1911 text *The Mind of Primitive Man*, Boas directly questioned the assumption that "the white race [is] the highest type of man." He pointed out that none of the allegedly higher races could attribute its success solely to its own contributions, since each race borrowed ideas and technologies from others. The rise of some races at the expense of others, he explained, could be attributed to accident and "the laws of chance." After reviewing his previous work on the statistically insignificant anatomical differences between Whites and Blacks, Boas concluded that "the identity of cultural achievement and of mental ability is founded on an error of judgment ... the variations in cultural development can as well be explained by a consideration of the general course of historical events," not "material differences of mental faculty in different races." Boas did not suggest that the races and social groups in the present were, in fact, equal or that they should be treated as equals. Rather, like Dewey, Boas merely argued that there was nothing innately inferior about people of color, and that the higher races were superior for contingent, accidental, and historical reasons.

Furthermore, in a critical article on eugenics, Boas carefully reviewed the recent evidence on heredity, biology, sociology, and anthropology to argue that "the anthropologist and the biologist are at odds." Rather than denounce the methods of the eugenicists altogether, Boas simply suggested that environment, education, and hygiene played a much larger role in racial development than eugenicists wanted to admit. "[N]o amount of eugenic selection will overcome those social conditions by means of which have raised a poverty and disease-stricken proletariat," Boas averred, "which will be reborn from even the best stock, so long as the social conditions persist that remorselessly push human beings into helpless and hopeless misery." He ultimately concluded: "the social stimulus is infinitely more potent than the biological mechanism," but did not completely dismiss the impact of heredity on sociological level.[8] Despite his major objections to eugenics, Boas's overall tone was one of caution rather than outrage.

Third, Boas and his associates challenged the innate inferiority of non-Whites. In an address to the American Folklore Society that was later published in *Science* and the *Journal of American Folklore*, Boas challenged the view that there were any major psychic divergences among races. "When we compare civilized people of any race with uncivilized people of the same race, we do not find any anatomical differences which would justify us in assuming any fundamental differences in mental constitution," he argued, "[therefore] . . . we are not inclined to consider the mental organization of different races of man as differing in fundamental points. " Boas traced divergent racial characteristics to differences in individual education, nutrition, environment, and economic and social opportunity. Yet, because Boas was working with the ethnocentric data of his time and speaking to his ethnocentric peers, he could not deny that a "number of anatomical facts point to the conclusion that the races of Africa, Australia, and Melanesia are to a certain extent inferior to races of Asia, America, and Europe." However, speaking in statistical terms, he argued that the differences among the inferior and superior races were so small that they did not come close to exceeding the variation within each race, and these anatomical differences themselves could not adequately explain differences in sociological level. Therefore, Boas confirmed his radical conclusion that "manifestations of the human mind in various stages of culture may be due almost entirely to the form of individual experience which is determined by the geographical and social environment of the individual." Echoing Dewey's iconoclastic conclusion in his 1902 essay on the savage mind, Boas concluded: "the development of culture must not be confounded with the development of mind."[9]

In 1909, Boas applied his radical anthropological views specifically to eugenics and race problems in America. Addressing the new immigrants from Eastern and Southern Europe, Boas confirmed that there were distinct racial types reflecting real physiological differences. "There is no doubt that these people of eastern and southern Europe represent a physical type distinct from the physical type of northwestern Europe," he explained, "and it is clear, even to the most casual observer, that their present social standards differ fundamentally from our own." Boas carefully described the social standard of recent immigrants as "present," implying that their status was contingent and temporary, not permanent. At the time, Boas was working on an intensive research project tracing the changes in the head shapes and sizes of recent immigrants and their children. He attributed the differences between immigrants and their children to their interaction with a new environment, not to heredity and race. This research confirmed his belief in the plasticity of racial types, especially when groups were immersed in new surroundings.[10]

Finally, Boas and his associates refuted the assertion that non-White savages were the psychological-sociological equivalent of White children, which was a major justification for child-centered education. For example, Wissler asserted in a 1912 review of the work of James Mark Baldwin that "the most notable American anthropologists have repudiated genetic conceptions," such as "the recapitulation theory" or the idea "that ontogenesis and the phylogenesis of consciousness are quite identical."[11] More forcefully, Kroeber dismantled the core principles of the theory of recapitulation in his 1915 article "Eighteen Professions," in which Kroeber sought to detach anthropology from biology completely, a step that even Boas was not willing to take. Kroeber boldly asserted, "The absolute equality and identity of all human races and strains as carriers of civilization must be assumed by the historian. . . . All men are totally civilized." Kroeber's proclamation continued, "The so-called savage is no transition between the animal and the scientifically educated man," and, as such, "The estimation of the adult savage as similar to the modern European child is superficial and prevents his proper appreciation either biologically or historically." Finally, Kroeber insisted, "There are no social species or standard cultural types or stages."[12] Kroeber outlined the most radical version of the cultural relativity position affiliated with Boas and his associates.

The work of Boas, Goldenweiser, Kroeber, and Wissler was largely outside the purview of progressive educators, although it was recognized and cited by G. Stanley Hall, Harold Rugg, Charles, Ellwood, and Dewey (see Chapter 6). However, the scholar who most directly addressed the general public and the theories of emerging progressive education was Margaret Mead. In 1928, Mead published her bestselling book, *Coming of Age in Samoa*. Mead's study was the most widely read and empathetic depiction of a primitive, non-White culture to date, and it represented the fruition of Boas's relativistic approach to premodern cultures. Based on a year of ethnographic work on the island, Mead used her findings to weigh in on two scholarly debates at the center of progressive education: First, to what extent was the "stormy, turbulent, unlovely" stage of adolescence biologically derived, and to what extent was it socially acquired and constructed? Second, to what extent are racial and cultural attributes biological and to what extent were they socially acquired and constructed? Consistent with her former teacher, Boas, who wrote the foreword to the study, Mead concluded that education, development, and racial attributes were contingent and relative to its cultural context. Pitting herself directly against the biological perspective presented by G. Stanley Hall in *Adolescence* (see Chapters 1 and 4), Mead explained how, in contrast to Hall, "the anthropologist . . . grew to realize the tremendous role played in an individual's life by the social environment in which each is born and reared," and accepted the "determinism of culture, plasticity of human beings." Mead concluded that neither "race nor common humanity can be held responsible for many of the forms which even such basic human emotions as love and fear and anger take under different social conditions."[13] The final two chapters of *Coming of Age in Samoa* contrasted the education and acculturation of the Samoans with the modern, Western educational system, and suggested that the "storminess" of adolescent in the United States was a contingent product of Western culture, not an inevitable psychological stage.

By challenging Hall's theory that all humans progressed linearly through biologically determined global stages, Mead further undermined the biological theory of recapitulation, which had more or less been rejected as a legitimate biological theory by the 1920s. She also provided more evidence against the determinism of inherited racial instincts, thus pointing to the significance of environment and education in the formulation of humans. Mead wished to spread her egalitarian views on race to the general public and, to do so, took an immediate interest in public education. She attacked the use of intelligence testing in an article for *School and Society* and provided free lectures to teachers on non-White cultures, so that they might "step outside their own civilizations and view them objectively" as she had modeled in *Coming of Age in Samoa*.[14]

The position of Boas and his associates was well outside the mainstream thinking of most scholars prior to World War I, and it would not become fully absorbed in the field of anthropology until the 1930s. However, the relativistic ideas of the Boasians provided a sympathetic ideological context for the construction of a new pluralistic approach to culture and race that would help launch the cultural gifts education movement in the 1920s (see Chapter 6). Scholars such as W.E.B. Du Bois, Carter Woodson, Horace Kallen, and Randolph Bourne constructed a dynamic, relational approach to race and culture that served as an alternative to the overt racism of the eugenicists, but avoided the relativity of the Boasians.

CULTURAL PLURALISM

Pluralists believed that in the United States all social groups had made and would continue to make contributions to a pluralistic, transnational culture. W.E.B. Du Bois, Carter Woodson, Horace Kallen, and Randolph Bourne constructed the idea of cultural pluralism as an alternative to the notion that Northern Europeans had contributed everything that was good and beneficial to humanity and, therefore, all other social groups ought to assimilate to their ways. The pluralists shared an antagonism to eugenics and biological racism with the Boasian cultural relativists, but diverged from them in two fundamental ways. First, unlike the Boasians, pluralists maintained a belief in universal sociological stages and pointed to transnationalism as the final, highest stage of development. Second, the pluralists focused their discussion of culture on the contributions of the educated, urban elite of each marginalized group, but were dismissive of their agrarian, premodern populations. In other words, pluralists argued that immigrants ought to be proud of their cultural heritage, but they ought to maintain only those aspects that contributed to the progress of the transnational culture, and abandon those that did not.

The first scholar to suggest the position of cultural pluralism was W.E.B. Du Bois because in the 1890s, Du Bois authored two of the most important essays on race of the twentieth century, "The Conservation of Races" and "Of Our Spiritual Strivings" from *The Souls of Black Folk*. While incorporating many of the racialist arguments about the biological distinctions among races, Du Bois nevertheless constructed a dynamic, pluralist vision of racial identity. In the 1897 essay "The Conservation of Races," Du Bois accepted the conventional wisdom of the period that "human beings are divided into races . . . the whites, Negroes, possibly the yellow race," but he challenged the idea that these races could be arranged in a permanent hierarchy of cultures. Anticipating Boas's position years before he heard Boas speak, Du Bois insisted that anatomical similarities among the races far exceeded their differences, and that racial identity was largely a matter of common history and lifestyle. He defined race as "a vast family of human beings, generally of common blood and language, always of common history, traditions, impulses, who are both voluntarily and involuntarily striving together." Du Bois argued that "the advance guard" of the race must accept that their destiny "was not a servile imitation of Anglo-Saxon culture, but a stalwart originality which shall unswervingly follow Negro ideals."[15] Du Bois's rejection of assimilation to Anglo-Saxonism as an overt goal of racial uplift was unprecedented in American life in 1897, and the seeds of cultural pluralism can be traced to the ideas expressed in this essay. However, this vision put him in direct opposition to the Booker T. Washington and the Hampton-Tuskegee model. When Du Bois openly and unequivocally attacked the position of Washington in speeches and in his classic 1903 book *The Souls of Black Folk,* he earned a reputation as a radical.

In the opening chapter of *The Souls of Black Folk,* "Of Our Spiritual Strivings," Du Bois employed the term *double-consciousness* to describe the feeling he had of recognizing his own intrinsic worth while simultaneously internalizing how others perceived him as Negro—a perception "which yields [the Negro] no self-consciousness, but only lets him see himself through the revelation of the other world . . . this sense of always looking at one's self through the eyes of others, of measuring one's soul by the tape of a world that looks on in amused contempt and pity." He reiterated his position that Americans Blacks "would not bleach his Negro soul in a flood of white Americanism, for he knows that Negro blood has a message for the world."[16] These two essays outlined a new vision not only for the ideological liberation of African Americans, but for any minority group seeking to earn respect and acceptance by a dominant culture. He challenged cultural assimilation as an overt goal, and championed the cultural preservation of marginalized social groups at a time when very few were doing so.

Du Bois pointed the way toward a new approach to African and African American history, and he aligned a race's self-esteem with its sense of history. The scholar who pursued this idea to its fullest extent was Carter G. Woodson, the second African American historian after Du Bois to receive his doctoral degree from Harvard University. "If a race has no history, if it has no worth-while tradition," Woodson explained, "it becomes a negligible factor in the thought of the world, and it stands in danger of being exterminated."[17] Writing in 1919, Woodson criticized the current state of research on African Americans. He accused Northern history teachers of accepting "the southern white man's opinion of the Negro and endeavor[ing] to instill the same into the minds of their students." This practice, he reasoned, "has had the effect of promoting the increase of race prejudice to the extent that the North has become about as lawless as the South in the treatment of the Negro." Like Kelly Miller, Woodson argued that a better understanding of the African Americans would lead to a "wide degree of cooperation between the best elements of both races, to emphasize the best rather than the worst features of interracial relations."[18]

In 1915, Woodson founded the Association of Negro Life and History dedicated to the scientific study of its subject, and he established the *Journal of Negro History* in 1916 to disseminate some of this work. More significantly, he made education a central aim of his intellectual and social agenda. His most successful reform was the launching of Negro History Week in 1926, an effort that was not merely aimed at boosting the self-image of African American children, but also at challenging the racist assumptions of Whites. Woodson authored textbooks on African American history for college, high school, and elementary students that gained wide dissemination in Black schools in the 1920s and 1930s.

Alain Locke, who also graduated from Harvard, was the first African American Rhodes scholar selected for study at Oxford University. Locke allegedly first coined the term *cultural pluralism* in talks about dual identity with his Jewish friend Horace Kallen, while the two were undergraduates at Harvard. Like Boas and Du Bois, Locke rejected the biological basis of race, which he considered an "ethnic fiction" based on the "historical record of success or failure of an ethnic group." However, despite the fact that racial categories were socially constructed, Locke recognized that race had a real impact on socialization and self-identity because "modern systems are systems that require social assimilation."[19] Thus, Locke viewed ethnic identity as an inevitable outcome of living in a multiethnic nation such as the United States, yet he doubted the idea that American society really belonged to a monolithic Anglo-Saxon culture.

American Jewish intellectuals were at the forefront of the movement to challenge cultural assimilation. The anthropologists who formulated the position on cultural relativity, Boas and Goldenweiser, were Jewish, and the leading philosopher of cultural pluralism, Horace Kallen, was Jewish as well.[20] Drawing upon his discussions at Harvard with Locke, Kallen constructed a pluralist vision in his 1915 essay "Democracy Versus the Melting Pot." Kallen contrasted his views with the culturally aggressive imperialism of Russia and Germany because Kallen did not want to see America adopt the same policy of forced assimilation. Instead, Kallen suggested, "'American civilization' may come to mean the perfection of 'European civilization,' the waste, the squalor, and the distress of Europe being eliminated—a multiplicity in a unity, an orchestration of mankind . . . so in society each ethnic group is the natural instrument, its spirit and culture are its theme and melody, and the harmony and dissonances and the discords of them all make the symphony of civilization."²¹ Kallen's vision did not necessarily support racial egalitarianism and social mobility of all peoples. Rather, his vision suggested that all Americans should accept and celebrate their role and should play the metaphorical instrument they were given to the best of their ability. The acceptance of all types, Kallen argued, instead of the movement toward Anglo-Saxonism, is what made America's brand of civilization exceptional.

Kallen's cultural pluralism accepted that the characteristics of racial and ethnic types were fixed, but he wanted to remove these groups from a limited hierarchical view. In other words, he did not go as far as Boas and Du Bois had done in arguing that all cultures had something to teach one another. Instead, each contributed to a larger intercultural American society, which no single race or ethnicity owned. In a letter to Kallen, Dewey expressed his approval of Kallen's "Melting Pot" essay. "I quite agree with your orchestration idea," Dewey explained, "but upon condition we really get a symphony and not a lot of different instruments playing simultaneously. I never did care for the melting pot metaphor, but genuine assimilation to one another—not to Anglo-saxondom—seems to be essential to an America."²² Dewey rejected the idea of the White Protestant as the archetype of culture, but he did not yet fully commit to the pluralist view, even though he did move beyond Kallen in recommending cultural "assimilation to one another." Instead, Dewey confirmed his pre-1916 view of culture as linear movement toward civilization, a democratic, accumulating process that would lead society toward a broader and more cosmopolitan view.

Similarly, in 1916, Randolph Bourne published a provocative essay entitled "Trans-national America," in which he declared that Americanization as it had been conceived by Anglo-Saxons had failed. "The foreign cultures have not been melted down or run together, made into some homogenous Americanism," Bourne explained, " but have remained distinct by contributing to the greater glory and benefit not only of themselves but of all the native Americanism around them." Bourne viewed the failure of racial and ethnic assimilation as a strength of American society, not a weakness. Praising the public schools for accommodating the multiple nationalities, Bourne celebrated the geographic, ethnic, and cultural diversity of the United States for creating a "unique sociological fabric." Like Kallen, Bourne suggested that the true "cosmopolitan" and "intellectual international" American culture lay in the future, as the multiethnic society constructed its own unique pathway to modernity. Bourne was, nevertheless, dismissive of the culture of Eastern Europeans who, after spending time in America, allegedly returned to their home nations "with an entirely new critical outlook, and sense of superiority of American organization to the primitive living around them."²³ Like Kallen, Bourne saw little value in the preindustrial, "primitive" lifestyle of agrarian immigrants because the cosmopolitan and international future he envisioned lay in the urban milieu.

The pluralists rejected the idea that the sociological level of each social group was a deterministic product of their biological instincts, and they rejected Anglo-Saxonism as the cultural end point of sociological development. All national and racial groups had contributed to American society, and its progress was dependent upon the further harnessing of their cultural gifts. In this sense, the pluralists rejected the hierarchical thinking that was embedded in the theory of recapitulation. However, unlike the Boasians, they had little to say about the cultural value of premodern social groups, they emphasized only the elite and vanguard of each cultural group, and they continued to conceive of progress in terms of moving through sociological stages, reflecting the residual effects of the theory of recapitulation. The preeminent voice of the new education, John Dewey, addressed these issues directly between 1916 and 1923, during which his views shifted from the cultural pluralism of Kallen and Bourne toward the cultural relativity of the Boasians. He absorbed these discussions of race, culture, and nationality into his evolving position on education in a democracy.

POST-1916 DEWEY

In Dewey's final years at the University of Chicago and his first years at Columbia University, he began to write more openly about the role of education in a democracy. In doing so, he focused more on issues of race, sociology, and education in democratic schools, although he failed to address race directly until 1922. Dewey largely ignored race during this time, because to acknowledge race was to acknowledge the idea of a latent biological potential, something he had spent the 1890s attacking. Race was largely insignificant to his pragmatic philosophy, because anyone, regardless of biological background, could achieve the highest level of civilization if exposed to an adequate social environment and education. For Dewey, all of the peoples of the world, regardless of skin color, could potentially be placed at any level along the linear scale of sociological development based on their lifestyle, education, and cultural opportunity. Some people just happened to have been left behind.

In his essay "The School as Social Centre," Dewey first considered the pluralistic makeup of American society and first dealt directly with issues of racial and religious intolerance. He did so, however, with his recapitulation approach intact. "We find our political problems involve race questions, questions of assimilation of diverse types of language and custom," Dewey explained. "The contents of the term citizenship is broadening; it is coming to mean all the relationships of all sorts that are involved in membership in a community." He recognized that the notion of citizenship needed to be broadened beyond the traditional view of White Anglo-Saxon Protestants, because the modern world had evolved. However, this democratic process still involved "assimilation." Dewey recognized that the new urban environment forced different social groups to interact with one another whether they liked it or not. "The centralization of industry had forced members of classes into closest association with, and dependence upon, each other," Dewey explained. "Bigotry, intolerance, or even an unswerving faith in the superiority of one's own religious and political creed, are much shaken when individuals are brought face-to-face with each other, or have the ideas of others continuously and forcibly placed before them."[24] Cultural isolation, not reason or human nature, caused bigotry, Dewey boldly suggested. Therefore, the role of schools in a democracy was to force different social groups to assimilate with one another. He specifically named religion, language, and custom as potential impediments to assimilation, but he failed to identify skin color as a factor. This strongly suggests that he was referring only to recent White immigrant groups.

In Dewey's commonly cited 1916 essay "Nationalizing Education," he reiterated his linear approach to sociological-psychological development. He argued that democracy would "fall to pieces" if schools did not do their part to assuage inherited "divisions of interests, class, and sectional ideas." Dewey outlined two forms of nationalism that he thought should be fostered in the United States by carefully distinguishing his American brand of nationalism from the European. The first American form, he explained, "was interracial and international in its makeup" and constituted a "unity created by drawing out and composing into a harmonious whole the best, the most characteristic which each contributing race and people has to offer." This position was consistent with Dewey's definition of culture as those attributes that contributed to the new and progressive growth of humankind. In fact, for Dewey the "interracial and international" stage was an outgrowth of sociological development of the nation; it was the final, highest stage of cultural development. Dewey encouraged the mixing of social groups, but like Kallen and Bourne, only so that the best traits from each could contribute to the greater, transracial fund of progress. Only those social traits that could potentially contribute to progress and growth would be considered "culture." Dewey's second form of nationalism reinforced his notion that the hyphenated identities, such as Jewish or Polish American, should connect rather than separate Americans from one another. "The other point in the constitution of a genuine American nationalism," Dewey explained, ". . . is that we have been occupied during the greater part of our history in subduing nature."[25] Dewey was convinced that society, if it was to move forward, must continue its ability to subordinate the environment cooperatively through the creation of more generic, transracial knowledge. Thus, Dewey's second form of nationalism restrained him from arriving at a position that embraced cultural difference, because it still reflected Dewey's linear, ethnocentric definition of culture outlined above.

In *Democracy and Education*, Dewey even implied that certain social groups were inhibiting progress because of their premodern ways. Any antisocial or self-serving clique was counterproductive to the evolutionary process because "its prevailing purpose is the protection of what [the clique] has got, instead of reorganizations and progress through wider relationships." Dewey insisted that such a tendency could be seen in "savage tribes" who have "identified their experience with rigid adherence to their past customs."[26] Because Dewey's coauthor, James Tufts, had elucidated in their *Ethics* text that he considered native, Black, and American Indian populations as "savage" just a few years earlier, many readers of the time would likely have read the term as if Dewey were referring to these social groups.

Dewey's pragmatism reflected a contingent and evolutionary approach to knowledge. Instead of appealing to static laws and unchanging first principles, Dewey and his pragmatic peers accepted that conclusions could and should change to meet the needs of new environments and new problems. Social issues should be taken on their own terms and approached through the latest, most up-to-date research because new questions emerged, even before the old ones were ever fully solved. As Dewey explained, "intellectual progress usually occurs through sheer abandonment of questions . . . an abandonment that results from their decreasing vitality and a change of urgent interest. We do not solve them; we get over them."[27] All knowledge needed to be reevaluated and retested against a shifting, changing reality. Accordingly, Dewey abandoned much of the historicist language of savagery-barbarianism-civilization around 1916 because it no longer served as a useful lens through which to view racial difference. Dewey's views on race evolved with the times, but the evolution of his views did not reflect a sense of confusion or contradiction; rather, it demonstrated his pragmatism in action.

Over the course of the first two decades of the twentieth century, Dewey subtly but significantly revised his cultural view from a linear, hierarchical one—one that was affiliated with the theory of recapitulation and subsumed all societies past and present within a single narrative of progress—to a pluralist view that recognized the necessity of interaction among diverse but equivalent ways of living. Dewey's transformation was the result of both internal and external developments. The gradual acceptance of the research challenging neo-Lamarckianism led most social scientists to reject any recapitulation theories. Dewey was never a neo-Lamarckian, and he never believed in the biological differentiation of racial and ethnic groups. However, he still arranged his Laboratory School curriculum as a linear historical reenactment of the stages of race history that he attempted to coordinate with the emerging native capacities and interests of the child, which were biologically based. Thus, the complete abandonment of the theory of recapitulation by biologists and psychologists must have cast some doubt on the effectiveness of the curriculum he enacted in Chicago. Furthermore, the positive reception of the functional psychology of Thorndike and the behavioral psychology of John Watson underscored the significance of observable, immediate reinforcements in the lifetime of the individual and shifted attention away from long-term biological and cultural-institutional explanations of mind and behavior. Specifically, most psychologists abandoned attempts to link the biologically inherited instincts of individuals with the social inheritance of cultures and instead focused on immediate environmental factors and stimuli of Thorndike.[28] Overall, as the evolutionary psychology of Wundt, Hall, and Baldwin became less significant, the more immediate conditions outlined by social psychology, behavioral psychology, and cultural anthropology grew in influence. As a result of this important paradigm shift, and in accordance with the pragmatic approach to knowledge, Dewey reconsidered his philosophical views on the necessity of a diverse, pluralistic environment for actualizing potentials.

During the years in which Dewey was reconstructing his cultural views, the field of social psychology emerged as a distinct area of study. Dewey also confirmed the significance of Tarde and Baldwin in his entry on "imitation" for the *Cyclopedia of Education*. "Largely under the influence of Tarde," Dewey explained in 1914, "imitation was made the chief, if not sole, category of social psychology." Dewey, however, agreed more with "Baldwin's account" of imitation that man "is dealing with the various processes by which one person arrives at a community of beliefs and ideas with others," but according to Dewey, Baldwin had not gone far enough in appreciating the interactional nature of socialization.[29] What appeared to be similar cultural behaviors brought about by imitation, Dewey reasoned, were actually similar habitual and socially mediated responses to the same cultural environment. "What is called the effect of imitation," Dewey later explained, "is mainly the product of conscious instruction exercised by the unconscious confirmations and ratifications of those with whom one associates."[30] For Dewey, imitation was inherently conservative if not accompanied by some means of progress and reform, an aspect that Tarde and Baldwin had not fully appreciated.

To remedy this shortcoming, Dewey introduced an important factor to social psychology, which would become crucial to his later pluralist views on culture: the necessity of diversity of viewpoints. "The intellectual and moral progress of the human race," Dewey insisted, "has come through first tolerating and then encouraging divergencies and diversities of thought."[31] That is, progress occurred when individuals of diverse backgrounds and thoughts aligned with a similar idea through imitation, not passively, but actively by consciously realizing that their own viewpoint aligned with the cultural idea. Thus, individuals arrived at the imitated, social perspective through the means of their own pluralistic perspective.

The idea of applying the Darwinian notion of natural variation to the thoughts, viewpoints, and societies of the present could be traced to the cognitive pluralism of William James. But Dewey, having arrived at his version of the theory of recapitulation through Hegel, had previously emphasized the movement toward convergent, generic, and objective knowledge. As the twentieth century progressed, Dewey began to emphasize and appreciate the other side of the equation. In other words, Dewey recognized the necessity of pluralism to achieving a meaningful unity. In a 1903 letter to William James, Dewey implored James to "state your Plurality as a matter of historic significance as well as the universal unity" and recognized that James's "Plurality as it now stands is aesthetic rather than logical."[32] That is, Dewey wanted James to recognize that historical progress was a necessary outcome of pluralistic interaction and that current problems organically contained the historical solutions of the past. Likely influenced by James and his colleague at the University of Chicago William I. Thomas, Dewey slowly began employing a more pluralistic language in 1915–1916. For example, in 1915 Dewey declared that "science is always a plurality of diverse interacting and changing existences."[33] Two years later, in reference to the evolution and growth of the individual, Dewey wrote that "the organism is in and of the world, and its activities correlated with those of other things in multiple ways . . . these connexions

[sic] are of diverse kinds. . . . *In this sense,* pluralism, not monism, is an established empirical fact [italics in original]."³⁴ As Dewey explained by drawing upon and citing James, the reconstruction of knowledge that occurred as a result of these environmental interactions was dependent upon a diversity of native capacities emerging from the individual, as well as a plurality and heterogeneity of ideas in the social environment.

At approximately the same time that Dewey began using the phrase "associated form of living" to describe democracy, he began referring to "cultures" in the plural—first in *Democracy and Education* in 1916 and again that year in his essays on "Nationalizing Education" and "Education and Culture." In the first essay, Dewey insisted that there was a danger in refusing to accept "what other cultures have to offer" and in trying to accept one component of culture as the "pattern to which all other strains and cultures are to conform."³⁵ In the second essay, Dewey insisted on the importance of liberating modern society from the "class cultures of the past."³⁶ Likewise, in *Democracy and Education,* Dewey demanded that a reformation of education required that "the ideas and ideals which are inherited from older and unlike cultures" be reevaluated.³⁷ It is not likely that Dewey consciously started using *culture* in the plural, but it is, nevertheless, very suggestive that the term suddenly appeared in 1915–1916, when he began reconsidering the necessity of pluralistic interaction. By 1915, Dewey even accepted the label of "pluralist," but only after some coaxing by a peer.

Scudder Klyce, a former naval officer and eccentric independent scholar, wrote a lengthy letter to Dewey in 1915 explaining how he planned to use Dewey's work in a philosophical research project on which he was currently working. As he bluntly informed Dewey in a letter, "you are an infinite pluralist, explicitly; Kant was one, James was one: . . . most scientists are very vaguely but actually pluralists."³⁸ After reflection upon Klyce's description of his pragmatic position, Dewey replied with the following revelation:

> I . . . have everywhere made prominent that the only end or aim of education is capacity for more education, or widening and refining the scope of perception of meanings. I have also identified this, as extended all the way around, with a democratic society. The further I go the more I see that I have become a confirmed infinite pluralist. . . . I am grateful for having the *infinite* part of the pluralism made obvious.³⁹

Dewey's acceptance of "infinite pluralism" can be seen in an important essay on social psychology, in which he not only endorsed some of his emerging ideas, but also subtly reconstructed some of his older ones.

In 1916, Dewey was asked to speak to the American Psychological Association on the occasion of its twenty-fifth anniversary, and he chose the topic of social psychology because he believed the sub-discipline offered the most promise for the future of the field, which by 1916 was moving toward the mechanistic approach of Thorndike. Dewey argued that psychologists should approach the mind from a "pluralistic basis: the complexity and specific variety of the factors of human nature, each operating in response to its own highly specific stimulus, and each subject to almost infinite shadings and modulations as it entered into combinations and competition with others." Essentially endorsing the pragmatic approach to psychology, Dewey underscored the significance of social and cultural environment on mental development. Subtly denouncing the excessively genetic and/or comparative approaches of social psychology of the 1890s (perhaps including his own modified recapitulation approach to curriculum at the Dewey School), he reiterated that the mind "is no remote inference from speculative reconstruction of the primitive mind." That is, the mind was not merely a deductive distillation to its essential, pristine form—or what he called misguided idea of "progressive unfolding of original potencies latent in a ready made mind." Instead, it was the product of native tendencies realized in the plurality of associated living—a conclusion, he insisted, that was "confirmed by the development in the life of every infant now observable."[40] Dewey stated forcefully a conviction that he had always held, but which now had immediate consequences for the education of non-Whites: that social environment and education trumped biological inheritance. For Dewey, the most significant factor in explaining the development of the mind, especially as his "infinite pluralism" was emerging, was the interaction among different social ideas. Growth for the individual and society occurred "in connection with interaction with new elements in its surroundings."[41]

Dewey's new pluralistic view of society and culture was best and most fully on display in Chapter 7 of *Democracy and Education*, one of the most original and influential passages he ever wrote. In it, Dewey outlined the necessity of diversity to democracy and progress. Because democratic citizens ultimately had to rule themselves instead of depending upon the traditional ruling elite and its prescribed knowledge, they not only had to be informed about the present situation, but they needed the tools to envision a better future. According to Dewey, such a progressive vision was dependent upon the ability of a plurality of ideas and attributes to be "mutually interpenetrating," and upon having an educational system that fostered and modeled these ideals. The Dewey School had not engaged in this kind of cultural intermixing. Although Dewey's experimental school was indeed set up as an embryonic community reflective of the larger social world, its focus was on social occupations based upon Dewey's old recapitulation view of culture, whereas the vision he outlined in Chapter 7 of *Democracy and Education* was based upon his new, pluralistic view. In theory, the vision outlined by Dewey would require a diverse student population within the school and classroom. An education that broke down "barriers of class, race and national territory," Dewey insisted—in a rare instance of clearly using the word race in a pluralistic way instead of in reference to the broader notion of the "human race"—would lead to "the liberation of a greater diversity of personal capacities which characterize a democracy." Dewey concluded that "only diversity makes change and progress," because diversity broadened the environment and allowed for cultural interpenetration to take place.[42]

In addition to Dewey's emphasis on social psychology, his reconsideration of the significance of environmental interactionism for actualizing potentials, and his transformative travels to the nations of Japan and China, Dewey revised his views on culture and race in response to changes within the field of anthropology itself.[43] Specifically, Dewey reconsidered the significance of the innovative work of Thomas. Dewey biographers Steven Rockefeller and Alan Ryan both attribute a change in Dewey's cultural perspective to his exposure to the work of Boas. However, with a few exceptions, there is little evidence directly connecting the two.[44] The influence of Thomas on Dewey, however, was much more direct and easier to trace. Dewey's admiration for Thomas was first expressed in a letter in 1898 in which he proclaimed, "Mr. Thomas, to my mind, is without any doubt opening a distinct new field in Sociology . . . he will at once command recognition as a pioneer in a most important direction." According to Dewey, Thomas's work represented "the attempt to discover concrete laws of social growth through the application of modern psychological methods to historical material."[45] Dewey had cited Thomas in his 1904 essay, "Interpretation of the Savage Mind" (see Chapter 2), an influence so great that Dewey considered the essay a "joint contribution."[46] Like Dewey, Thomas combined sociological, psychological, and anthropological elements into a historicist theory of cultural and racial development.

As described earlier, Thomas had become a leader in race and social psychology. In a fifty-page article cataloguing the mental capacities of immigrants and people of color, Thomas drew on the empirical work and theories of Tarde, James, Boas, Du Bois, Dewey, and many others to establish the fact that "individual variation is of more importance than racial difference"[47]—a view that directly challenged Thorndike and other eugenicists. In an essay on "The Mind of Woman and the Lower Races," Thomas insisted that "difference in natural ability, is in the main, a characteristic of the individual, not of the race or of sex." Drawing upon his extensive ethnographic readings, Thomas reached an iconoclastic conclusion about the cultural value of Western civilization. As early as 1907, Thomas suggested the radical idea that woman and the so-called inferior races could potentially contribute to Western culture by contributing to a diverse, pluralist environment. "The instinct to belittle outsiders is perhaps at the bottom of our delusion that the white race has one order of mind and the black and yellow races have another," Thomas asserted. "It is certain at any rate, that our civilization is not the highest type possible . . . the participation of woman and the lower races will contribute new elements, change the stress of attention, disturb the equilibrium, and force a crisis which will result in the reconstruction of our habits on more sympathetic and equitable principles."[48] In this passage, Thomas, in essence, suggested the position of cultural pluralism years before Dewey fully appreciated and embraced the position. There is no direct evidence suggesting that Dewey read these specific essays, but there is evidence of intellectual contact between Dewey and Thomas and expressions of their mutual admiration. So, it is more likely that Dewey was influenced by Boas-via-Thomas than he was influenced directly by Boas. In fact, Dewey's position of emphasizing the importance of environment on social development and the benefits of cultural interaction was much closer to Thomas's position than Boas's when Dewey addressed race most directly in his 1922 essay, "Racial Prejudice and Friction." The argument Dewey presents in this essay is almost identical to the views Thomas presented in his various essays on race and race prejudice in years prior.

In Dewey's "Race Prejudice" essay, which was first delivered as a speech to the Chinese Social and Political Science Association, he revealed a new perspective on the topic that had been in gestation since 1915. Like Thomas, Dewey attributed race prejudice to biological and social inheritance, to "biases that originally spring from instincts and habits which are deep set in our natures." As he did in his 1909 address to the National Negro Conference, Dewey insisted that "Race is an abstract thing; according to science it is largely a mythical idea, since all peoples now powerful in the world are highly mixed."[49] So if scientists had determined that race was a social construction largely correlated with nationalism and social inequality, why were people still racist? Dewey traced racial prejudice to an instinctual sense of abhorrence that historically emerged when different tribes and groups first encountered one another. The habitual instinct to resist and fear someone different was embedded in the nature of individuals and fostered by threatened social groups. For example, Dewey explained, Anglo-Saxons first resisted the Irish, then the Chinese, then the Southern Europeans, before they eventually grew accustomed to each social group. However, the group that was previously discriminated against became the most active in opposing the next group; for example, the Irish were the most vigilantly prejudiced against the Chinese. Prejudice, Dewey again argued, was an instinctual response, not the application of the intellect. However, the prejudice instinct could be overcome through continued exposure to alternative social groups and reflective thinking.

In the "Race Prejudice" essay, Dewey again used the term cultures in the plural, pointing to his newer conception of the term, but he still had not entirely transcended his ethnocentric historicism of its original definition. The world was still characterized by a linear narrative of social progress. "The simple fact of the case is that at present the world is not sufficiently civilized to permit close contact of peoples of widely different cultures without deplorable consequences," Dewey admonished. "This deficiency of civilization is much more than a personal matter; it may be and is readily overcome in many individual cases."[50] Significantly, in this passage Dewey defined civilization not as the ability to understand and contribute to industrial progress as he had earlier, but rather as the ability to tolerate and assimilate multiple social groups. His new definition was both a refutation of his earlier Eurocentric definition of culture affiliated with the theory of recapitulation and simultaneously an affirmation of culture as a means of developmental distance from primitiveness. As Dewey further explained, using the term *types of culture* for the first time, the authentic adjustment of cultures to one another would be a difficult and drawn-out process. Dewey concluded that the unavoidable yet difficult solution to the problem of racial friction was "mutual adjustment to one another."[51] While espousing this culturally pluralist, interactionist view, Dewey also endorsed the outright restriction of immigrants to the United States in order to give the world "rest and recuperation." Dewey argued that World War I had put an unnatural stress on the nation, and so postwar society was not the best context in which to test his "mutual adjustment" proposal. Dewey's position on limiting immigrants also could have been viewed as supportive of segregation in the American South because it confirmed that authentic interaction took a long time, although Dewey did not comment specifically on the issue.

Overall, the "Race Prejudice" essay reflected Dewey's change of cultural perspective from a linear, Eurocentric view of culture to a transactional, infinite pluralistic one as espoused by Kallen and Bourne. But, like Thomas, Dewey proposed that "mutual adjustment to one another" required time. However, it was not the matter of letting one social group catch up with the other that required time, as the theory of recapitulation implied, but rather a matter of allowing the social groups to interact slowly and organically with one another so as to derive the best aspects of each from one another. Such a process required a constant replenishing of fresh cultural insights, ideas, and contributions. This process was the application of pluralistic-interactionism to the associated living of democratic society. Nevertheless, it should be noted that Dewey again failed to state explicitly whether African Americans and American Indians had the "types of culture" to which the White groups should adjust. In contrast, Thomas had specifically identified these oppressed groups in his characterization of racial diversity. By 1922, it was likely that Dewey included these groups in this scheme as well, but he never stated it outright. For example, later that year in an essay on inferiority and superiority, Dewey wrote, "Inferior races are inferior because their successes lie in different directions, though possibly more artistic and civilized than our own."[52] Thus, Dewey implied that so-called inferior groups could "possibly" have artistic cultural contributions to make, a position very similar to that expressed by Hall. Art was not a component of Dewey's previous, historicist definition of culture.

In an essay critiquing the kind of intelligence testing endorsed by Thorndike and the psychometricians, Dewey insisted: "At present superior races are superior because of their own conspicuous achievements," not because of an innate, hereditary, and/or genetic advantage that destined them to greatness. In fact, Dewey bluntly asserted, "The idea of abstract, universal superiority and inferiority is an absurdity." Although they were useful in some situations, all intelligence tests did was arbitrarily determine a set of acquired traits deemed useful by those in power and then identify the individuals who, largely through forces outside of their control, already possessed those traits. Intelligence testing reinforced misguided ideas of predetermined superiority, mediocrity, and inferiority, and it also ignored the significance of educational process, context, contingency, and growth. In a more sinister vein, Dewey alleged, the type of intelligence testing espoused by Thorndike, Yerkes, Goddard, and Brigham was a way to reinforce social inequalities by denying certain individuals the opportunity to fulfill their potentials and express their creativities. This was undemocratic: "Democracy will not be democracy until education makes it its chief concern to release distinctive aptitudes in art, through companionship." Dewey called for an education that valued qualitative diversity and the fostering of individual strengths and talents.[53] In other words, he argued on behalf of cultural plurality.

Pluralistic interaction was also a central concern of Dewey's *Human Nature and Conduct*, published in 1922 so Dewey could weigh in on the nature-nurture controversy. "The problem of social psychology is not how either the individual or collective mind forms social groups and customs," Dewey argued, "but how different customs, established interacting arrangements, form and nurture different minds." Dewey was pointing to the limitations of both the individualist approach of Watson's behavioral psychology and the sociological group approach of Tarde's imitation suggestion. Neither approach focused adequately on the interaction among instinct, environment, and culture. Because the native stock of instincts "is practically the same everywhere," Dewey insisted, the native differences between social groups had been exaggerated. Dewey listed the Patagonians, Greeks, Sioux Indians, Hindus, Bushmen, and Chinese as evidence of the strength of acquired habits, "not the growth of customs in terms of instincts."[54] The next year, in an essay on schools and social consciousness, Dewey suggested that "We need a curriculum in history, literature and geography which will make the different racial elements in this country aware of what each has contributed," as well as inspire "feelings of respect and friendliness for other nations and peoples of the world."[55] Again, these passages suggest the significance of cultural diversity, but like fellow pluralists Kallen and Bourne, Dewey never explicitly identified American Indian and African American cultures as potential contributors to the transnational and transracial associated form of culture he outlined.

*****

Resistance and criticism of monoculturalism and White supremacy came in many forms and from many angles during World War I, as scholars sought to redefine democracy in contrast to German imperialism. These critics did not necessarily adhere to a single ideology or state a single objective. Yet, they made their voices known and, in some cases, changed the minds of those around them. It is no accident that, with the exception of Dewey, those scholars who forged an alternative to cultural assimilation to Anglo-Saxonism were outside the White, male, Protestant, able-bodied hegemony. Boas, Goldenwiesen, and Kallen were Jewish; Du Bois, Locke, and Woodson were Black; Mead was female; and Bourne was disabled—he had a hunched back from a childhood bout of tuberculosis. Thus, they had all experienced firsthand what it meant to be underestimated, excluded, or dismissed for who they were, instead of what they had accomplished. To combat the idea of superiority as an inherited trait or static essence, these scholars and activists forged an approach to cultural identity grounded in a dynamic, historically contingent orientation to race and ethnicity. At the same time, they were also careful to praise and celebrate the greatest accomplishments of American civilization, because they were all self-consciously products of it. Rather than reject the inherent superiority of American culture, the Boasians pointed to its accidental, contingent, evolving nature, and the cultural pluralists viewed American culture as not yet having reached its full multiethnic potential.

Despite their shared status as outsiders, the marginalized individuals often pitted themselves against other marginalized groups. For example, in launching Negro History Week, Woodson chided American Indians for their lack of a recorded history, asking, "The American Indian left no continuous record . . . and where is he today?"[56] Earlier, Kelly Miller had cast American Indians as a race destined for extinction, compared with African Americans who were demographically thriving. Furthermore, nearly every critic of racial hierarchy still employed racialist language reflecting a biological, spiritual, and/or essentialist definition of race, demonstrating the residual effects of the theory of recapitulation. Most pluralist scholars ignored the radicalism of Boas's cultural relativism and maintained the savagery-barbarianism-civilization terminology. For example, Bourne was certain that immigrants would reject the "primitive" culture of their past once they were exposed to the American brand of civilization. Similarly, Black and American Indian elites did not romanticize their premodern lifestyles as sociologically valuable, but rather they resented their public depiction as being stuck in their savage past instead of progressing rapidly toward civilization. Even Mead pointed out how Samoa represented a "simpler" lifestyle than that of the United States, yet she was careful to refer to the Samoans as a "civilization," reflecting Kroeber's assertion that all peoples were equally civilized. In other words, it was difficult to leave the linear, hierarchical language of race and culture completely behind, even while challenging some of its racist manifestations.

Perhaps Dewey best demonstrates the difficulty of abandoning the hierarchical language of race in *Democracy and Education*—the single most significant, respected, and articulate statement on progressive education ever published. Dewey wrote that in *Democracy and Education*, which was released in 1916 to glowing reviews, his philosophical outlook "was most fully expounded," because the book was "the closest attempt I have made to sum up my entire philosophy."[57] As discussed earlier, Dewey outlined his pluralistic view on American culture in Chapter 7 of the book. "A modern society is many societies more or less loosely connected," he explained. "The intermingling in the school of youth of different races, differing religions, and unlike customs creates for all a new and broader environment." Dewey insisted that democratic citizens associated "in all kinds of ways and for all kinds of purposes . . . in a multitude of diverse groups" that created "varied and free points of contact with other modes of association." Such "back and forth play" and "diversity of stimulation" among the social groups, he averred, were essential to bringing forth novel ideas that would contribute to American progress.[58] Yet, outside of Chapter 7, *Democracy and Education* was filled with references to the psychological-sociological stages of culture affiliated with the theory of recapitulation. As early as page two, Dewey introduced the savage as the antithesis of all things *democratic* and *scientific*, terms that Dewey essentially used as synonyms for the civilized world. Accordingly, Dewey introduced the savage as an example of all that was undemocratic, unscientific, and uncivilized, and as a symbol of the distant undeveloped past of Western ideas and institutions. In other words, savagery represented everything that needed to be overcome in a democratic society.

By the end of the 1920s, many progressive educators adopted Dewey's view that non-Whites were contingently and sociologically inferior, but they mostly ignored Boas's argument that all cultures were sociologically equivalent. However, by removing the language of racial inferiority from innate, permanent traits to the language of cultural deprivation, Dewey effectively reoriented the discussion of non-Whites from racism to ethnocentrism. Yet, his ethnocentric belief in the sociological inferiority of people of color allowed progressive educators to ignore or even justify segregated schools and the political disenfranchisement of Blacks and American Indians. Even Boasian Ruth Benedict, who in the 1930s fought scientific racism as vigilantly as anyone of her generation, nevertheless admitted, "great numbers of negroes are not ready for full citizenship."[59] As we shall see in the next chapter, in the 1920s leading progressive educators maintained Dewey's orientation on the social deficiency of nonwhites, or continued to espouse the biological and hereditary basis for racial inequality.

CHAPTER 6

Refashioning

After World War I, there were essentially three positions to take on race. The first, and perhaps most influential, group included those scholars who continued to believe in the innate, hereditary, or biological basis for the inferiority of people of color. Psychometricians such as H. H. Goddard, Robert Yerkes, Carl Brigham, and Edward Thorndike replaced the language of inherited impulses and instincts of non-Whites with data from eugenics and intelligence tests to demonstrate the inherited cognitive inferiority of marginalized groups. The second position took Lester Frank Ward's and Dewey's position on the sociological deficiency of non-Whites. Leading cultural pluralists believed that all humans, regardless of race, had the potential to reach civilization, but at present most people of color were stuck in an earlier sociological stage, where they would remain until they could be brought up to speed via education and extended exposure to an enhanced social environment. Finally, the third group, represented by Boas and his cultural relativist associates, argued that all humans were equally civilized. People of color were in no way sociologically deficient, but instead they reflected different, fully developed lifestyles based upon their own unique histories and traditions. As G. Stanley Hall explained in 1908, "Weissman, Boas, and many other anthropologists have shown that in native gifts, primitive people are hardly inferior to us; but it is just as essential that they should evolve along the lines of their own heredity and traditions as it is for us to do so."[1]

After World War I, leading educators more or less rejected (or ignored) the radical cultural relativity of the Boasians, and either maintained their belief in the innate-biological inferiority of students of color, or they adopted Dewey's pre-1916 position of the sociological deficiency of non-Whites. In both cases, progressive educators maintained the entrenched belief that had been established by the previous generation, that non-Whites represented a previous, less developed step toward Western civilization. In other words, even as leading educators phased out explicit references to the theory of recapitulation in the 1920s, the underlying belief in the sociological inferiority of non-Whites remained embedded in the idea of child-centeredness, and shaped the subsequent reforms of progressive education. Thus, progressive educators refashioned the theory of recapitulation into alternative theories of sociological development in which students of color were, nevertheless, approached as sociologically deficient.

CHILD-CENTERED PROGRESSIVES

After World War I, the *new education* morphed into *progressive education*, although educators used both terms interchangeably. The new education originated with an ethnocentric focus on child-centeredness that originated with the theory of recapitulation. After the war, educators built upon this foundation by maintaining the focus on child-centeredness, but they focused less on the psychological-sociological stages of humankind and more on the generic aspects of nurturing the cognitive, vocational, and artistic needs of the developing child. However, scholars had different views about what was meant by individuality. As curriculum historian Herbert Kliebard explains, "To some in the 1920s, individuality meant building a curriculum around the individual child's spontaneous creative interests; to others, individuality meant adapting the pace of instruction to the differences in individuals learning capacities."[2] In other words, to some progressive educators individuality was internally determined and aimed toward self-expression, but for others individuality was externally determined and aimed at identifying and sorting students into their appropriate social roles. Historians have commonly referred to the first group as pedagogical or child-centered progressives and to the second group as administrative progressives. This distinction is useful for contrasting the educational visions of the two groups. However, in a consideration of their racial views, this distinction perhaps obscures more than it reveals, because, with few exceptions, both groups maintained the belief that immigrants and non-Whites were sociologically deficient.

Although the new education was concerned with matching the appropriate curriculum with the emerging instincts of children based on their race, progressive education was essentially a movement aimed exclusively at White, middle-class students. The Progressive Education Association (PEA), founded in 1919, showed no immediate concern for non-White students whatsoever. In its founding statement, the PEA identified "Freedom to Develop Naturally; Interest the Motive of All Work; The Teacher as Guide, Not as Task Master"; and "Scientific Study of Pupil Development" as four of its founding principles, demonstrating its focus on child-centered pedagogy.[3] Many of the earliest members of the PEA worked in private schools, and its most significant early member, Marietta Johnson of the Organic School in Fairhope, Alabama, worked in a racially segregated school in the South. Seeking to draw in Southern support, the founders of the PEA likely overlooked the issue of race deliberately. Furthermore, the early concerns of the PEA had little to do with correcting social injustices. The leading scholars of the new child-centered progressive education, William Heard Kilpatrick and Harold Rugg, initially ignored race and the racial implications of the work they cited, instead focusing on meeting the developmental needs of children. When leading educational scholars such as Alexander Inglis addressed race, they conflated the views of Thorndike and Dewey into a generic focus on student-centeredness. Likewise, Kilpatrick and Rugg both drew equally upon the ideas of Thorndike and Dewey in constructing their educational approaches, despite the divergent views Thorndike and Dewey held on race.

Two of the most significant publications in the history of child-centered progressivism were Kilpatrick's "The Project Method" and Rugg and Ann Shumaker's *The Child-Centered School*. Both ignored race and both ignored the theory of recapitulation, confirming that by the 1920s the field had largely moved beyond concern for the stages of psychological-sociological development. In addition, Kilpatrick's and Rugg's publications drew equally upon Dewey and Thorndike to make a case for a relevant, child-centered approach to curriculum. Kilpatrick's article, published in *Teachers College Record* in 1918, was immediately and immensely popular; the press had to run off 60,000 reprints to meet the intense demand for the paper. Kilpatrick argued that the student-centered project could unify "important related aspects of the educative process." To make his case, he employed Deweyan language such as "the important generalization that education is life," and centered his proposal on Deweyan concepts such as the "purposeful act" and "wholehearted vigorous activity." Furthermore, Kilpatrick also referenced Thorndike's "laws of learning," including the assumption that "any conduct consists of a response to the existing situation . . . because there existed in the nervous system a bond or connection joining the stimulus of that situation with that response." Educators embraced the project method because Kilpatrick had successfully reconciled the two major strands of the new education—the humane, holistic, relevant, democratic vision of Dewey and the proto-behaviorist scientific approach of Thorndike. "[A]ny plan of educational procedure which does not aim consciously and insistently at securing and utilizing vigorous purposing on the part of pupils," Kilpatrick insisted, ". . . is founded essentially on an ineffective and unfruitful basis."[4]

Kilpatrick developed his ideas further in his 1925 book *Foundations of Method*, a series of lectures based on a course by the same name that he taught at Teachers College. In the preface, Kilpatrick reiterated that Spencer, James, Dewey, Thorndike, and Woodworth had all influenced his ideas, but the ideas that influenced him most were "particularly those of Dewey and Thorndike." Despite the author's claim that his educational philosophy looked the "demands of modern life squarely in the face," his book failed to address race, immigration, eugenics, urbanization, or any of the broader social issues facing educators.[5] These concerns were beyond the purview of the new breed of child-centered advocates. Kilpatrick suggested that the project method would not only interest children and lead to a more fulfilling educational experience, but it would also make the curriculum more efficient because the approach aligned with the laws of learning. What was missing from Kilpatrick's project method, however, was a set of criteria for selecting what content ought to be taught. The theory of recapitulation had provided a sequence of content based upon the history of the human race. However, when the new breed of child-centered educators abandoned the theory of recapitulation as a basis for the selection of content, there was little consensus about what to use in its place.

Rugg and Shumaker, teachers at the Lincoln School of Teachers College, issued their own suggestions for how the curriculum ought to be reconstructed in their 1928 coauthored book, *The Child-Centered School*. In the book, Rugg and

Shumaker enthusiastically traced the rise of experimental child-centered teaching. The authors identified Dewey as the leading prophet of the new education throughout the text, because he "ignited the first flame of the current educational revolution." As they further explained, "[T]he proponents of freedom in education under the revolutionary leadership of John Dewey have focused attention upon the continuous growth of the child, upon freedom, initiative, spontaneity, vivid self-expression."[6] Although they were not inaccurate, Rugg and Shumaker offered a simplistic characterization of Dewey's pedagogy, ignoring his rigorous, but subtle refashioning of the theory of recapitulation as the basis for the curriculum at the Dewey School. They also completely ignored Dewey's important discussions on race and pluralism as key components of his democratic and educational vision.

In their study, Rugg and Shumaker cited Thorndike less frequently, but praised him as much as they had praised Dewey. "Under the leadership of Thorndike the learning process was explored indirectly by the statistical method of measuring products of learning," they explained. "This contribution to the learning of the skills and to the philosophy of the inductive method of learning will live in the history of education." Drawing upon Dewey and Thorndike, Rugg and Shumaker argued that the new education could ultimately be reduced to two major concepts: "tolerant understanding" and "self-expression."[7] Dewey and Thorndike would not have been comfortable having their views reduced to these two principles. Nevertheless, like Kilpatrick, Rugg was hoping to translate the dense, scientific language of Thorndike and Dewey into simpler methods and procedures that could be easily understood and implemented by teachers. If progressive education was to reach its full potential in the schools, then the technical language of its leading theorists needed to be synthesized and simplified. Kilpatrick's "The Project Method" and Rugg and Shumaker's *The Child-Centered School* successfully performed that function. In the process, these progressives stripped child-centeredness of its ethnocentric baggage by ignoring the stages of psychological-sociological development as expressed by Dewey and circumventing the eugenicist language of Thorndike. As a result, Kilpatrick, Rugg, and Shumaker marginalized race as a major concern for the second wave of child-centered progressives emerging in the 1920s.[8]

Another important progressive thinker who saw no contradictions in the views of Thorndike and Dewey was Harvard professor Alexander J. Inglis, whose seven-hundred-page magnum opus *The Principles of Secondary Education* exerted an influence on the contents of the NEA's Commission on the Reorganization of Secondary Education report. Like most of his contemporaries in 1918, Inglis did not draw upon the theory of recapitulation. Instead, he drew upon the research of both Dewey and Thorndike to support a focus on the intellectual diversity of expanding the high school population and how students needed a more relevant curriculum that catered to their needs. In a section on human development, Inglis explained that there were two conflicting approaches to the topic: the theory of serial development and the theory of concomitant development. Inglis identified Bagley as a proponent of the former, and Dewey and Thorndike as proponents of the latter. Inglis included lengthy quotations from Dewey's *How*

We Think, followed by an equally long quotation from Thorndike's *Notes on Child Development* to demonstrate how Thorndike and Dewey agreed that "the development of efficiency is more dependent on growth as effected by experience than on a serial development of capacities determined by the forces of inner growth."[9] That is, Dewey and Thorndike both viewed learning as the development of specific psychological capacities of the mind through interaction, not the unraveling of a latent potentials brought on by maturation.

If Inglis recognized the similarities in the psychological outlooks of Dewey and Thorndike, he did not recognize the divergence in their approaches to race. Interestingly, while quoting Thorndike, Inglis essentially expressed Dewey's position that education and socialization trumped biology and heredity: "In general we can say that individual differences among secondary school pupils due to biological heredity are relatively unimportant, but that individual differences due to social heredity are great and important."[10] Drawing on Marion J. Mayo's 1913 study comparing the mental efficiencies of Black and White children in New York City (see Chapter 4), Inglis argued that biological and racial backgrounds of students made little difference because the statistically measured capacities of both groups of students overlapped more than they diverged. Nevertheless, Inglis explained how sociological differences could be problematic for immigrant children because of their sociological deficiencies, which prevented many of them from reaching high school. However, he also presented data suggesting that the children of these students would achieve higher educational attainment because they would be better socialized to American life. Ultimately, Inglis concluded that teachers and administrators ought to focus on the wide variety of ability levels within each sociological group; emphasis should be on the individual difference of students, not their racial and ethnic background.

For Kilpatrick, Rugg, Shumaker, and Inglis, individual student difference was something to be embraced and incorporated into a humane but scientific approach to teaching. The new breed of child-centered advocates abandoned the theory of recapitulation as a justification for a curriculum that catered to the inherited instincts of the child. In its place, they offered a vague, generic appeal to child interests based upon the Dewey-Thorndike consensus, which nevertheless traced its origins to the theory of recapitulation. At the elementary level, scientific curriculum making meant a focus on hands-on activities. At the secondary level, scientific curriculum making meant a multitrack differentiated curriculum as recommended by the 1918 Commission on the Reorganization of Secondary Education.

ADMINISTRATIVE PROGRESSIVES

In 1936, Harold Rugg proudly proclaimed that "The subservience to morphology . . . is beginning to be replaced by dynamic interest in contemporary life."[11] By "morphology," Rugg meant the field's early focus on the stages of psychological-sociological evolution, which was giving way to a more recent interest in transforming the present through behavioral psychology and the empirical study of children and the curriculum. Indeed, Rugg was correct that in the 1920s progressive educators were replacing developmental, historicist, and evolutionary theories of psychology and curriculum with more presentist, functional, and technocratic ones. Drawing on this context, educational sociologists and administrative-minded progressives viewed the school from an institutional standpoint and believed that the public school system needed to be modernized through more efficient management techniques. In particular, they believed that students needed to be identified early for their academic potential, sorted into appropriate classes and tracks, and provided with a differentiated curriculum that aligned with their likely future occupation. Under the banner of scientific study and increased social efficiency, administrative progressives viewed schools as a means of social control and administrative improvement. They proposed a utilitarian curriculum that aligned with each student's projected future.

One of the first educators to draw attention to the inefficiency of educational instruction was Leonard Ayers in his text *Laggards in Our Schools*. Ayers, the former superintendent of schools in Puerto Rico, had gained firsthand experience with allegedly retarded students overseas. Ayers argued that the modern school system was still aimed at bright students and had not adequately accounted for the influx of less capable children. He cited a recent study of 20,000 New York City children, discovering that 23 percent of them were below age level in intelligence. Broken down further by race, the study found that 36 percent of Italian immigrant children were retarded, as well as 29 percent of Irish children, 24 percent of the English, and 23 percent of the Russians. All of these immigrants demonstrated a higher retardation rate than American-born students, whose rate was 19 percent. "The question of how to handle a Scotch immigrant," Ayers concluded, "is very different from how to handle an Italian."[12] Ayers promoted a school system that identified and segregated these laggards into separate classes where they could be taught more efficiently. Thus, he identified student difference as a major concern of the progressive educator.

Another scholar who followed educational debates closely was sociologist Charles A. Ellwood of the University of Missouri. Ellwood wrote more consistently and openly about race than perhaps any other figure during the period covered in this book. Like Bagley and Hall, Ellwood's views on race evolved through the 1910s in relation to emerging biological and anthropological research, yet he never fully abandoned his belief in the biological origins of sociological stages. A prolific reader and writer, Ellwood reviewed many works that were published on the race problem in the 1910s and 1920s. Through these reviews, Ellwood painted himself as a moderate between authors who offered "too optimistic" a view of "the negro character" and those authors who failed to depict accurately "the indifference and unfairness of the superior race toward the inferior" in the South.[13] Scientific detachment from the race problem was highly valued by Ellwood, as demonstrated by his brief review of recent literature on the "Negro Problem" in 1913. Notably, in this essay Ellwood recognized the work of Black authors including Booker T. Washington and what he called the "non-conciliatory" research of W.E.B. Du Bois and Kelly Miller, who "both demand for the negro full social and political rights." Not impressed by the overall quality of this work, he concluded that an "adequate, scientific work dealing with the relations between the negroes and the whites" had "yet to be published."[14]

Throughout his early career, Ellwood consistently argued that races were distinguished from one another by their inherited instincts and habits. For example, in 1901 Ellwood insisted that the socialization of Blacks was "at every turn limited, controlled, and modified by a series of instinctive impulses which have become relatively fixed," a point exemplified by "the negro child, [who] even when reared by a white family under the most favorable conditions, fails to take on the mental and moral characteristics of the Caucasian race." The reappearance of "voodooism" and "fetishism" in Southern Blacks, Ellwood argued, confirmed that biological inheritance exerted a powerful force upon individuals that could not be completely overcome by social forces and education.[15] Elsewhere, Ellwood insisted that "the average negro is still a child of nature."[16] In his 1912 book *Sociology in Its Psychological Aspects*, Ellwood asserted that "man's instincts are more adapted to the barbarous and savage condition than to civilization." Still to some degree a recapitulationist at this point, Ellwood insisted that social scientists could learn much from the study of "present savage and barbarous peoples." For this reason, education was so important to civilized societies because only through schooling could students gradually learn to overcome their inherited savage tendencies.

Ellwood traced racial differences to divergences in inherited impulses and instincts that were formed over hundreds of years of interaction with different physical environments. Citing Thorndike, Ellwood asserted: "There can be no doubt that instinctive reactions are somewhat unlike in different races.... While the fundamental mental traits of the negro and white for example, are the same ... differences in native reactions to similar stimuli are patent even to the ordinary observer." This position distinguished Ellwood from Dewey, Thomas, and Boas who all believed that the inherited instincts of all people were more or less the same, regardless of race. Consequently, Ellwood also openly endorsed eugenics, which along with education, he believed, could provide "charity" for the unfit. Clearly a Darwinian, Ellwood cited "mutations" as the driving force in evolution, as opposed to the transmission of acquired traits.[17] Accordingly, he was skeptical that the race problem would be solved any time in the near future for two reasons. First, he felt that the different instincts of the Black and White races made "harmonious adjustment to each another and to the same environment difficult." Second, he believed that all humans inherited an instinctual "race antipathy." Recall that Dewey, drawing upon Thomas, had also traced racism to an inherited instinct to resist those who are different. Despite these problems, Ellwood was optimistic about the power of education to overcome these irrational instincts and he also believed that "proper education ... can unquestionably overcome the slight differences between the negro and the white by training and modifying these impulses."[18]

After traveling to England to study with cultural anthropologist R. R. Merritt in 1914, Ellwood began to place less emphasis on biological difference and environmental determinism and more emphasis on cultural difference. By 1920, he was starting to absorb and cite the research for Boas's students, "the new school of anthropologists... such as Goldenweiser, Lowie, and Wissler." As a result, he deemphasized the biological and geographic determinism of his early years and considered the fact that "cultures appear to be entirely independent of one another."[19] By 1927, Ellwood had aligned himself directly with Dewey on the issue of culture. In an article on the origins of cultural patterns, he quoted extensively from Dewey's 1902 article "Interpretation of the Savage Mind" to conclude that "the occupation of hunting not only furnished most of the patterns for primitive culture but also laid the basis for the cultural patterns of civilized man." Thus, Ellwood approached culture pragmatically as a mostly learned attribute. "Culture as a learning process," Ellwood explained, "is necessarily an expanding process." Nevertheless, like Dewey, Ellwood believed that culture took place through a linear process of psychological-sociological stages. As a result, he considered savages the psychological-sociological equivalent of children. As Ellwood explained, "[T]he mind of primitive man must have been like the mind of the child.... It had, however, qualitatively the same powers and capacities, so far as we can judge, as our own minds."[20] Although Dewey's prewar interactionist position on culture was radical in 1896, by 1927 it was moderate because Boas's students had completely removed culture from the savage-barbarism-civilization rubric altogether. Wissler had suggested in *Man and Culture* that culture could be distilled to nine ahistorical categories that all societies, past and present, shared. Nevertheless, Ellwood dismissed Wissler's position as too arbitrary and drew upon Dewey's 1902 position to reassert the linear developmental nature of culture as passing through cumulative, qualitative sociological stages. Apparently, Ellwood was not aware that by 1916 Dewey had himself moved beyond his earlier hierarchical position toward the more pluralist outlook of Wissler and Boas. Thus, by the 1920s Ellwood distanced himself somewhat from the overtly deterministic views that he had expressed in 1901, but he still traced racial differences to biologically inherited instincts.

In 1914, Ellwood authored an article for the journal *Education* that echoed Ayers's concerns that schools were not doing enough to identify and segregate "retarded" students. The article argued that mandatory attendance laws in schools were outdated because they were tied to chronological age, instead of mental age. Impressed by Goddard's use of the Binet-Simon test to identify feeble-minded children, Ellwood thought children should be retained in schools as long as it took until they had mastered a minimum level of efficiency, regardless of chronological age. Indefinite retention would prevent feeble-minded students from entering society without adequate training in citizenship. "An indeterminate compulsory education law would have a eugenic value for the race," Ellwood argued in one of the first instances of linking eugenics directly to school administration, "as well as a social and economic value for individual success and good citizenship."[21] Ellwood agreed with Goddard that schools could be used to reduce the number of feeble-minded students in the general population.

Despite his turn toward Dewey's more egalitarian view of culture and race by 1920, Ellwood still looked to schools as a means of social control. In an article on citizenship, he identified "the harmonious adjustment of the negro and the white" and "the control of the immigration" as issues to be addressed by public schools. He endorsed a social studies curriculum that made up no less than a third of the overall curriculum because such pressing social issues required an informed and intelligent citizenry. Ellwood optimistically concluded that a modernized approach to schooling would, "make our democracy someday so startlingly efficient that the boasted efficiency of autocracy will look small in comparison."[22]

By World War I, David Snedden, Massachusetts commissioner of education (and later a professor at Teachers College), was the leading proponent of curriculum utilitarianism in the United States. Snedden had studied under leading eugenicist Edward A. Ross at Stanford University. Ross has authored *Social Control* and *The Old World in the New*. Both of Ross's books presented a defensive posture toward the diversifying nation, and argued on behalf of education as a means of fostering an orderly transition to the modern world. As Ross explained in *Social Control*, the non-White races were particularly resistant to the kind of reform that was needed for civilization. As a result, they required a multiple-front attack. Quoting Sire Henry Maine, Ross explained:

> The entire Mohammedan world detests [reform]. The multitudes of colored men who swarm in the great continent of Africa detest it; and it is detested by that large part of mankind, which we are accustomed to leave on one side as barbarous or savage. The millions upon millions of men who fill the Chinese empire loath it.... The enormous mass of the Indian population hates and dreads change.[23]

Ross explained how schooling, churches, industry and/or contact with Whites could not by themselves reform the "American negro," yet all of these factors working in cooperation could possibly change the "backward portion of the race."[24] In *The Old World in the New*, Ross offered an exhaustive catalogue of the physical, cultural, mental, and biological characteristics of multiple waves of U.S. immigrants, including the Celtic Irish, Germans, Scandinavians, Italians, Slavs, Eastern European Hebrews, and the "lesser immigrant groups" such as Africans, Mongolians, and Magyars. Ross expressed his concerns that "the pioneer breed [was] being swamped and submerged by an overwhelming tide of latecomers from the old world hive." These newer immigrants were not representative of their race, but in fact had come from the lowest rungs of their respective societies. He warned that "race suicide" awaited the United States as the fertility rate of the well-born continued to decline in relation to that of the newer immigrants.[25]

Although Snedden shared a similarly dismissive disposition toward non-Whites and immigrants, his views on race were only partially shaped by Ross because geographer Ellsworth Huntington equally influenced Snedden's views. In his 1915 text, *Civilization and Climate*, Huntington proposed a geographically deterministic argument similar to Ellwood's that racial groups were largely formed through interactions with their geographic regions, and so the Teutonic race engendered the civilized world because of its historical climatic advantages. Focusing specifically on the White and Black races, Huntington opened his book with an overview of existing data to confirm "every exact test which has been made on a large scale indicates mental superiority on the part of the white race, even when the two races [White and colored] have equal opportunity." The racial differences, he argued, were biological and had been acquired through generations of living in a particular climate. "Initiative, inventiveness, and the power of leadership are the qualities which give favor to the Teutonic race," Huntington explained. "Good humor, patience, loyalty, and the power of self-sacrifice give flavor to the negro."[26] For Huntington, it was not that Whites were essentially and necessarily superior to African Americans; it was just that the racial qualities of Whites, acquired through interaction with their geography and climate, happened to have led to civilization, while the characteristics of non-Whites happened to have left them better suited for a precivilized world. This was essentially the same conclusion as the theory of recapitulation, but without the linear developmental aspect.

Drawing on Huntington's theories, Snedden argued in *Educational Sociology* that it "is improbable that within the next few hundred years any considerable advances can be made in the purposeful adaptation of man ... [in] adverse environments such as those of the tropics or of highly developed urban life." That is, American Blacks were not cognitively equipped to assimilate to civilized, democratic life because they had developed specifically for life in the tropics. Regarding eugenics, Snedden provided a lukewarm endorsement for the movement, reporting, "Ideals of eugenics are increasingly prevalent among better educated classes in the formation of marital unions." Citing Ross, he reported that the most prosperous Americans were reproducing at a slower rate than the less prosperous, which could possibly lead to "race suicide." However, Snedden stopped short of endorsing government interventions such as "denying marriage to those of poor stock." Instead, he supported voluntary compliance and the use of schools to educate the public about race betterment. For one of his discussion questions, Snedden posed: "Eugenics may yet bring it about that people will be born into a world more nearly equal in endowment than now. Can education be now employed as means of furthering such eugenic policies?"[27] Snedden was sincerely posing this as an open-ended question, because he was unsure of the answer, given the current state of racial science.

Educational sociologists and the administrative progressives with whom they were allied viewed the racial problem from the systemic level. Rather than base their assumptions on irrational racial stereotypes as Ross had done, Ellwood and Snedden took a quantitative, functional approach to the issue. "Ethnology does not find pure races to any extent," Snedden explained. "Racial intermixtures have taken place so often that even supposedly unblended peoples like the Jews, Scandinavians, or the Arabs prove to be racially very composite."[28] Races could not be reduced to their essences, Snedden argued, and the potentials of each race could not be reduced to absolute terms. Instead, races could only be understood in statistical, quantitative terms as averages because there was variation within each group. In one of his book reviews, Ellwood rebuked an author for not citing "the results of experimental study" and for referencing "the 'negro' when he should have said 'the average negro.'" In other words, Ellwood was chiding the author for not employing quantitative methods and language in an age when quantitative was synonymous with scientific. (Accordingly, Ellwood dismissed Du Bois's *The Souls of Black Folks* as "a literary work of subjective psychological analysis, rather than a scientific treatise."[29]) Thus, administrative progressives used science as a shield against subjectivity. Drawing on this scientific work, Ellwood, Huntington, and Snedden argued that through historical contingencies, most of the individuals in certain races were not equipped to be successful in a civilized democracy. This inequality was not necessarily because of each race's essential or innate inferiority, but simply because their racial traits were not a good fit for the modern world. Science had allegedly proven this. From an administrative level, true social equality could only be achieved by reducing variation through eugenics. In the meantime, education informed by science could be used to sort students into their appropriate roles. This was the essence of social control during the high tide of administrative progressivism. As Ellwood confirmed, "our complex urban world demands a maximum of control."[30]

SOCIOLOGICAL DEFICIENCY AND CULTURAL PLURALISM

As the child-centered and administrative progressives sought to expand their vision to all American schools, they reached a general consensus that immigrant and non-White populations would need to learn to be American by adopting the English language and swiftly rejecting their premodern ways. Overlooking the cultural relativity of Boasians, both child-centered and administrative progressives agreed that immigrant and non-White groups were sociologically deficient and needed to be taught how to behave in a civilized nation. Most progressive educators embraced the teaching of tolerance and sought to reduce racial prejudice, but they did so while working through the cultural pluralist orientation focused on the celebration of the cultural gifts and contributions. In other words, leading educators rejected Boasian cultural relativity and embraced the pluralists' emphasis on recognizing only those cultural aspects that were perceived to contribute to sociological progress.

One of the most celebrated experiments of the new education prior to World War I was the "platoon system" or "Gary Plan" of Gary, Indiana. Designed, implemented, and led by Dewey's former student William Wirt, the platoon system allowed students to study academic content and acquire industrial skills in two alternating shifts, and also allowed the community to utilize the school to provide evening classes for adults. The purpose of the plan, according to Wirt, was to have teachers "render the greatest service with the least expenditure of energy, and that the maximum use may be secured from the school plant and other child-care facilities."³¹ Wirt's plan was nationally recognized and praised for its efficient use of time and finances, and for its fusing of academic and industrial content. Specifically, John and Evelyn Dewey celebrated the Gary schools in *Schools of To-morrow*, and the leading theorist of cultural pluralism, Randolph Bourne, did the same in *The Gary Schools*, published in 1916. Bourne titled his chapter on the Gary curriculum "Learn by Doing," a phrase that the Deweys had first introduced in *Schools of To-morrow* the previous year. For the next century, "learn by doing" became the shorthand distillation of progressive education itself, a pedagogical approach that was affiliated with the hands-on learning of the movements' two most celebrated experiments, the Dewey School and the schools of Gary, Indiana.

Educators considered Wirt's platoon system so successful with the students of Gary—who were mostly the children of immigrants and destined for factory work—that in 1914 Mayor John Purroy Mitchell doubled Wirt's salary to bring him to New York City to implement the Gary Plan in New York's urban schools. In the summer of that year, Wirt converted two overcrowded schools in Brooklyn and the Bronx to the Gary Plan. Both schools were located in communities of mostly Eastern European Jewish immigrants. The Jews viewed the Gary Plan as a watering down of the curriculum and an attempt to funnel their children into factory work by diverting attention away from academic content toward vocational training. In addition, the longer school day required by the Gary Plan displaced time spent in after-school Hebrew schools, and thus was interpreted as an attack on Jewish religious freedom. One articulate critic of the time cast the Gary Plan as "capitalistic intrigue" designed to "widen the gulf between the classes by providing one kind of education for the children of the poor while the rich were giving their children a training that would result in higher intelligence, broader culture and consequently social and industrial supremacy."³² Mayor Mitchell ignored this dissent and expanded the Gary Plan to dozens of other schools across the city. However, after years of relentless meetings, public hearings, protests, boycotts, and walkouts by the Jewish community and other opponents of the Gary Plan, the issue came to the attention of all New Yorkers. As a result, the election of 1917 became a referendum on the recent school reforms. Mayor Mitchell was soundly defeated and the Gary Plan was slowly phased out, marking a partial victory for the efforts of the grassroots Jewish organizations.³³

Additional dissent by ethnic minorities was aimed at the contents of textbooks. In 1922, when New York City officials conducted hearings on David Muzzey's popular *American History* text, Jewish and Black leaders voiced their objections to the book for its failure to recognize and the contributions of their ethnic heroes. Similar hearings erupted in Chicago, Boston, Baltimore, Seattle, and San Francisco, prompting journalist Walter Lippman to comment in 1928, "it seems as if there were hardly an organization in America which has not set up a committee . . . to rewrite the textbooks."³⁴ Catholic, Irish, German, Italian, Jewish, and African American interest groups all demanded revised textbooks and a greater presence of their own ethnic heroes in the curriculum. However, as argued by historian Jonathan Zimmerman, these ethnic groups did not necessarily support the pluralistic history of Du Bois, Kallen, and Bourne, nor did they endorse a critical, issue-based curriculum as suggested by the new historians and the 1916 Committee on Social Studies. Rather, these groups supported a traditional, patriotic brand of history that celebrated the contributions of all "true" Americans, which, they argued, necessarily included their own ethnic heroes. Zimmerman's conclusion was confirmed by Jeffrey Mirel's study of foreign-language newspapers and educational materials produced by immigrant groups themselves. These materials reflected a perspective that Mirel dubbed "patriotic pluralism," in which the immigrants' desire to assimilate coexisted with their effort to retain many cultural attributes of their native country.[35] In other words, many ethnic and racial groups celebrated their cultural attributes while at the same time supporting a traditional, pre-progressive curriculum that emphasized rigor and discipline over student-centeredness and the teaching of social issues.

A disconnect between intellectual elites and the immigrant communities they represented can be seen in the case of Gary Plan. As the Jewish immigrants were mobilizing their effort to resist the implementation of the Gary Plan in New York City, Randolph Bourne was praising the very same plan in his book on the schools. In his essay "Trans-national America," Bourne boasted how the Slav "is the raw material to be educated, not into a New Englander, but into a socialized American along such lines as those thirty nationalities are being educated in the amazing schools of Gary."[36] The Gary Plan represented the quintessence of progressive education with its hands-on learning, use of administrative efficiency, fusing of academic and industrial curriculum, focus on the whole child, and engagement with the community. Yet, this holistic educational approach left little room for the cultural, religious, and intellectual identity of the Jewish immigrants to be maintained, and it replaced the kind of traditional pedagogy to which the Jews were accustomed and had specifically sought out in American schools. For this reason, the Jews resisted the reforms.

Similarly, W.E.B. Du Bois was a proponent of progressive education in its focus on social reform and cultural pluralism, but, when it came to his own children, he prescribed a traditional pedagogy based on the outdated psychology of the mental faculties. "Read some good, heavy, serious books just for discipline," Du Bois instructed his daughter. "... Make yourself do unpleasant things, so as to gain the upper hand of your soul." Learning, Du Bois later wrote, "is a matter of blunt, hard, exercise of memory, done so repeatedly and for so many years, that it becomes second nature, so that it cannot be forgotten."[37] This was exactly the kind of outdated pedagogy that progressive educators were hoping to replace.

Unfortunately for Blacks, the new focus on educating recently arrived White immigrants shifted attention away from the issue of teaching non-Whites. By 1919, Franklin Lane, secretary of the interior, considered the job of incorporating American Indians and Blacks into the fabric of American society an ongoing but largely completed process. "The Indian we feel we are responsible for as a Nation, and we give him an education—a most practical one," he explained, and "the Negro ... is slowly, very slowly coming into that knowledge ... of developing into a growing national asset—the knowledge of the way of making a living."[38] Indeed, by the 1920s, there was still a general consensus among Whites that the Hampton-Tuskegee model of industrial education was still the most effective route for American Indians and Blacks. For example, a 1921 study by Adolph Rigast at the University of Wisconsin traced the rise and fall of high-quality industrial education for Negroes in the South. He reported on gross disparities in the educational spending between both groups—$10.32 per pupil for Whites, $2.89 for Blacks—and he regretted the continual institutional and political disenfranchisement of African Americans by Southern Whites.

Throughout his study, Rigast related a sense of outrage at the African American condition in U.S. society, and he expressed frustration over the failed promise of industrial education for the race. He even insisted that Blacks would one day demand legal and political equality, although that day would be in the future. Nevertheless, Rigast never questioned that fact that industrial education was the best means for racial, sociological, and moral uplift in the meantime. Industrial education, he insisted, "trains the heart because . . . the negro is made more amiable neighbor, a better citizen, husband, and friend" and it "trains the head . . . mak[ing] him a more intelligent and efficient citizen and stuart [sic] of his home." In a position similar to what the Deweys had outlined in *Schools of To-morrow*, Rigast concluded that "It must be clearly understood that industrial education is not the solution of the race question in itself, but a medium through which the solution is arrived at." Ultimately, even the most vocal White advocates for improved education for Blacks still viewed industrial, not academic, education as the most appropriate for Black students, especially in the South. As Rigast explained, "It is up the whites to extend a helping hand to their black brother in his struggle for improvement."[39] Progressive educators considered Southern Blacks to be so deficient that they required an educational approach catered specifically to their sociological level.

With rising high school enrollments, progressive educators began to focus more on the American high school. In 1922, George Counts published what would ultimately become one of the most innovative books ever written on education, *The Selective Character of American Secondary Education*. In the study, Counts concluded that the American high school was not the engine of social mobility, egalitarianism, and democracy that proponents had claimed. In reality the high school reproduced rather than alleviated the socioeconomic inequalities because parental occupation was the biggest predictor of student graduation rates. Based on quantitative data from four U.S. cities (St. Louis, Seattle, Bridgeport, and Mount Vernon), Counts's conclusion on the selective character of American schools was curt and pithy. "Misfortune, as well as fortune, passes from generation to generation," he argued, and as a result, "secondary education . . . reflects the inequalities of family means and ambition."[40] Counts was not weighing in on the nature-nurture, heredity-environment debate; he was ignoring the debate altogether. For Counts, innate biological or cognitive potential did not necessarily dictate one's success, nor did exposure to education and the civilized sociological stage; it was the socioeconomic structure of American society itself that largely dictated one's outcome in life. Counts in essence turned the whole nature-nurture question inside out and pointed to the broader influences of American society and how they framed and dictated the lives of students. He would continue to explore this theme throughout his career.

Significantly, Counts's book was the first major survey of American school since the Deweys' *Schools of To-morrow* to include a segregated "negro high school" as part of its sample, the Sumner "Colored" High School in St. Louis. According to Counts, the vast majority of the Black students he surveyed had parents in occupations "requiring little skill." He repeatedly noted the instability of the Negro family; Black parents died at a greater rate than their White counterparts, a point, Counts argued, that had "not received adequate recognition." Blacks had a larger median family size (3.1) than Whites (2.8), and Black females attended high school at a higher comparative rate than White females. Although most Black males enrolled in the four-year commercial track, more Black females elected to take the home economics curriculum track than Whites, who tended to enter the clerical track. Counts attributed this to the "inferior opportunities to enter into the clerical occupations on the part of colored girls." Most of the Black females reported that they planned to attend college in hopes of acquiring a teaching job. In conclusion, Counts speculated that Blacks did not value secondary education as much as Whites because they were largely destined for low-skill jobs, "the standard of living is low, . . . the home is not a center of stimulation and inspiration, [and] . . . the family is notoriously unstable." Counts recognized that no other social group in America faced so many barriers to education, yet he ended on an optimistic note by noting that many Black families expressed ambition and desire for social betterment that exceeded Whites' in the same economic condition.[41]

Published at the peak of eugenics, Counts's depiction of Black students was striking in its failure to suggest that their unfortunate situation was in any way the result of innate inferiority or lower intelligence. In fact, Counts never suggested that the Black community in St. Louis was any different from their White counterpart in terms of sociological potential; Blacks' inferiority was mainly a result of their oppressive history and economic deprivation. His assessment of the Black community was empathetic and humane, even if some of his speculations about their homes lacking stimulation and ambition came close to blaming the victim. Nevertheless, just as the Deweys had done in *Schools of To-morrow*, Counts chose to include Blacks in his vision for American schools, at a time when most progressive educators simply ignored them. Yet, again as the Deweys had done, Counts failed to openly critique the segregated schools of St. Louis, an oversight made more conspicuous by his book's focus on the selective character of the high school. Furthermore, Counts made no references whatsoever to the theory of recapitulation, demonstrating that most postwar educators had completely abandoned the theory.

In the 1920s, White Protestant educators launched programs specifically aimed at reducing racial tension and prejudice. This included the "cultural gifts" assembly programs of New Jersey teacher Rachel Davis DuBois, the Committee on Goodwill between Jews and Christians, and the Commission on Interracial Cooperation in the South. Despite their reliance on shifting and inconsistent streams of funding, these groups experienced positive responses and reported moderate levels of success in the 1920s and 1930s. Grassroots reformers such as DuBois, Leonard Covello, and the Reverend Everett Clinchy collaborated directly with one another and with pluralist scholars such as Dewey, Du Bois, and Ruth Benedict. These educators drew directly upon the latest social scientific research challenging the rationality of racism. In particular, almost every White educator involved in the cultural gifts movement cited the innovative research of psychologist Bruno Lasker.

Lasker's groundbreaking book *Race Attitudes in Children*, published in 1929, argued that racial attitudes were learned unconsciously through socialization. Lasker drew attention to the role of textbooks in creating and perpetuating racial stereotypes, because textbooks were "apt to create antipathies which cannot always later in life be traced to their sources and so, with others, are carried along as seemingly innate." In particular, Lasker suggested that photographs had a more powerful influence than artistic portrayals because textbooks presented these images as "objective statements." Lasker directly challenged the common depiction of non-Whites in the context of linear development because of the subtle, unconscious message these images sent about African Americans. "Heroes of history may merge with those of legend and fiction," Lasker explained, "but the naked savage pictured, in contrast with a fully dressed white man, as representative of the Negro race will have produced a mental impression which returns as the word Negro is mentioned."[42] In 1929, Carter Woodson's *Journal of Negro History* cited this passage from Lasker as justification for the work of the Association of Negro Life and History to combat misinformation about African Americans.[43]

Rachel Davis Du Bois established the cultural gifts movement to challenge the stereotypes revealed by Lasker in his research on children and to introduce young students to positive images of non-Whites and recent immigrant groups. Using assemblies, cultural fairs, and classroom activities, DuBois emphasized the cultural contributions of all ethnic and racial groups. Despite its successes, the leaders of the cultural gifts movement often misread the social science research, tended to overgeneralize and exaggerate the contributions of certain cultural groups, and failed to address the larger socioeconomic causes of racism and inequality. For example, teachers who participated in Du Bois's cultural gifts program continued to espouse ethnocentric views, and some even used the new information to reinforce their preexisting stereotypes. As one teacher commented, "before taking this course I could not understand why he [the Jew] was so aggressive—after hearing the history of Jews ... I understand the reasons."[44] The cultural gifts movement stressed tolerance and patience toward those groups who were still assimilating to American life, but did not completely embrace the cultural relativity of the Boasians.

One progressive educator who incorporated the ideas of the cultural gifts movement was Harold Rugg. While coauthoring his book on child-centered education, Rugg was also working on a far more ambitious project: to reconstruct the social studies curriculum. Although *The Child-Centered School* ignored race, Rugg's famous series of textbooks on social problems did not. In the early 1920, Rugg argued that traditional content in history and social sciences should be replaced with material of "social worth"; specifically, historical facts should be replaced with historical generalizations that could be applied immediately to social problems. For Rugg, the recommendations of the 1916 NEA Committee on Social Studies report were too conservative, because they had been based upon "armchair philosophy" and "the opinion and *a priori* judgment of a small group of specialists in subject-matter." He saw little distinction between the Committee on Social Studies report and the recommendations of the 1893 Committee of Ten because both reports approached the curriculum as "piecemeal—subject by subject" without bringing itself "to view in close juxtaposition the total American scene and the whole school curriculum," and both reports had not been based upon the "measurement of results attained in current instruction."[45] To design his own curriculum, Rugg's methodology included a systematic analysis of leading frontier thinkers in the social sciences, from which generalizations were drawn. After compiling these generalizations from the leading authors of the period, Rugg constructed an interdisciplinary, problem-based social studies curriculum. Based on this work, he issued several pamphlets based on this analysis in the 1920s and eventually authored a series of bestselling textbooks in the 1930s.

Rugg's doctoral student Neal Billings performed the analysis of frontier thinkers. He compiled 888 generalizations from 61 books by leading scholars, including Franz Boas, Charles Beard, James Harvey Robinson, Charles Ellwood, and John Dewey. Because the project was descriptive rather than prescriptive in nature, it is no surprise that some of the generalizations addressed race. For example, citing Boas and others, generalization number 612 stated that "Differences in racial types, social conditions, modes of life, religious beliefs, etc. make assimilation much more difficult." Citing Ellwood, generalization number 613 stated, "The crossing of races had undoubtedly added to the variation of human types." Generalization number 622 concluded, "The very fact of the immigrants' number will make difficult their assimilation," and number 655 concluded, "Race antagonisms prevent close cooperation." These statements tell us very little about Rugg's views on race but, nevertheless, convey the sense that in 1929 leading scholars still generally viewed recent immigrants and racial diversity as social problems. Despite his view of racial diversity as a social problem, Billings had identified fostering "tolerance" as one of the major goals of the social studies.[46]

When Rugg published his textbook *An Introduction to Problems of American Culture* two years later, he followed through on Billings's objective of fostering tolerance. In a chapter on assimilation of different nationalities and races, Rugg celebrated the cultural contributions of all ethnic groups. He viewed the problems of foreign-born Americans through a pluralist perspective, aiming "[t]o teach the immigrants the fine things of American life," but also "[t]o learn from immigrants the fine things in their own culture." Likely influenced by Dewey, Kallen, and the cultural gifts movement, Rugg's treatment of racial diversity offered a balanced but contradictory approach to immigrants and Blacks. Regarding assimilation, he insisted that immigrants needed to learn to speak English, dress like an American, and "live in a thoroughly representative American neighborhood of his community." Rugg concluded, "As long as the immigrant reads, speaks, and thinks only in the language of his native land, he can never become truly American." Notably, Rugg made no mention of eugenics or intelligence testing. Presumably, omitting these topics was a conscious choice by Rugg to avoid giving these movements legitimacy. Regarding learning from immigrants, Rugg followed the cultural gifts approach to listing the major social and artistic accomplishments of individuals from different ethnicities and races, particularly in music. Rugg devoted a section to the "darker-skinned races . . . Negroes, Mexicans, Chinese, and Japanese," including a three-page discussion of the artistic and musical accomplishments of African Americans, the only book by a White author of the time to address such a topic. He cited the work of Black scholars Booker T. Washington, W.E.B. Du Bois, and Alain Locke.[47]

Rugg overlooked (or ignored) the racial theories of many of the frontier thinkers he cited in his list of generalizations and clearly aligned himself with Kallen, Dewey, and the cultural pluralists. Rugg's discussion of the artistic accomplishments of non-Whites and his refusal to recognize the legitimacy of eugenics placed him as one of the more egalitarian thinkers on race at the time. However, like Rachel Davis Du Bois and the proponents of the cultural gifts movement, Rugg limited his definition of culture to the specific contributions of individuals from each group. Despite the fact that Boas was cited in the original list of generalizations by frontier thinkers compiled by Billings, Rugg made no references to the work of the Boasians in his discussion of culture. As a result, Rugg divorced language from culture and insisted, as most did at the time, that immigrants adopt American speech and dress as soon as possible in order to assimilate. He called for tolerance, but did not necessarily celebrate cultural difference. As a result, despite his pluralistic rhetoric, Rugg rejected the cultural relativity of Boas and supported the "melting pot" metaphor of cultural assimilation, proclaiming: "America is indeed becoming the melting pot of the world."[48]

Advances in racial theory in the 1920s further supported the emerging focus on the socially constructed nature of racial inequality and the learned, not instinctual, nature of racial prejudice. In addition to Lasker's *Race Attitudes in Children*, two major books were published that challenged the rational, scientific basis of racial inequality and suggested that tolerance was indeed something that could be taught. The first was by the radical behaviorist John Watson who argued in his 1924 book *Behaviorism* that "We have no sure evidence of inferiority in the negro race," an assertion fully consistent with his insistence that "racial habit systems are bred into people" by socialization to family values. In this same work, Watson issued his famous boast that, if he were given a dozen healthy babies, he could "take any one at random and train him to become any type of specialist I might select—doctor, lawyer, artist, merchant-chief, and yes, even beggar-man and thief, regardless of his talents . . . and race of his ancestors."[49] The same year, Horace Kallen published the term *cultural pluralism* for the first time in his book *Culture and Democracy in the United States* (see Chapter 5), providing an alternative to the cultural assimilation model for immigrants. Cultural pluralism was underscored by Lasker's four-hundred-page empirical study, published in 1929, confirming that racial prejudice was socially learned as Watson argued, not instinctual as Thomas and Dewey had suggested. Lasker argued, "children learn most of all through the observation of adult attitudes in circumstances when grown-ups are least conscious of being studied."[50] Lasker shared his ideas in popular periodicals such as *Parents' Magazine, Child Study*, and *Woman's Press*. In fact, by the late 1920s, sociologists had largely replaced "the race problem" with the idea of "race relations," due in large part to the work of sociologist Robert Park.

Prior to his appointment at the University of Chicago, Park had served as secretary and publicist for the Congo Reform Association and had worked as a staff writer for Booker T. Washington. Based on this experience, Park was convinced that "whenever a sophisticated people invades the territories of a more primitive people in order to exploit their lands, and, incidentally, to uplift and civilize them," the result was "a terrible thing . . . destructive and wasteful." As an academic sociologist, Park authored a groundbreaking study of immigrant socialization in which he outlined three universal stages of race relations: competition and conflict, accommodation, and assimilation. "The race relations cycle," he explained, "is apparently irreversible . . . immigration restriction and racial barriers may slacken the tempo of the movement . . . but cannot change its direction."[51] Like the transnational vision of the cultural pluralists, Park's race relations cycle reinforced American exceptionalism by placing the United States at the forefront of an inevitable, unraveling process of global development. Park's race relations approach ignored the innate and deterministic racial language of the eugenicists, and it avoided the savagery-barbarism-civilization hierarchy of the recapitulationists by approaching race and culture from a pluralist perspective. However, like the cultural pluralists, Park introduced assimilation itself as the final developmental step on a universal scale of sociological development. Thus, from an ontological standpoint, Park still approached non-White and immigrant races who sought to maintain their own cultural characteristics as less developed and as prior steps in a linear global process.

*****

As numerous educational historians have noted, by the 1920s progressive educators had essentially divided into two camps.[52] Educational psychologists such as Kilpatrick and Rugg focused on humanizing the curriculum to be interdisciplinary, student-centered, and relevant. Educational sociologists such as Ellwood and Snedden sought to use the schools as a lever of social control by focusing on enhanced administrative techniques and policies. Although they occasionally clashed on issues—for example, Dewey's debate with David Snedden over the role of vocational education in a democracy—for the most part, these two groups worked in tandem. In fact, both groups largely drew upon the Dewey-Thorndike consensus to argue for a modernized, relevant curriculum that addressed student differences and aimed schooling at social reform.

Regarding race, the child-centered progressives leaned toward a more egalitarian and pluralist perspective, while the administrative progressives espoused theories of innate racial difference. Nevertheless, with the exception of post-1916 Dewey, there is little evidence to suggest that by the end of the 1920s any of these major progressive educators embraced the relativistic approach to culture espoused by Boas and his associates. In other words, even when progressive educators denied the innate-biological differences among races, they still believed in the sociological deficiency of non-Whites and immigrants. As historian James McKee argued, "If more sociologists [in the 1920s] were moving from biology to culture in the analysis of the race problem, they were still deaf to the anthropological argument for the equal status of human cultures."[53] For example, when Ellwood revised his eugenics outlook to adopt Dewey's pre-1916 approach to race and culture in 1927, he still relegated non-Whites to the psychological-sociological equivalent of children by reverting back to the savage-barbarian-civilization hierarchy affiliated with the theory of recapitulation. When Counts traced racial inequality to broader socioeconomic conditions instead of innate differences, he nevertheless viewed the Black students as being sociologically deficient by pointing out how their homes were "not a center of stimulation and inspiration." Furthermore, when Rugg celebrated the cultural contributions of immigrants and non-Whites, he made it clear that all of these groups needed to learn how to dress, speak, and act like Americans. None of them approached non-White and immigrant cultures as equal but different; instead, they continued to approach culture through a hierarchical lens of sociological deficiency—as prior steps toward modern Western civilization.

Epilogue

By the 1930s, scholars more or less overturned the idea that non-White social groups were innately, cognitively, biologically, or anatomically inferior.[1] Because of the rise of fascism in Europe, the onset of the Great Depression—which underscored the economic, not biological origins of social inequality—and the accumulation of scientific research expressing skepticism about racial hierarchies, most leading social scientists abandoned the biological-anatomical deficit model regarding people or color. Neo-hereditary arguments about the inferiority of non-Whites emerged from time to time, but by the late 1930s most mainstream scholars had replaced the innate deficit model with new models of sociological deficiency and acquired pathology, culminating in Oscar Lewis's "culture of poverty" thesis in 1959.[2] In other words, scholars shifted focus from the biological deficiency to the environmental and cultural deficiency of non-Whites. The new cultural deficiency studies argued that, because of the damaging effects of slavery, a century of institutional racism, and generational poverty, many people of color were culturally deprived and/or deficient. Books such as *The Culturally Deprived Child* and *Compensatory Education for Cultural Deprivation* popularized the cultural deficit model with educators in the 1960s.[3]

Psychologist Richard R. Valencia defines deficit thinking in education as "an endogenous theory that 'blames the victim' ... [and] posits that students of color who experience academic achievement problems do so because they, their cultures, and their families have deficits or deficiencies."[4] By the 1930s, cultural deficiency became the new approach to educating non-Whites, "a way of thinking about difference that reifies and essentializes culture rather than genetic endowment," historian George Fredrickson explains, and "makes culture do the work of race."[5] Although the cultural deficit thinking orientation was certainly preferable to the anatomical theory of recapitulation and eugenics, it nevertheless allowed White supremacy to remain in place for the next thirty years, as non-White children were treated as ontologically less formed than their White counterparts.

The anthropological idea of the cultural deficit of non-White students predated the fall of scientific racism by about three decades. In fact, as argued in this study, the real origins of the cultural deficit thinking began with sociologist Lester Frank Ward and pre-1916 John Dewey. Historians correctly identify Ward and Dewey as having an egalitarian approach to race, culture, and education, especially when compared with most of their peers.[6] However, scholars fail to recognize that, although these scholars were ahead of their time, they nevertheless espoused a belief in the sociological inferiority of non-White groups. When Dewey published his provocative article "Interpretation of the Savage Mind" in 1902, he boldly argued that leading sociologists, anthropologists, and psychologists were wrong to dismiss non-White savages as anatomically or psychically deficient. Dewey challenged the innate or biological deficiency of non-Whites, and instead argued that premodern men and women were merely sociologically deficient because of their lack of education and exposure to a civilized social environment. In 1902, this was a humane and innovative anthropological argument. Dewey's essay was cited and praised by William James, Albion Small, William I. Thomas, and Charles Ellwood. Yet by the 1910s, Dewey's sociological deficiency argument was challenged by Boas and his former students, who argued that people of color had a *different* culture, not necessarily an inferior one. After World War I, even Dewey himself began to question his sociological deficiency thesis, as he constructed and espoused a pluralistic outlook toward all races. Despite Dewey's ideological shift, however, most mainstream educators adopted his earlier sociological deficit model toward non-Whites, which more or less remained in place until the 1970s. Thus, Ward's and Dewey's idea of the sociological-cultural deficiency of non-Whites was considered radical in the 1890s, innovative in the 1920s, mainstream by the 1930s, but dismissive and ethnocentric by the 1970s. Despite Dewey's egalitarian, even radical, views on race, Dewey inadvertently played a role in the establishment of deficit thinking and its relationship to progressive education for the next thirty years.

Why did most progressive educators choose the cultural deficit approach of Dewey and Ward over the cultural pluralist approach of the Boasians? The first reason is that in the 1920s the innate-biological explanation for racial disparity in achievement was not only supported by leading psychometricians such as Thorndike, but it was also reinforced by policymakers. The passage of sterilization laws pertaining to the "feeble-minded" and immigration restriction for non–Northern Europeans provided legal legitimization for biological racism, even though these policies were directed at the alleged inferiority of certain White populations. Second, although the discipline of anthropology had more or less adopted Boas's relativistic approach to culture by the 1930s, most sociologists adopted Ward's and Dewey's cultural deficit approach. Led by Edward Ross, David Snedden, and Charles Ellwood, educational sociology became a more influential subfield than cultural anthropology in the 1920s, especially in the area of educational administration. Before World War I, educators looked to anthropologists because they were considered the authorities on racial difference, but after the war sociologists such as Robert Park took the lead in explaining race and race relations. Because most sociologists espoused the psychological-cultural deficiency of non-White students, most educators simply followed their lead.

Although scholars abandoned the literal application of the theory of recapitulation to education by the 1920s, many of the core ideas remained. For example, the educational belief in the sociological deficiency of many people of color continued until the 1960s and beyond. In addition, the application of genetic psychology and stage theory to curriculum—most notably, the research of Jean Piaget, Lawrence Kohlberg, and Erik Erikson—remained, although these stage theories have largely been stripped of their cultural-sociological correspondence. In fact, Piaget cited leading recapitulationist James Mark Baldwin as an early influence on his thinking.[7] The teaching and reenacting of Native American culture in the K–3 curriculum can also, to some degree, trace its historical roots to the theory of recapitulation. Although now the inclusion of Native American culture in the early elementary curriculum is largely justified by multiculturalism, it originally earned its place in the schools because young children were believed to be in the same psychological-sociological stage as the savages they were studying. Ultimately, the progressive educational idea that teachers should nourish a child's natural and instinctual curiosity (i.e., child-centeredness) never disappeared, and it is still the leading approach espoused by most colleges of education.[8]

The objective of my study was not to dismiss progressive education outright nor to imply that current progressive educational theory is somehow ethnocentric, but rather to reveal the deep-seated, unconscious nature of ethnocentrism and racism in American education and society, an ideology so all-encompassing that it extended to the heart of one of the most humane, radical, justice-oriented movements of the twentieth century. Unfortunately, as demonstrated by the persistent achievement gap between Whites and students of color in American schools today, we are a long way from overcoming the long-term effects of cultural deficit thinking, the roots of which stretch back to progressive education, a movement self-consciously defined by its alleged commitment to social reform and justice.[9]

Notes

Introduction

1. Quoted in Adam Hochschild, *Kind Leopold's Ghost: A Story of Greed, Terror, and Heroism in Colonial Africa* (New York: Houghton Mifflin, 1998), 175.
2. Ernst Haeckel, *Die Lebenswunder* (Stuttgart, Germany: Kroner, 1904), 450.
3. John Dewey, "Address to National Negro Conference (1909)," in *Middle Works*, vol. 4, 157.
4. John Dewey, "Contributions to Cyclopedia of Education (1911)" in *Middle Works*, vol. 6, 399; John Dewey, *How We Think* (Mineola, NY: Dover Publications, 1997-Originally published in 1910), 160; John Dewey, *Democracy and Education: An Introduction to Philosophy of Education* (New York: Free Press, 1916), 217.
5. See Lawrence Cremin, *Transformation of the School: Progressivism in American Education 1876–1957* (New York: Knopf, 1961); Robert L. Church and Michael W. Sedlak, *Education in the United States: An Interpretive History* (New York: Free Press, 1976); Merle Curti, *The Social Ideas of American Educators* (New York: Charles Scribner and Sons, 1935); Kieran Egan, *Getting it Wrong form the Beginning: Our Progressive Inheritance from Herbert Spencer, John Dewey, and Jean Piaget* (New Haven: Yale University Press, 2002); Herbert Kliebard, *The Struggle for the American Curriculum 1893–1958*, 2nd ed. (New York: Routledge, 1995); Edward Krug, *The Shaping of the American High School, 1880–1920* (Madison, WI: University of Wisconsin Press, 1964); Diane Ravitch, *Left Back: A Century of Battles over School Reform* (New York: Touchtone, 2000); William J. Reese, *Power and Promise of School Reform: Grassroots Movements during the Progressive Era* (Boston: Routledge and Kegan, 1986); Daniel Tanner and Laurel Tanner, *History of the School Curriculum* (New York: Macmillan, 1990); Arthur Zilversmit, *Changing Schools: Progressive Education and Practice, 1930–1960* (Chicago: University of Chicago Press, 1993). See also the themed issue of *Paedagogica Historica* 29 (August 2003) on progressive education, especially Jeffrey Mirel, "Old Educational Ideas, New American Schools: Progressivism and the Rhetoric of Educational Revolution": 477–497.
6. Arthur Zilversmit, *Changing Schools*, 3; Diane Ravitch, *Left Back*, 60; Herbert Kliebard, *The Struggle for the American Curriculum*, 11.
7. On the origins and essence of progressive education see the references in note 5. In addition, see Patricia Albjerg Graham, *Progressive Education: From Arcady to Academe: A History of the Progressive Education Association, 1919–1955* (New York: Teachers College Press, 1967); David Labaree, "Progressivism, Schools, and Schools of Education: An American Romance," *Paedagogica Historica*, 41 (February 2005): 275–288; Susan F. Semel and Alan R. Sadovnik, *Schools of Tomorrow, Schools of Today: What Happened to Progressive Education?* (New York: Peter Lang, 1988); William J. Reese, "The Origins of Progressive Education," *History of Education Quarterly*, 41 (Spring 2001): 1–24.

8. Graham, *Progressive Education*, 8, 9.

9. See Egan, *Getting it Wrong form the Beginning*; Cremin, *Transformation of the School*, Kliebard, *The Struggle for the American Curriculum*. Notable exceptions are Charles Strickland, "The Child, the Community, and Clio: The Use of Cultural History in Elementary School Experiments in the Eighteen-Nineties," *History of Education Quarterly* 7 (Winter 1967): 474–492 and Christine Woyshner and Chara Bohan, eds. *Histories of Social Studies and Race: 1865–2000* (New York: Palgrave Macmillan, 2012).

10. David Wallace Adams, *Education for Extinction: American Indians and the Boarding School Experience* (Lawrence, Kansas: University Press of Kansas, 1995); James D. Anderson, *The Education of Blacks in the South, 1860–1935* (Chapel Hill: University of North Carolina Press, 1988); Cherry McGee Banks, *Improving Multicultural Education: Lessons from the Intergroup Education Movement* (New York: Teachers College Press, 2005); Zoe Burkholder, *Color in the Classroom: How American Schools Taught Race 1900–1954* (New York: Oxford University Press, 2011); Jeffery E. Mirel, *Patriotic Pluralism: Americanization Education and European Immigrants* (Cambridge, MA: Harvard University Press, 2010); Michael R. Olneck, "American Public Schooling and European Immigrants in the Early Twentieth Century: A Post Revisionist Synthesis," in *Rethinking the History of American Education*, ed. William. J. Reece and John L. Rury (New York: Palgrave Macmillan, 2008), 103–141; Steven Selden, *Inheriting Shame: The Story of Eugenics and Racism in America* (New York: Teachers College Press, 1999); Diana Selig, *Americans All: The Cultural Gifts Movement* (Cambridge, MA: Harvard University Press, 2008); Vanessa Siddle Walker, "Organized Resistance and Black Educators' Quest for School Equality, 1878–1938," *Teachers College Record 107* (March 2005): 355–388; William Watkins, *The White Architects of Black Education: Ideology and Power in America, 1865–1954* (New York: Teachers College Press, 2001); Melissa F. Weiner, *Power, Protest, and the Public Schools: Jewish and African American Struggles in New York City* (New Brunswick, NJ: Rutgers University Press, 2010); Ana G. Winfield, *Eugenics and Education in America* (New York: Peter Lang, 2007); Jonathan Zimmerman, *Whose America? Culture Wars in the Public Schools* (Cambridge, MA: Harvard University, 2002).

11. See Elazar Barkan, *The Retreat of Scientific Racism: Changing Conceptions in Britain and the United States between the World Wars* (New York: Cambridge University Press, 1992).

12. William Bagley, *Determinism in Education: A Series of Papers on the Relative Influence of Inherited and Acquired Traits in Determining Intelligence, Achievement, and Character* (Baltimore: Warwick and York, Inc., 1925), 16.

13. See Daryl Michael Scott, *Contempt and Pity: Social Policy and the Image of the Damaged Black Psyche, 1880–1996* (Chapel Hill: University of North Carolina Press, 1997); Richard R. Valencia, "Genetic Pathology Model of Deficit Thinking," in *The Evolution of Deficit Thinking: Educational Thought and Practice*, ed. Richard R. Valencia (Washington DC: Falmer Press): 41–113, and Russell Skiba, "'As Nature Has Formed Them': The History and Current Status of Racial Difference Research," *Teachers College Record, 114* (2012): 1–49.

14. Arthur Lovejoy, *The Great Chain of Being: A Study of the History of an Idea* (Cambridge, MA: Harvard University Press, 1936), 7.

15. See note 5.

16. James Sully, "The New Study of Children," in *Mind: Little Masterpieces of Science*, ed. George Iles (New York: Doubleday, 1902), 26.

17. Alexander Francis Chamberlain, *The Child: A Study in the Evolution of Man*, 2nd ed. (New York: Walter Scott Publishing, 1907), 52.

18. Olive Hide Foster, "An Experiment in Education; Professor Dewey's Theories and Methods as Exemplified in a School Conducted by the Pedagogical Department of the University of Chicago," *The Sunday Times-Herald Chicago* (June 3, 1900): 1.

19. For examples of his dichotomous language, especially as it relates to eugenics, in what are otherwise excellent studies, see Burkholder, *Color in the Classroom*; Selig, *Americans All*; Selden, *Inheriting Shame*; A. J. Angulo, *Empire and Education: A History of Greed and Goodwill from the War of 1898 to the War on Terror* (New York: Palgrave Macmillan, 2012); and Barkan, *The Retreat of Scientific Racism*. Studies with more dynamic views of ethnicity, race, and society include Hamilton Cravens, *The Triumph of Evolution: American Scientists and the Heredity-Environment Controversy 1900–1941* (Philadelphia: University of Pennsylvania Press, 1978) and Robert Richards, *Darwin and the Emergence of Evolutionary Theories of Mind and Behavior* (Chicago: University of Chicago Press, 1989); in anthropology, see George Stocking Jr., *Race, Culture and Evolution: Essays in the History of Anthropology* (Chicago: University of Chicago Press, 1968); in sociology see James McKee, *Sociology and the Race Problem: The Failure of a Perspective* (Chicago: University of Illinois Press, 1993); in the broader social sciences, see Dorothy Ross, *The Origins of American Social Science* (New York: Cambridge University Press, 1991); Thomas Gossett, *Race: The History of an Idea in America* (New York: Schocken Books, 1963) and Nell Irvin Painter, *The History of White People* (New York: Norton and Company, 2010); in law and public policy, see Matthew Frye Jacobson, *Whiteness of a Different Color: European Immigrants and the Alchemy of Race* (Cambridge, MA: Harvard University Press, 1998) and *Barbarian Virtues: The United States Encounters Foreign Peoples at Home and Abroad, 1876–1917* (New York: Hill and Wang, 2000).

20. See Ben Burks, "Unity and Diversity through Education: A Comparison of the Thought of W.E.B. Du Bois and John Dewey," *The Journal of Thought* (Spring 1997): 99–110; S. F. Stack, "John Dewey and the Question of Race: The Fight for Odell Walker," *Education and Culture, 25*(2009): 17–35; Laurel Tanner and Daniel Tanner, "Environmentalism in American Pedagogy: The Legacy of Lester Ward," *Teachers College Record 88*, no. 4 (1987): 537–547.

21. George Frederickson, *Racism: A Short History* (Princeton, NJ: Princeton University Press), 158.

22. Ronald Butchart made a similar observation, by drawing parallels between the "culturally responsive pedagogy" of today and the racist theories that led to the differentiated curriculum of the Hampton-Tuskegee model in the nineteenth century. See "Race, Social Studies, and Culturally Relevant Curriculum in Social Studies' Prehistory: A Cautionary Meditation," in *Histories of Social Studies and Race*, 19–36.

Chapter 1

1. Arthur Lovejoy, *The Great Chain of Being: A Study of the History of an Idea* (Cambridge, MA: Harvard University Press, 1936), 59.

2. Eric Hobsbawm, *The Age of Empire: 1897–1914* (New York: Vintage, 1987); Charles Mills, *The Racial Contract* (Ithaca, NY: Cornell University Press, 1997).

3. Darwin's idea that aboriginal populations were destined for extinction was common throughout the nineteenth century. See Patrick Brantlinger, *Dark Vanishings: Discourse on Extinction of Primitive Races, 1800–1930* (Ithaca, NY: Cornell University Press, 2003).

4. Charles Darwin, *The Descent of Man, and Selection in Relation to Sex* (New York: D. Appleton and Co., 1871), 193, 171.

5. Lewis Henry Morgan, *Ancient Society: Researchers in the Lines of Human Progress from Savagery through Barbarianism to Civilization* (Chicago: Charles H. Kerr, 1877), xxxi.

6. Edward Burnett Tylor, *Anthropology: An Introduction to the Study of Man and Civilization* (New York: D. Appleton and Co., 1881), 24, 25.

7. See Stephen Jay Gould, *Ontogeny and Phylogeny* (Cambridge, MA: Harvard University Press, 1977).

8. This argument was anticipated by George Stocking Jr. in *Race, Culture, and Evolution: Essays in the History of Anthropology* (Chicago: University of Chicago Press, 1968).

9. Robert Wiebe, *The Search for Order, 1877–1920* (New York: Hill and Wang, 1967), xiii, 111.

10. Hobsbawm, *The Age of Empire*, 56–73.

11. Morton White, *Social Thought in America: The Revolt Against Formalism* (New York: Oxford Press, 1947); Eric Bredo, "Evolution, Psychology, and John Dewey's Critique of the Reflex Arc Concept," *Elementary School Journal* 98 (1998): 449. See also the introduction to James T. Kloppenberg, *Uncertain Victory: Social Democracy and Progressivism in European and American Thought, 1870–1920* (New York: Oxford University Press, 1986).

12. Herbert Spencer, "Progress: Its Laws and Cause," in *Seven Essays: Selected From the Works of H. Spencer* (London: Watts and Co., 1907), 33.

13. Dewey, "The Influence of Darwinism on Philosophy (1909)" in *Middle Works*, vol. 4: 7.

14. Dewey, "The Evolutionary Method as Applied to Morality (1902)," in *Middle Works*, vol. 2: 14.

15. John Dewey, *Democracy and Education: An Introduction to Educational Philosophy* (New York: Free Press, 1916), 73.

16. Robert Brandom, "When Philosophy Paints Its Blue on Grey: Irony and the Pragmatist Enlightenment," in *Pragmatism, Nation and Race: Community in the Age of Empire*, eds. Chad Kautzer and Eduardo Mendieta (Bloomington: Indiana University Press, 2009), 20.

17. Quoted in Louis Menand, *The Metaphysical Club: A Story of Ideas in America* (New York: Farrar, Straus, and Giroux, 2001), 109.

18. Edward Burnett Tylor, *Primitive Culture: Researches into the Development of Mythology, Philosophy, Religion, Language, Art and Custom* (New York: Putnam and Sons, 1871), 360.

19. Quoted in *Stocking, Race, Culture, and Evolution*, 116.

20. Tylor, *Primitive Culture*, 101, 6.

21. Morgan, *Ancient Society*, 3–4.

22. Tylor, *Primitive Culture*, 295.

23. Quoted in Stocking, *Race, Culture, and Evolution*, 124.

24. A. C. Haddon, *The Study of Man* (London: Bliss, Sands, & Co, 1898), xxii.

25. See Kliebard, *The Struggle for the American Curriculum;* Tanner and Tanner, *History of the School Curriculum*; and Krug, *The Shaping of the American High School*.

26. Herbert Spencer, *First Principles* (London: Williams and Norgate, 1864), 158.

27. Herbert Spencer, *Education: Intellectual, Moral, and Physical* (London: John Childs and Son, 1861), 75.

28. Lester Frank Ward, *Dynamic Sociology, or Applied Social Science* (New York: D. Appleton and Co., 1883), 593.

29. Ibid., 594.

30. Lester Frank Ward, *The Psychic Factors of Civilization* (New York: Ginn and Co., 1893), 49, 317.

31. Ibid., 141.

32. Lester Frank Ward, *Haeckel's Genesis of Man, or History of the Development of the Human Race* (Philadelphia: Phillip Stern and Company), 1879.

33. Franklin Giddings, *Principles of Sociology: An Analysis of the Phenomenon of Association and of Social Organization* (New York: Macmillan, 1896), 138, 155, 264.

34. Albion Woodbury Small, *General Sociology: An Exposition of the Main Development in Sociological Theory From Spencer to Ratzenhofer* (Chicago: University of Chicago Press, 1905), 198.

35. Emile Durkheim, *The Elementary Forms of Religious Life* (London: G. Allen and Unwin, 1915), 3.

36. John Dewey and James Tufts, *Ethics* (New York: Henry Holt and Co, 1908), 21.

37. Wilhelm Wundt, *Outlines of Psychology*, trans. Charles Judd (New York: G. E. Stechert and Co, 1896), 336.

38. G. Stanley Hall, "The New Psychology as Basis of Education," *The Forum 17* (March–August 1894): 716.

39. Georg Wilhelm Frederich Hegel, *Hegel as Educator*, ed. Frederic Ludlow Luqueer (New York: Macmillan, 1896), 112.

40. William Torrey Harris, *Psychologic Foundations of Education: An Attempt to Show the Genesis of Higher Faculties of the Mind* (New York: D. Appleton Press, 1898), xi, vii, 8, 9, 378, 359, 313, 265.

41. Quoted in Cornell West, *The American Evasion of Philosophy: A Genealogy of Pragmatism* (Madison: University of Wisconsin Press, 1989), 29, 31.

42. See Harvey Cormier, "William James on Nation and Race," in *Pragmatism, Nation and Race: Community in the Age of Empire*, ed. Chad Kautzer and Eduardo Mendieta (Bloomington: Indiana University Press, 2009), 142–162.

43. William James, *Principles of Psychology* (New York: Henry Holt and Co, 1890), 435. I thank Jim Garrison for pointing me to this passage.

44. Quoted in Menand, *The Metaphysical Club*, 145.

45. James, *Principles of Psychology*, 368–369.

46. Charles H. Judd, *Genetic Psychology for Teachers* (New York: D. Appleton Press, 1909), xii, 199, 203.

47. G. Stanley Hall, *Adolescence: Its Psychology and Its Relation to Physiology, Anthropology, Sociology, Sex, Crime, Religion and Education* (New York: D. Appleton Press, 1905), vii, vii, x, xi, 179, 216, 122, 215.

48. James Mark Baldwin, *Mental Development in the Race and Child: Methods and Processes* (New York: Macmillan, 1895), 16.

49. James Mark Baldwin, *Darwin and the Humanities* (Baltimore: Review Publishing, 1909), 93, 91.

50. Hugo Münsterberg, *Psychology and the Teacher* (Baltimore: Review Publishing, 1909), 284.

51. John Stuart Mill, *Principles of Political Economy: With Some of Their Applications to Social Philosophy* (New York: Longmans, Green and Co., 1909—Originally published in 1848), 144, 273, 157, 439.

52. Thorstein Veblen, *The Theory of the Leisure Class: An Economic Study of Institutions* (New York: Macmillan, 1899), 240, 215, 218, 289.

53. See Michael Knoll, "From Kidd to Dewey: The Origin and Meaning of Social Efficiency," *Journal of Curriculum Studies, 41* (2009): 361–391.

54. Benjamin Kidd, *Social Evolution* (New York: Macmillan, 1894), 293.

55. See Thomas Fallace and Victoria Fantozzi, "Was There Really a Social Efficiency Doctrine? The Uses and Abuses of an Educational Idea," *Educational Researcher* (May 2013): 142–150.

56. Benjamin Kidd, *The Control of the Tropics* (New York: Macmillan, 1898), 52, 53, 53, 54.

57. Herbert Baxter Adams, "The Germanic Origin of New England Towns," *Johns Hopkins University Studies in Historical and Political Science, 1* (1883): 8.

58. Quoted in Gossett, *Race*, 113.

59. John Fiske, *Darwinism and Other Essays* (New York: Houghton Mifflin, 1902—Originally published 1879), 157, 114, 38.

60. Albert Bushnell Hart, *School History of the United States* (New York: American Book Company, 1918), 110.

61. Peter Novick, *That Noble Dream: The Objectivity Question and the American Historical Profession* (New York: Cambridge University Press, 1988), 88.

62. Frederick Jackson Turner, *The Frontier in American History* (New York: Henry Holt and Company, 1921), 4.

63. Ibid., 15, 144, 269.

64. James Harvey Robinson, *New History: Essays Illustrating the Modern Historical Outlook* (New York: Macmillan, 1912), 252, 108.

65. Robinson, *Medieval and Modern Times* (New York: Ginn and Company, 1916), 221, 431.

66. See John Dewey's collected reviews of books by scholars who employed the theory of recapitulation in Dewey, "Review of The Psychic Factors of Civilization by Lester F. Ward" Boston: Ginn and Co., 1893; *Social Evolution*, by Benjamin Kidd. New York and London: Macmillan Co., 1894; *Civilization During the Middle Ages*, by George B. Adams. New York; Charles Scribner's Sons, 1894, and *History of the Philosophy of History*, by Robert Flint. New York: Charles Scribner's Sons, 1894 (1894)," in *Early Works*, vol. 4, 200–213; and Dewey, "Review of Harris's Psychological Foundations of Education" and "Review of Social and Ethical Interpretations in Mental Development: A Study in Social Psychology by James Mark Baldwin, New York: Macmillan Co, 1897 (1897)," in *Early Works*, vol. 5, 372–421.

67. G. Stanley Hall, "The New Psychology as Basis of Education," *The Forum, 17* (March 1894), 719.

68. John Dewey and Albion Small, *My Pedagogic Creed and the Demands of Sociology Upon Pedagogy* (New York: E. Kellogg and Co., 1897), 18.

Chapter 2

1. Frank Forest Bunker, "Reorganization of the Public School System," *U.S. Office of Education Bulletin 1916*, no. 8 (Washington DC: US Government Printing Office, 1916), 116.

2. John Dewey, "Plan of Organization of University Primary School (1900)" in *Early Works*, vol. 5, 224.

3. Harriet Scott and Gertrude Buck, *Organic Education: A Manual for Teachers in Primary and Grammar Grades* (Boston: DC Heath and Co., 1899), 13.

4. Quoted in Chamberlain, *Child*, 293.

5. See references in notes 6 and 12 of Introduction.

6. John Dewey and Evelyn Dewey, "Schools of To-morrow (1916), " in *Middle Works*, vol. 8, passim.

7. Jean Jacques Rousseau, *Discourse Upon the Origin of the Inequality* (Indianapolis: Hackett Publishing Co, 1992—Originally published in 1755), 50.

8. Frederich Froebel, *Education of Man*, trans. W. N. Hailman (New York: D. Appleton Press, 1906), 160, 18.

9. Quoted in Gould, *Ontogeny and Phylogeny*, 138.

10. Quoted in C. C. Van Liew, "The Educational Theory of Culture Epochs Viewed Historically and Critically," in *The First Yearbook of the Herbart Society for the Scientific Study of Teaching* (Bloomington, IL: National Herbart Society, 1895), 82.

11. Marie Montessori, *The Montessori Method*, trans. Anne George (New York: Frederick Stokes Co., 1912), 149–153.

12. Marie Montessori, *Pedagogical Anthropology*, trans. Frederic Taber Cooper (New York: Frederick Stokes Co., 1912), 218–219.

13. Cremin, *Transformation of the School*, 129.

14. Francis Wayland Parker, *Talks on Pedagogics: An Outline of the Theory of Concentration* (New York: E. L. Kellogg, 1894), 457, 238.

15. Ibid., 92–93.

16. Thomas J. Morgan, "A Plea for the Papoose," *Baptist Home Mission Monthly 18* (December 1896): 404.

17. Margaret Jacobs, *White Mother to a Dark Race: Settler Colonialism, Maternalism, and the Removal of Indigenous Children in the American West and Australia, 1800–1940* (Lincoln: University of Nebraska Press), 96–103.

18. Ibid., 75–76, 112, 135.

19. Ibid., 132, 136.

20. Quoted in Anderson, *The Education of Blacks*, 38, 39.

21. Thomas Jesse Jones, *Social Studies in the Hampton Curriculum* (Hampton, VA: Hampton Institute Press, 1908), 4.

22. William Archibald Dunning, *Reconstruction: Political and Economic, 1865–1877* (New York: Harper and Brothers, 1907).

23. Jones, *Social Studies*, 5, 47.

24. Ibid., 47.

25. Quoted in Ruth Spack, "English, Pedagogy, and Ideology: A Case Study of the Hampton Institute, 1878–1900," *American Indian Culture and Research Journal 24* (2001): 18, 15.

26. Quoted in Lee D. Baker, *From Savage to Negro: Anthropology and the Construction of Race, 1896-1954* (Berkeley: University of California Press, 1998), 57.

27. Ibid., 60.

28. Quoted in Eugene F. Provenzo Jr., *Culture as Curriculum: Education and the International Expositions* (1876–1904) (New York: Peter Lang, 2012), 78.

29. Quoted in Elliott M. Rudwick and August Meier, "Black Man in the 'White City': Negroes and the Columbian Exposition, 1893," *Phylon 26* (4th Quarter 1965): 359, 354.

30. Quoted in Jacobs, *White Mother to a Dark Race*, 384, 407.

31. Quoted in Anne Paulet, "To Change the World: The Use of American Indian Education in the Philippines," *History of Education Quarterly 47* (May 2007): 198.

32. G. Stanley Hall, "How Far Are the Principles of Education along Indigenous Lines Applicable to American Indians?" *Journal of Proceedings and Addresses of the Forty-Sixth Annual Meeting of the National Education Association, 46* (1908): 1161.

33. Quoted in Roland Sintos Coloma, "'Destiny Has Thrown the Negro and Filipino Under the Tutelage of America' Race and Curriculum in the Age of Empire," *Curriculum Inquiry, 39* (2009): 508, 507.

34. William T. Harris, Address Delivered at the Inauguration of the Reverend John Gordon, D.D. (Washington, DC: US Government Printing Office, 1904), 28.

35. Louis Dalrymple, "School Begins," *Puck* (January 1898): 8–9.

36. Eric Hobsbawm, *The Age of Empire: 1897–1914* (New York: Vintage, 1987).

37. In addition to Coloma, "Destiny Has Thrown the Negro" and Paulet, "To Change the World," see David H. Kim, "The Unexamined Frontier: Dewey, Pragmatism, and America Enlarged" in *Pragmatism, Nation and Race*, ed. Chad Kautzer and Eduardo Mendieta (Bloomington: Indiana University Press, 2009), 46–72.

38. William Torrey Harris, *Educational Review*, Vol. XVI, June–December, ed. Nicholas Murray Butler (New York: Henry Holt and Company, 1898): 204, 205.

39. Quoted in Paulet, 185.

40. Charles Bartlett Dyke, "Essential Features in the Education of the Child Races," in *Addresses and Proceeding: National Education Association of the United States* (Chicago: University of Chicago Press, 1909), 929, 930.

41. Ibid., 932.

42. Frank. H. Ball, "Some Phases of Industrial School Work in Porto Rico," in *Proceedings of the Eastern Manuel Training Association* (Allegheny, PA: John C. Park, 1903), 118, 120, 116.

43. See Spack, "English, Pedagogy and Ideology," 5.

44. William Torrey Harris, "An Educational Policy for Our New Possessions," *Educational Review 18* (September 1899): 114–15.

45. William James, "The Philippine Tangle (1899)," in *The Works of William James: Essays, Comments and Reviews*, ed. Fredson Bowers (Cambridge, MA: Harvard University Press, 1987), 157.

46. G. Stanley Hall, "The Point of View Toward the Primitive Races," *The Journal of Race Development 1* (July 1910): 5.

47. See Thomas Fallace, "Repeating the Race Experience: John Dewey and the History Curriculum at the University of Chicago Laboratory School," *Curriculum Inquiry 39* (June 2009): 381–405.

48. John Dewey, *Democracy and Education: An Introduction to Philosophy of Education* (New York: Free Press, 1916), 217.

49. John Dewey, "Some Stages of Logical Thought (1900)," *Middle Works*, passim.

50. See Thomas Fallace, "'The Mind at Every Stage Has Its Own Logic': John Dewey as Genetic Psychologist," *Educational Theory 60* (April 2010): 129–146.

51. Dewey, *How We Think*, 31, 32.

52. John Dewey, *Democracy and Education*, 184, 191, 195.

53. John Dewey to Clara Mitchell, November 29, 1895 (record 00272) in *The Correspondence of John Dewey*, Vol. 1: 1871–1918, 3rd ed., CD-ROM version, ed. Larry Hickman (Carbondale: Center for Dewey Studies, Southern Illinois University, 2005).

54. John Dewey, *The Child and the Curriculum and The School and Society*, 10th ed. (Chicago: University of Chicago Press, 1969), 9.

55. John Dewey and James H. Tufts, "Ethics (1908)," in *Middle Works*, vol. 5, 23.

56. Ibid., 6.

57. See Chapter Six, "The Dark Skinned Savage: The Image of Primitive Man in Evolutionary Anthropology," in Stocking, *Race, Culture, and Evolution*.

58. John Dewey, "The School as Social Centre (1902)," in *Middle Works*, vol. 2, 85–86.

59. Jane Addams, *Twenty Years at Hull-House* (New York: Macmillan, 1911), 237, 243, 236. See also Anne Durst, *Women Educators in the Progressive Era: The Women Behind Dewey's Laboratory School* (New York: Palgrave Macmillan, 2010).

60. Jane Addams, *Democracy and Social Ethics* (New York: Macmillan, 1902), 229, 182.

61. Quoted in Anna Lasch-Quinn, *Black Neighbors: Race and the Limits of Reform in the American Settlement House Movement, 1890–1945* (Chapel Hill: University of North Carolina Press), 15, 21.

62. See Harvey Cormier, "William James on Nation and Race," in *Pragmatism, Nation, and Race: Community in the Age of Empire*, ed. Chad Kautzer and Eduardo Mendieta, 142–162.

63. John Dewey, "Interpretation of the Culture-Epoch Theory (1896)," in *Early Works*, vol. 5, 248.

64. See Small, *General Sociology*, 642; William Isaac Thomas, *Source Book for Social Origins* (Chicago: University of Chicago Press, 1909), 173; William James to John Dewey, September 28, 1902 (rec. 00746), in *The Correspondence of John Dewey*.

65. John Dewey, "Interpretation of the Savage Mind (1902)," in *Middle Works*, vol. 2, 39.

66. John Dewey, "Address to National Negro Conference (1909)," in *Middle Works*, vol. 4, 157.

67. See Peter Bowler, *The Eclipse of Darwinism: Anti-Darwinian Evolution Theories in the Decades around 1900* (Baltimore: Johns Hopkins Press, 1983), 240; Louis Menand, *The Metaphysical Club: A Story of Ideas in America* (New York: Farrar, Straus, and Giroux, 2001), 382.

68. Dewey, "Address to National Negro Conference," 157.

69. John Dewey, "Contributions to Cyclopedia of Education, vols. 1 and 2 (1911)," in *The Middle Works*, vol. 6, 406.

70. John Dewey, "The Philosophical Work of Herbert Spencer (1904)," in *Middle Works*, vol. 3, 196.

71. Chamberlain, *Child*, 353, vii.

72. Ibid., vii, 51, 229, 232.

73. Charles McMurry, *Elements of General Method: Based on the Principles of Herbert* (New York: Macmillan, 1903), 61, 62.

74. Dewey, "History for the Educator (1909)," *Middle Works*, vol. 4, 195.

75. Wilbur Samuel Jackman, *Nature Study and Related Studies for Common Schools* (Chicago: Normal School Publishing, 1898), 11.

76. John Ward Stimson, *The Gate Beautiful: The Philosophy of Beauty* (Trenton, NJ: Albert Brandt, 1903), 156.

77. Quoted in Dorothy McMurray, *Herbartian Contributions to History Instruction in American Elementary Schools* (New York: Bureau of Publications, Teachers College, Columbia University, 1946), 77, 78, 86.

78. L. C. Marshall and Charles Judd, "An Introduction to Social Studies," in *The Twenty Second Yearbook of the National Society for the Study of Education: Part II, The Social Studies in the Elementary and Secondary School*, ed. G. M. Whipple (Bloomington, IL: Public School Publishing Company, 1923), 87–88.

79. Scott and Buck, *Organic Education*, 3, 13, 291.

80. Catherine Isabel Dodd, *Introduction to the Herbartian Principles of Teaching* (New York: Macmillan, 1898), 42, 44.

81. Katherine Elizabeth Dopp, *The Tree-Dwellers: Age of Fear* (New York: Rand McNally, 1904), 9–10, 11.

82. Katherine Elizabeth Dopp, "Some Steps in the Evolution of Social Occupations," *The Elementary School Teacher and the Course of Study*, 3 (1903): 625, 626.

83. Walter Schell, "The Value of Play in the Development of the Child," *The Inland Educator*, 9 (5): 214–215.

84. Edwin Ashbury Kirkpatick, *Genetic Psychology: An Introduction to the Objective and Genetic View of Intelligence* (New York: Macmillan, 1910), 357.

85. James Sully, *Studies in Childhood* (New York: D. Appleton, 1895), 168.

86. C. C. Van Liew, "The Educational Theory of Cultural Epochs: Viewed Historically and Critically," in *The Yearbook of the Herbart Society for the Scientific Study of Teaching* (Chicago: Herbart Society, 1895), 106.

87. George Edgar Vincent, *The Social Mind and Education* (New York: Macmillan Company, 1897), vii–viii.

Chapter 3

1. Charles DeGarmo, "Social Aspects of Moral Education," in *Forgotten Heroes of American Education: The Great Tradition of Teaching Teachers*, ed. J. Wesley Null and Diane Ravitch (Greenwich, CT: Information Age Publishing, 2006), 293.

2. Sidney Hook, *John Dewey: An Intellectual Portrait* (New York: John Day Company, 1939), 15. On the curriculum for the Dewey School, see Durst, *Women Educators in the Progressive Era*; Ellen C. Lagemann, "Experimenting with Education: John Dewey and Ella Flagg Young at the University of Chicago," *American Journal of Education*, 104 (1996), 171–185; Laurel Tanner, *Dewey's Laboratory School: Lessons for Today* (New York: Teachers College Press, 1997).

3. John Dewey, *The Child and the Curriculum and The School and Society*, 20, 19, 53. Evidence of application of the theory of recapitulation at the Dewey School can also be found in Katherine Camp Mayhew and Alice Camp Edwards, *The Dewey School: The Laboratory School of the University of Chicago, 1896–1903* (New York: Appleton-Century, 1936).

4. Ibid., 21.

5. John Dewey, "Some Stages of Logical Thought (1900)," in *Middle Works*, vol. 1, 151.

6. Susan Blow to William Torrey Harris, June 12, 1896 (record 01247) in *The Correspondence of John Dewey*, vol. 1: 1871–1918, 3rd ed., CD-ROM version, ed. Larry Hickman (Carbondale: Center for Dewey Studies, Southern Illinois University, 2005).

7. Laura Runyon, "A Day with the New Education," *Chautauquan: Organ of the Chautauqua Literacy and Science Circle* 30 (1900): 591.

8. Elizabeth Langley and Annette Butler, *Elementary School Record*, 3 (1900): 377.

9. H. M. Hodgman, "A New Departure in Education," *Education*, 21 (December 1900): 235.

10. Laura Runyon, *The Teaching of Elementary History in the Dewey School* (Master's thesis, University of Chicago, 1906), 49, 55.

11. John and Evelyn Dewey, "Schools of To-Morrow (1915)" in *Middle Years*, vol. 8, 244, 260, 269–270, 391.

12. Ibid., 340, 351.

13. Anonymous, "Review of Schools of Tomorrow," *The Southern Workman*, 45 (1916): 123–124.

14. See Walter Feinberg, *Reason and Rhetoric: Intellectual Foundations of Twentieth Century Liberal Educational Policy* (New York: John Wiley, 1975); Frank Margonis, "John Dewey's Racialized Visions of the Student and Classroom Community," *Educational Theory*, 59 (2009): 17–39.

15. Ibid., 244, 260, 369–370.

16. Department of the Interior, Bureau of Education, *Educational Survey of Elyria, Ohio, Bulletin No. 15* (Washington, DC: US Government Printing Office, 1918), 174.

17. Ibid., 191.

18. Ibid.

19. Ibid., 194.

20. Arthur Dunn, *The Community and the Citizen* (New York: Heath and Company, 1907), vi.

21. See Fallace, *Dewey and the Dilemma of Race: An Intellectual History, 1895–1922* (New York: Teachers College Press, 2012).

22. Dunn, The Community and the Citizen, 153–154.

23. Department of the Interior, Bureau of Education, *Educational Survey of Elyria, Ohio* (Washington, DC: US Government Printing Office, 1918), 181.

24. Quoted in Luther V. Hendricks, *James Harvey Robinson: Teacher of History* (New York: King's Crown Press, 1946), 37.

25. See Thomas Fallace, "John Dewey's Influence on the Origins of the Social Studies: An Analysis of the Historiography and New Interpretation," *Review of Educational Research,* 79 (2009): 601–624.

26. John Dewey, *The Child and the Curriculum and the School and Society*, 151, 158–159.

27. Department of the Interior, Bureau of Education, *The Social Studies in Secondary Education,* Bulletin No. 28 (Washington, DC: US Government Printing Office, 1916), 34, 44.

28 Ibid., 40.

29. Ibid., 21, 32.

30. See Thomas Fallace, "Did Social Studies Really Replace History in American Secondary Schools?" *Teachers College Record, 110* (2008): 2245–2270.

31. *The Social Studies in Secondary Education*, 9.

32. See Kliebard, *The Struggle for the American Curriculum*, 83; Wayne Au, "Teaching under the New Taylorism: High-stakes Testing and the Standardization of the 21st Century Curriculum," *Journal of Curriculum Studies, 43* (2011): 25–45; and Raymond Callahan, *Education and the Cult of Efficiency* (Chicago: University of Chicago Press, 1962).

33. Quoted in Knoll, "From Kidd to Dewey," 367, 368, 369.

34. Ira W. Howerth, "The Social Aim of Education," in *The Fifth Yearbook of the National Herbart Society for the Scientific Study of Teaching* (Chicago: University of Chicago press, 1899), 99, 69.

35. William Bagley, *The Educative Process* (New York: Macmillan, 1905), 103, 156, 27, 197, 201.

36. Ibid., 62–65.

37. Samuel Train Dutton, *Social Phases of Education in the School and the Home* (New York: Macmillan Co., 1907), 102, 231, 217–218.

38. Michael O'Shea, *Education as Adjustment: Educational Theory Viewed in Light of Contemporary Thought* (New York: Longman, Green and Co., 1903), 177.

39. Michael O'Shea, *Dynamic Factors in Education* (New York: Macmillan, 1906), 69.

40. Charles William Eliot, *Education for Efficiency: And The New Definition of Cultivated Man* (New York: Houghton Mifflin, 1909), 1, 6, 11, 27, 29, 21–22.

41. Irving King, *The Psychology of Child Development: With An Introduction by John Dewey* (Chicago: University of Chicago Press, 1903), xvii, 158, 162, 173.

42. Irving King, *Social Aspects of Education: A Book of Sources and Original Discussions with Annotated Bibliographies* (New York: Macmillan, 1912), vii, 18, 17, 7.

43. Irving King, *Education for Social Efficiency: A Study in the Social Relations of Education* (New York: D. Appleton Press, 1913), 284, 286, 292.

44. Runyon, "A Day with the New Education," 591.

45. W. W. Charters, *Methods of Teaching: Their Basis and Statement Developed From a Functional Standpoint*, Revised and Enlarged 3rd ed. (Chicago: Row, Peterson, and Co., 1912), 137.

46. W. W. Charters, *Teaching the Common Branches: A Textbook for Teachers of Rural and Graded Schools* (New York: Houghton Mifflin, 1913), 124.

47. W. W. Charters, *Curriculum Construction* (New York: Houghton Mifflin, 1918), 11, 40.

48. J. M. Barrie, *Peter Pan* (Stilwell, KS: Digireds.com Publishing, 2005—Originally published in 1911), 6

49. Johann David Wyss, *The Swiss Family Robinson: Edited for Use in the Schools* (Boston: Ginn and Company, 1885), 137.

50. Daniel Defoe, Robinson Crusoe: Edited after the Original Editions with a Bibliographic Introduction by Henry Kingsley (London: Macmillan, 1868).

51. Henry Wadsworth Longfellow, *The Song of Hiawatha* (Boston: Tickner and Fields, 1855), 7.

52. W.E.B. Du Bois, "Dusk of Dawn," in *W.E.B. Du Bois: Writings*, ed. Nathan Huggins, (New York: Library of America, 1986), 625.

53. Francis Appleton, *Elementary Geography* (New York: American Book Company, 1880), 16, 82.

54. Alex Everett Frye, *Elements of Geography* (Boston: Ginn and Co., 1990), 108.

55. Charles Francis King, *Elementary Geography: A Textbook for Children* (Boston: Lothrop Publishing Company, 1903), 136, 84.

56. Henry Justin Roddy, *Elementary Geography* (New York: American Book Company, 1902), 85.

57. David Saville Muzzey, *An American History* (New York: Ginn and Company, 1911), 23, 619.

58. Philip Van Ness Myers, *A Short History of Medieval and Modern Times* (New York: Ginn and Company, 1906), 3–5.

59. Quoted in Burkholder, *Color in the Classroom*, 29, 25.

60. Milton Bennion, *Citizenship: An Introduction to Social Ethics* (Yonkers-on-Hudson, NY: World Book Company, 1917), 9, xvi.

61. Ellwood Kemp, *An Outline of Method in History* (Terre Haute, IN: Inland, 1897), 17, 30.

62. Ibid., 42.

63. For more on this ideology of "social control," see Barry Franklin, *Building the American Curriculum: The School Curriculum and the Search for Social Control* (Philadelphia: Falmer, 1986).

64. Royal Dixon, *Americanization* (New York: Macmillan, 1916), 17.

65. Ibid., 192.

66. Ibid., 194.

67. Kate Upson Clark, *Teaching the Child Patriotism* (Boston: Page Company, 1918), 11, 114, 154.

68. William R. Hood, compiler, *State Laws Relating to Education: Enacted in 1915, 1916, and 1917*, Department of the Interior, Bureau of Education, Bulletin 1918, No. 23 (Washington, DC: US Government Printing Office, 1919), 164; "Americanization Through Education," in *Report of the Commissioner of Education for The Year Ended June 30, 1918*, Department of the Interior, Bureau of Education (Washington, DC: US Government Print-

ing Office, 1918), 42–49. For more on the Americanization campaign, see Mirel, *Patriotic Pluralism*.

69. See McKee, *Sociology and the Race Problem*.

70. These texts were selected because they were the most popular in the North Central States according to a 1922 survey. This region was not necessarily representative of the entire nation. See Walter Monroe and I. O. Foster, *The Status of the Social Sciences in High Schools and the North Central Association* (Urbana, IL: University of Illinois Press, 1922), 30–36.

71. Howard Copeland Hill, *Community Life and Civic Problems* (New York: Ginn and Company, 1922), 333.

72. Ray Oswald Hughes, *Community Civics* (New York: Allyn and Bacon, 1917), 403.

73. Charles A. Ellwood, *Sociology and Modern Social Problems* (New York: American Book Company, 1919), 249.

74. Henry Reed Burch and S. Howard Patterson, *American Social Problems: An Introduction to the Study of Society* (New York: Macmillan, 1920), 126, 128, 129, 136.

Chapter 4

1. Frederickson, *Racism: A Short History*, 6.

2. Walker, "Organized Resistance and Black Educators," 363–368.

3. Jennifer Ritterhouse, *Growing Up Jim Crow: How Black and White Children in the South Learned Race* (Chapel Hill, NC: University of North Carolina Press, 2006), 9.

4. See Richards, *Darwin and the Emergence of Evolutionary Theories of Mind and Behavior*.

5. Carl Kelsey, *The Physical Basis of Society* (New York: D. Appleton and Co., 1916), 215.

6. Quoted in Stocking, *Race, Culture, and Evolution*, 255.

7. William I. Thomas, *Source Book on Human Origins: Ethnological Materials, Psychological Standpoint, Classified and Annotated Bibliographies for the Interpretation of Savage Society* (Boston: Gorham Press, 1909), 316, 26.

8. Charles Ellwood, "The Theory of Imitation in Social Psychology," *American Journal of Sociology*, 6 (May 1901): 721.

9. Thomas, Source *Book on Human Origins*, 26.

10. Carl Kelsey, "The Influence of Heredity and Environment upon Race Improvement: An Introductory Paper upon the Significance of the Problem," *Annals of the American Academy of Political and Social Science* (July 1909): 8.

11. Francis Galton, "Eugenics: Its Definition, Scope and Aims," *The American Journal of Sociology*, 10 (July 1904): 1.

12. Ellwood P. Cubberley, *Changing Conceptions of Education* (New York: Houghton Mifflin, 1909), 13–15.

13. Cravens, *The Triumph of Evolution*, 53.

14. See Chapter 4 of Selden, *Inheriting Shame*, 63–83.

15. Charles Davenport, "Suggested Classification of Writings on Eugenics," *Science* 37 (March 7, 1913): 370.

16. Quoted in Painter, *History of White People*, 275.

17. William Z. Ripley, *The Races of Europe: A Sociological Study* (New York: D. Appleton and Co., 1899), 437, 37, vi, 457.

18. Ibid., 108.

19. Ibid., 119, 120.

20. Kelly Miller, "Eugenics and the Negro Race," *The Scientific Monthly*, 5 (July 1917): passim.

21. Kelly Miller, *Out of the House of Bondage* (New York: Neale Publishing, 1914), 17, 31, 32.

22. Quoted in George S. Counts, *The Selective Character of American Secondary Education* (Chicago: University of Chicago, 1922), 114.

23. Marion Jacob Mayo, *The Mental Capacity of the American Negro* (New York: Science Press, 1913), 10.

24. Ibid., 29, 38, 29, 55.

25. Lewis Terman, *Measurement of Intelligence: An Explanation and Complete Guide for the Use of the Stanford Revision and Extension of the Binet-Simon Intelligence Scale* (New York: Houghton Mifflin 1916), vii, xi, 92.

26. Ibid.

27. Lewis Terman, *The Intelligence of School Children: How Children Differ in Ability, the Use of Mental Tests in School Grading and the Proper Education of Exceptional Children* (Boston: Houghton Mifflin, 1919) and *Intelligence Tests and School Reorganization* (Yonkers-on-Hudson, NY: World Book, 1922).

28. See Paula Fass, "The IQ: A Cultural and Historical Framework," *American Journal of Education*, 88 (August 1980): 431–458; Paul D. Chapman, Schools as Sorters: Lewis M. Terman, *Applied Psychology, and the Intelligence Testing Movement, 1890–1930* (New York: New York University Press, 1988), and Valencia, "Genetic Pathology Model of Deficit Thinking." On the African American response to intelligence testing, see William B. Thomas, "Black Intellectuals' Critique of Early Mental Testing: A Little Known Saga of the 1920s," *American Journal of Education*, 90 (May 1982): 258–292.

29. Quoted in Painter, *History of White People*, 283, 285.

30. Selden, *Inheriting Shame*, 99.

31. King, *Education for Social Efficiency*, 295, 296, 304.

32. William Carl Ruediger, *The Principles of Education* (New York: Houghton Mifflin, 1910), 30, 33, 252.

33. Quoted in Stocking, *Race, Culture and Evolution*, 255. The literature on Hall's views on race, perhaps because Hall addressed it so directly and so often, is the most nuanced and accurate of all the scholarship addressing the racial views of progressive educators. See Dorothy Ross, *G. Stanley Hall: Psychologist as Prophet* (Chicago: University of Chicago Press, 1972), 414–415; Joshua Garrison, "A Problematic Alliance Colonial Anthropology, Recapitulation Theory, and G. Stanley Hall's Program for the Liberation of America's Youth," *American Educational History Journal*, 35 (2008): 131–147; Lester F. Goodchild, "G. Stanley Hall and an American Social Darwinist Pedagogy: His Progressive Educational Ideas on Gender and Race," *History of Education Quarterly*, 52 (Winter 2012): 62–98.

34. Edward Thorndike, "Biographical Memoir of Granville Stanley Hall, 1846–1924," *National Academy of Sciences Biographical Memoirs*, 12 (1925): 140.

35. G. Stanley Hall, *Adolescence*, 52, 53.

36. G. Stanley Hall, "The Underdeveloped Races in Contact with Civilization," *The Bulletin of the Washington University Association* (1905): 146.

37. Ibid., 148.

38. G. Stanley Hall, "How Far Are the Principles of Education along Indigenous Lines Applicable to American Indians?" *Journal of Proceedings and Addresses of the Forty-Sixth Annual Meeting of the National Educational Association*, 46 (1908): 1164.

39. Hall, "The Point of View Toward Primitive Races," *Journal of Race Development* (July 1910): 7.
40. William Bagley, *Craftsmanship in Education* (New York: Macmillan, 1912), 37, 38.
41. Bagley, *The Educative Process*, 10, 17, 219.
42. Quoted in Cravens, *The Triumph of Evolution*, 230.
43. William Bagley, *Educational Values* (New York: Macmillan, 1912), 3, 82, 94, 98.
44. William Bagley, "Educational Determinism, or Democracy and the IQ," *Educational Administration and Supervision, 8* (1922): 260, 271.
45. William C. Bagley, *Determinism in Education*, 5, 5, 46.
46. Edward Thorndike, *Educational Psychology, Vol. 1: The Original Nature of Man* (New York: Teachers College Press, 1913), 258.
47. Ibid., 279.
48. See Ellen Condliffe Lagemann, "The Plural Worlds of Educational Research," *History of Education Quarterly, 29* (Summer 1989): 183–214.
49. Quoted in Geraldine Joncich, *The Sane Positivist: A Biography of Edward Thorndike* (Middletown, CT: Wesleyan University Press, 1968), 273.
50. Edward Thorndike, "Darwin's Contribution to Psychology," *University of California Chronicle, 12* (1909): 65.
51. Edward Thorndike, *The Elements of Psychology* (New York: A. J. Seiler, 1905), 195–196.
52. John Watson, *Psychological Care of Infant and Child* (New York: Norton, 1928), 40.
53. Thorndike, *Educational Psychology: Vol. 1*, 234.
54. Edward Thorndike, *The Principles of Teaching: Based on Psychology* (New York: A. J. Seiler, 1911), 83.
55. Edward Thorndike, *Measurement of Twins* (New York: Science Press, 1905), iii.
56. John Dewey, "The Need for Social Psychology (1917)," *Middle Works*, vol. 10, 56.
57. Ibid., 57.
58. John Dewey, "The Subject-Matter of Metaphysical Inquiry (1915)," *The Middle Works*, vol. 8, 11.
59. Edward Thorndike, *Educational Psychology, Vol. III: Mental Work and Fatigue and Individual Differences and Their Causes* (New York: Teachers College Press, 1913), 309.
60. Ibid., 217, 220, 223.
61. Thorndike, *Elements of Psychology*, 195.
62. Quoted in Joncich, *The Sane Positivist*, 375.
63. Edward Thorndike, "Review of The Feebly Inhibited: Nomadism, or Wandering Impulse, with Special Reference to Heredity: Inheritance of Temperament by Charles B. Davenport," *Science, 43* (March 1916): 429.
64. William Bagley, *Determinism in Education*, 125.

Chapter 5

1. Du Bois, "Dusk of Dawn," 625, 627, 628.
2. Franz Boas, "The History of Anthropology (1904)," in *The Shaping of American Anthropology, 1883–1911: A Franz Boas Reader*, ed. George Stocking Jr. (New York: Basic Books, 1974), 36.
3. Quoted in Menand, *Metaphysical Club*, 384.
4. Franz Boas, "The Limitations of the Comparative Method of Anthropology," *Science, 4* 103 (December 18, 1896): 906, 907, 908.

5. Clark Wissler, "The Psychological Aspects of the Culture-Environmental Relation," *American Anthropologist, 14* (April–June 1913): 219.

6. Quoted in Cravens, *The Triumph of Evolution*, 108.

7. A. A. Goldenweiser, "The Principle of Limited Possibilities in the Development of Culture," *The Journal of American Folklore, 26* (July–September 1913): 290.

8. Franz Boas, "Eugenics," *Scientific Monthly, 3* (November 1916): 475, 477, 476.

9. Franz Boas, "The Mind of Primitive Man," *The Journal of American Folklore, 14* (January–March 1901): 3, 6, 3, 11.

10. Franz Boas, "Race Problems in America," *Science, 29* (May 1909): 840, 847, 844, 848.

11. Clark Wissler, "Review of Mental Development in the Child and the Race by James Mark Baldwin and Ethical Interpretation in Mental Development: A Study in Social Psychology by James Mark Baldwin," *American Anthropologist, 9* (January–March 1907): 194–196.

12. A. L. Kroeber, "Eighteen Professions," *American Anthropologist, 17* (April–June 1915): 285, 286.

13. Margaret Mead, *Coming of Age in Samoa: A Psychological Study of Primitive Youth for Western Civilization* (New York: HarperCollins, 2001—Originally published in 1928), 5.

14. Quoted in Burkholder, *Color in the Classroom*, 84.

15. Du Bois, "Conservation of Races," 816, 817, 820.

16. W.E.B. Du Bois, "Souls of Black Folk," in *W.E.B. Du Bois: Writings*, ed. Nathan Huggins (New York: Library Classics of the United States, 1986), 364–365.

17. Carter G. Woodson, "Negro History Week—The Eleventh Year," *The Journal of Negro History, 21* (April 1936): 105. For more on Woodson, see Sarah Bair, "The Early Years of Negro History Week, 1926–1922," in *Histories of Social Studies and Race: 1865–2000*, eds. Christine Woyshner and Chara Bohan (New York: Palgrave Macmillan, 2012), 57–78, and Agnes M. Roche, "Carter G. Woodson and the Development of Transformative Scholarship," in *Multicultural Education: Transformative Knowledge and Action: Historical and Contemporary Perspectives*, ed. James A. Banks (New York: Teachers College Press, 1996), 91–114.

18. Carter G. Woodson, "Negro Life and History in our Schools," *The Journal of Negro History, 4* (July 1919): 276, 280.

19. Quoted in Menand, *Metaphysical Club*, 397–398.

20. Barkan, *The Retreat of Scientific Racism*, 93.

21. Quoted in Menand, *Metaphysical Club*, 393.

22. John Dewey to Horace Kallen, March 31, 1915 (record 003222) and December 22, 24, 1895, in *The Correspondence of John Dewey, Vol. 1: 1871–1918*, 3rd ed. CD-ROM version, ed. Larry Hickman (Carbondale: Center for Dewey Studies, Southern Illinois University, 2005).

23. Randolph Silliman Bourne, *History of a Literary Radical and Other Essays* (New York: B. W. Huebsch, 1920), 278, 282, 291, 296.

24. John Dewey, "The School as Social Centre," 80–89.

25. John Dewey, "Nationalizing Education (1916)," in *The Middle Works*, vol. 10, 203, 204, 205, 206.

26. Dewey, *Democracy and Education*, 86.

27. Dewey, "The Influence of Darwinism," 14.

28. See Hamilton Cravens and John C. Burnham, "Psychology and Evolutionary Naturalism in American Thought, 1890–1940," *American Quarterly*, 23 (December 1971): 635–657.

29. John Dewey, "Contributions to Cyclopedia of Education, vols. 3, 4 and 5 (1914)," in *Middle Works*, vol. 7, 236.

30. Dewey, *Democracy and Education*, 35.

31. John Dewey, "Contributions to Cyclopedia of Education," 236.

32. John Dewey to William James, March 15, 1903 (record 00797) in *The Correspondence of John Dewey*, Vol. 1.

33. Dewey, "The Subject-Matter of Metaphysical Inquiry (1915)," in *Middle Works*, vol. 8, 7.

34. John Dewey, "The Need for Recovery of Philosophy (1917)," in *Middle Works*, vol. 10, 11–12.

35. Dewey, "Nationalizing Education," 205, 204.

36. John Dewey, "American Education and Culture (1916)," in *Middle Works*, vol. 10, 198.

37. Dewey, Democracy and Education, 331.

38. Scudder Klyce to John Dewey, April 4, 1915 (record 03511) in *Correspondence of John Dewey, Vol. 1*.

39. Dewey to Klyce, June 19, 1915 (record 03540) in *The Correspondence of John Dewey, Vol. 1*.

40. Dewey, "The Need for Social Psychology," 56, 58, 60, 59.

41. John Dewey, "The Subject-Matter of Metaphysical Inquiry," 11.

42. John Dewey, *Democracy and Education*, 87, 90.

43. See Fallace, *Dewey and the Dilemma of Race*.

44. For more on Boas's alleged influence on Dewey, see Thomas Fallace, "John Dewey and the Savage Mind: Uniting Anthropological, Psychological and Pedagogical Thought, 1894–1902," *The Journal of the History of Behavioral Sciences*, 44 (Fall 2008): 335–349.

45. John Dewey to Seth Low, June 16, 1898 (record 01886), in *Correspondence of John Dewey, Vol. 1*.

46. John Dewey, "Interpretation of the Savage Mind," 47n.

47. William I. Thomas, "Race Psychology: Standpoint and Questionnaire, With Particular Reference to the Immigrant and the Negro," *American Journal of Sociology*, 17 (May 1912): 726.

48. Ibid., 468–469.

49. John Dewey, "Race Prejudice and Friction (1922)" in *Middle Works*, vol. 13, 243, 246.

50. Ibid., 252.

51. Ibid., 254.

52. John Dewey, "Individuality, Equality, and Superiority (1922)," in *Middle Works*, vol. 13, 295.

53. Ibid., 295, 296, 300.

54. John Dewey, *Human Nature and Conduct: An Introduction to Social Psychology* (Carbondale: Southern Illinois University Press, 1976), 67.

55. Dewey, "The School as Means of Developing a Social Consciousness and Social Ideals in Children (1923)," in *Middle Works*, vol. 15, 155.

56. Carter G. Woodson, "Negro History Week," 239.

57. John Dewey, "From Absolutism to Experimentalism (1930)" in *John Dewey: The Later Works, vol. 5 of The Collected Works of John Dewey*, ed. Jo Ann Boydston (Carbondale: Southern Illinois University Press, 1984), 156; John Dewey to Horace Kallen, July 1, 1916 (record 03236) in *The Correspondence of John Dewey, Vol. 1: 1871–1918*, 3rd ed., CD-ROM version, ed. Larry Hickman (Carbondale: Center for Dewey Studies, Southern Illinois University, 2005).

58. John Dewey, *Democracy and Education*, 21, 82, 84–85.

59. Ruth Benedict, *Race: Science and Politics* (New York: 1940), 154.

Chapter 6

1. G. Stanley Hall, "How Far are the Principles of Education along Indigenous Lines Applicable to American Indians?" *Journal of Proceedings and Addresses of the Forty-Sixth Annual Meeting of the National Educational Association*, 46 (1908): 1163.

2. Kliebard, *Struggle over the American Curriculum*, 177.

3. Quoted in Cremin, *Transformation of the School*, 243–245.

4. William Heard Kilpatrick, "The Project Method," *Teachers College Record* (September 1918): 319–335. Available at http://historymatters.gmu.edu/d/4954. For more on the origins and evolution of the project method, see Michael Knoll, "I Made a Mistake: William Heard Kilpatrick and the Project Method," *Teachers College Record* (February 2012): 1–45.

5. William Heard Kilpatrick, *Foundations of Method: Informal Talks on Teaching* (New York: Macmillan, 1925), viii.

6. Harold Rugg and Ann Shumaker, *The Child-Centered School: An Appraisal of the New Education* (New York: World Book, 1928), 38, 35.

7. Ibid., 214, 9.

8. Interestingly, Rugg and Shumaker completely wrote G. Stanley Hall out of the history of child-centeredness.

9. Alexander James Inglis, *Principles of Secondary Education* (New York: Houghton Mifflin, 1918), 46. For more on Inglis, see William Wraga, *Progressive Pioneer: Alexander James Inglis and American Secondary Education, 1879–1924* (New York: Peter Lang, 2007).

10. Inglis, *Principles of Secondary Education*, 97.

11. Harold Rugg, *American Life and the School Curriculum: Next Steps toward Schools of Living* (New York: Ginn and Company, 1936), 208.

12. Leonard P. Ayers, *Laggards in Our Schools: A Study of Retardation and Elimination in City School Systems* (Philadelphia: Press of W. M. Fell, 1909), 106.

13. Charles A. Ellwood, "Review of *The Negro and the Nation: A History of American Slavery from Enfranchisement by George Merriam*," *American Journal of Sociology*, 12 (September 1906): 275; "Review of *Social and Mental Traits of the Negro by Howard W. Odum*," *International Journal of Ethics*, 21 (April 1911): 371.

14. Charles. A. Ellwood, "A Survey of Recent Literature upon the Negro Problem in the United States," *Weltwirtshcaftliches Archiv* (1913): 401.

15. Ellwood, "The Theory of Imitation in Social Psychology," 735.

16. Ellwood, "Review of *The Negro and the Nation*," 275.

17. Charles A. Ellwood, *Sociology in Its Psychological Aspects* (New York: D. Appleton & Co., 1912), 240, 49, 237.

18. Ibid., 785, 783, 787, 237–238.

19. Charles A. Ellwood, "Theories of Cultural Evolution," *American Journal of Sociology*, 23 (May 1918): 783, 785, 787.

20. Charles A. Ellwood, "Primitive Concepts and the Origins of Cultural Patterns," *American Journal of Sociology, 33* (July 1927): 7–8, 12, 4.

21. Charles A. Ellwood, "Our Compulsory Education Laws, and Retardation and Elimination in Our Public Schools," *Education: Devoted to Science, Art, Philosophy and Literature in Education, 34* (May 1914): 576.

22. Charles Ellwood, "Education for Citizenship in a Democracy," *American Journal of Sociology, 26* (July 1920): 75, 80.

23. Edward A. Ross, *Social Control: A Survey of the Foundations of Order* (New York: Macmillan, 1901), 187.

24. Ibid., 336.

25. Edward A. Ross, *Old World in the New: The Significance of Past, Present, Immigration to the American People* (New York: The Century Co., 1914), 282, 300.

26. Ellsworth Huntington, *Civilization and Climate* (New Haven, CT: Yale University Press, 1915), 12, 19.

27. David Snedden, *Educational Sociology* (New York: The Century Co., 1922), 289, 59, 63, 66.

28. Ibid., 108.

29. Ellwood, "Review of *Social and Mental Traits*," 371; Ellwood, "Review of a Survey of Recent Literature," 401.

30. Ellwood, "Education for Citizenship," 74.

31. William Wirt, "Introduction" to Randolph Silliman Bourne, *The Gary Schools* (New York: Houghton Mifflin, 1916), xix.

32. William Charles O'Donnell, "The Gary System in the Crucible of a Political Campaign," *Educational Foundations, 29* (January 1918): 271.

33. Between 1897 and 1923, African American groups resisted the introduction of segregated schools in several Northern cities through grassroots boycotts and lawsuits. However, because of internal divisions within the Black community, and the growing inertia of segregation across the nation, these efforts ultimately failed. See August Meier and Elliot M. Rudwick, "Early Boycotts of Segregated Schools: The Alton, Illinois Case, 1897–1908," *The Journal of Negro History, 36* (Autumn 1967): 394–402; "Early Boycotts of Segregated Schools: The East Orange, New Jersey, Experience, 1899–1906," *History of Education Quarterly, 7* (Spring 1967): 22–35; and "Early Boycotts of Segregated Schools: The Case of Springfield, Ohio, 1922–23," *American Quarterly, 20* (Winter 1968): 744–758.

34. Quoted in Zimmerman, *Whose America*, 18.

35. See Jeffrey Mirel, *Patriotic Pluralism*.

36. Bourne, *History of a Literary Radical*, 271.

37. Quoted in Alridge, *The Educational Thought of W.E.B. Du Bois*, 64, 105.

38. Department of the Interior, *America, Americanism, and Americanization* (Washington, DC: US Government Printing Office, 1919), 17, 14.

39. Adolph K. Rigast, *Industrial Education among the American Negroes* (Master's thesis, University of Wisconsin, 1921), 110, 123–124, 125, 110.

40. Counts, *Selective Character*, 148.

41. Ibid., 117, 119, 122.

42. Bruno Lasker, *Race Attitudes in Children* (New York: Henry Holt, 1929), 372–373.

43. See "Review of *Race Attitudes in Children* by Bruno Lasker," *Journal of Negro History, 14* (July 1929): 352–353.

44. Cited in Selig, *American All*, 110.

45. Harold O. Rugg, "How Shall We Reconstruct the Social Studies Curriculum?" *The Historical Outlook, 12* (May 1921): 184–189; Rugg, "A Century of Curriculum-Construction in American Schools," in *Making Past and Present: The 26th Yearbook of the National Society for the Study of Education* (Bloomington, IL: Public School Publishing Company, 1933), 39, 50, 62; Rugg, *Foundations for American Education* (New York: Yonkers-on-Hudson, 1947), 575n. See also Earl Rugg, "How the Current Courses in History, Geography, and Civics Came to Be What They Are," in *Social Studies in the Elementary and Secondary School: 22nd Yearbook for the National Society for the Study of Education* (Bloomington, IL: Public School Publishing Company, 1923), 48–75. Harold's brother Earl offered a similar assessment of the Committee on Social Studies report.

46. Neal Billings, *A Determination of Generalizations Basic to the Social Studies Curriculum* (Baltimore: Warwick and York, Inc., 1928), 179, 183, 180, 5.

47. Harold Rugg, *An Introduction to Problems of American Culture* (New York: Ginn and Company, 1931), 561, 566, 584.

48. Ibid., 590. For more on Rugg and race in his textbooks in the 1930s, see LaGarrett J. King, Christopher Davis, and Anthony Brown, "African American History, Race and Textbooks: An Examination of the Works of Harold O. Rugg and Carter G. Woodson," *The Journal of Social Studies Research, 36* (4): 359–386.

49. Watson, quoted in Selig, *Americans All*, 27.

50. Lasker, quoted in Selig, *Americans All*, 33.

51. Quoted in McKee, *Sociology and the Race Problem*, 107, 110.

52. See David Tyack, *The One Best System* (Cambridge, MA: Harvard University Press, 1974), 196–198; Church and Sedlak, *Education in the United States*, 255–260; Zilversmit, *Changing Schools*, 2–3.

53. McKee, *Sociology and the Race Problem*, 96.

Epilogue

1. See Barkan, *The Retreat of Scientific Racism*, and Cravens, *The Triumph of Evolution*.

2. See Michael B. Katz, *The Undeserving Poor: From the War on Poverty to the War on Welfare* (New York: Pantheon, 1990); Sylvia Martinez and John Rury, "From 'Culturally Deprived' to 'At Risk': The Politics of Popular Expression and Educational Inequality in the United States, 1960–1985," *Teachers College Record, 111* (2012): 1–31; Scott, *Contempt and Pity*; Russell Skiba, "'As Nature Has Formed Them': The History and Current Status of Racial Difference Research"; and Valencia, "Genetic Pathology Model of Deficit Thinking." The most cited cases of neo-hereditary arguments are Richard Herrnstein and Charles Murray, *The Bell Curve: Intelligence and Class Structure in American Life* (New York: Free Press, 1994) and Arthur A. Jensen, "How Much Can We Boost IQ and Scholastic Achievement?" *Harvard Educational Review, 39* (1969): 1–123.

3. Frank Riessman, *The Culturally Deprived Child* (New York: Harper, 1962); Benjamin S. Bloom, *Compensatory Education for Cultural Deprivation* (New York: Holt, Rinehart, and Winston, 1965).

4. Richard R. Valencia, "Contextualizing 'Rethinking Compensatory Education': The Value of a Temporal Continuity Analysis," *Teachers College Record, 114* (2012): 5.

5. Fredrickson, *Racism*, 141.

6. Ben Burks, "Unity and Diversity through Education: A Comparison of the Thought of W.E.B. Du Bois and John Dewey," *The Journal of Thought* (Spring 1997): 99–110; S. F. Stack, "John Dewey and the Question of Race: The Fight for Odell Walker," *Education and*

Culture, 25 (2009): 17–35; Laurel Tanner and Daniel Tanner, "Environmentalism in American Pedagogy: The Legacy of Lester Ward," *Teachers College Record, 88* (1987): 537–547.

7. See Jacques Voneche, "Reflections on Baldwin," *The Cognitive Developmental Psychology of James Mark Baldwin: Current Theory and Research in Genetic Epistemology*, ed. John M. Broughton and John Freeman-Moir (Norwood, NJ: Ablex Publishing Company, 1982), 80–86.

8. See David Labaree, "Progressivism, Schools, and Schools of Education," 275–288.

9. See Tyrone Howard, *Why Race and Culture Matters in Schools: Closing the Achievement Gap in America's Schools* (New York: Teachers College Press, 2010) and Richard R. Valencia, *Dismantling Contemporary Deficit Thinking: Educational Thought and Practice* (New York: Routledge, 2010).

Bibliography

COLLECTED PAPERS IN PRINT

Bulletins, Bureau of Education, Department of the Interior. Washington DC: US Government Printing Office, 1916–1919.

The Correspondence of John Dewey, Vols. 1–3. Third edition, CD-ROM version. Edited by Larry Hickman. Carbondale: Center for Dewey Studies, Southern Illinois University, 2005.

John Dewey: The Early Works, of *The Collected Works of John Dewey*. Edited by Jo Ann Boydston. Carbondale: Southern Illinois University Press, 1969–1972.

John Dewey: The Later Works, of *The Collected Works of John Dewey*. Edited by Jo Ann Boydston. Carbondale: Southern Illinois University Press, 1981–1990.

John Dewey: The Middle Works of *The Collected Works of John Dewey*. Edited by Jo Ann Boydston. Carbondale: Southern Illinois University Press, 1976–1983.

The Shaping of American Anthropology, 1883–1911: A Franz Boas Reader. Edited by George Stocking Jr. New York: Basic Books, 1974.

W.E.B. Du Bois: Writings. Edited by Nathan Huggins. New York: Library of America, 1986.

The Works of William James: Essays, Comments, and Reviews. Edited by Fredson Bowers. Cambridge, MA: Harvard University Press, 1987.

PUBLISHED PRIMARY WORKS

Adams, Herbert Baxter. "The Germanic Origin of New England Towns." *Johns Hopkins University Studies in Historical and Political Science* 1 (1883): 5–78.

Addams, Jane. *Democracy and Social Ethics*. New York: Macmillan, 1902.

———. *Twenty Years at Hull-House*. New York: Macmillan, 1911.

Anonymous. "Review of *Race Attitudes in Children* by Bruno Lasker." *Journal of Negro History* 14 (July 1929): 352–3.

Anonymous. "Review of Schools of To-Morrow." *The Southern Workman* 45 (1916): 123–4.

Appleton, Daniel. *Elementary Geography*. New York: American Book Company, 1880.

Ayers, Leonard P. *Laggards in Our Schools: A Study of Retardation and Elimination in City School Systems*. Philadelphia: Press of W. M. Fell, 1909.

Bagley, William. *Craftsmanship in Education*. New York: Macmillan, 1912.

———. *Determinism in Education: A Series of Papers on the Relative Influence of Inherited and Acquired Traits in Determining Intelligence, Achievement, and Character*. Baltimore, MD: Warwick and York, Inc., 1925.

———. "Educational Determinism, or Democracy and the IQ." *Educational Administration and Supervision* 8 (1922): 257–72.

———. *Educational Values*. New York: Macmillan, 1912.

———. *The Educative Process.* New York: Macmillan, 1905.
Baldwin, James Mark. *Darwin and the Humanities.* Baltimore: Review Publishing, 1909.
———. *Mental Development in the Race and Child: Methods and Processes.* New York: Macmillan, 1895.
———. *Social and Ethical Interpretations in Mental Development: A Study in Social Psychology.* New York: Macmillan, 1897.
Ball, Frank H. "Some Phases of Industrial School Work in Porto Rico." In *Proceedings of the Eastern Manual Training Association.* Allegheny, PA: John C. Park, 1903: 115–122.
Barrie, J. M. *Peter Pan.* Stilwell, KS: Digireds.com Publishing, 2005.
Benedict, Ruth. *Race: Science and Politics.* New York: Viking, 1940.
Bennion, Milton. *Citizenship: An Introduction to Social Ethics.* Yonkers-on-Hudson, NY: World Book Company, 1917.
Billings, Neal. *A Determination of Generalizations Basic to the Social Studies Curriculum.* Baltimore: Warwick and York, Inc., 1928.
Boas, Franz. "Changes in Bodily Form of Descendants of Immigrants." *American Anthropologist* 14 (July–September 1912): 530–62.
———. "Eugenics." *Scientific Monthly* 3 (November 1916): 471–78.
———. "The Limitations of the Comparative Method of Anthropology." *Science* 4 103 (December 18, 1896): 901–8.
———. "The Mind of Primitive Man." *The Journal of American Folklore,* 14 (January–March 1901): 1–11.
———. *The Mind of Primitive Man.* Revised 2nd edition. New York: Macmillan, 1938. Originally published in 1911.
———. "Race Problems in America." *Science* 29 (May 1909): 839–49.
Bourne, Randolph Silliman. *The Gary Schools.* New York: Houghton Mifflin, 1916.
———. *History of a Literary Radical and Other Essays.* New York: B. W. Huebsch, 1920.
Burch, Henry Reed, and S. Howard Patterson. *American Social Problems: An Introduction to The Study of Society.* New York: Macmillan, 1920.
Chamberlain, Alexander Francis. *The Child: A Study in the Evolution of Man.* 2nd ed. New York: Walter Scott Publishing, 1907.
Charters, W. W. *Curriculum Construction.* New York: Houghton Mifflin, 1918.
———. *Methods of Teaching: Their Basis and Statement Developed From a Functional Standpoint.* Revised and enlarged third edition. Chicago: Row, Peterson, and Co., 1912.
———. *Teaching the Common Branches: A Textbook for Teachers of Rural and Graded Schools.* New York: Houghton Mifflin, 1913.
Clark, Kate Upson. *Teaching the Child Patriotism.* Boston: Page Company, 1918.
Counts, George S. *The Selective Character of American Secondary Education.* Chicago: University of Chicago Press, 1922.
Cubberley, Ellwood P. *Changing Conceptions of Education.* New York: Houghton Mifflin, 1909.
Dalrymple, Louis. "School Begins." *Puck* (January 1898): 8–9.
Darwin, Charles. *The Descent of Man, and Selection in Relation to Sex.* New York: D. Appleton and Co., 1871.
Davenport, Charles. "Suggested Classification of Writings on Eugenics." *Science* 37 (March 1913): 370.
Defoe, Daniel. *Robinson Crusoe: Edited after the Original Editions with a Bibliographic Introduction by Henry Kingsley.* London: Macmillan, 1868.

DeGarmo, Charles. "Social Aspects of Moral Education." In *Forgotten Heroes of American Education: The Great Tradition of Teaching Teachers*. Edited by J. Wesley Null and Diane Ravitch. Greenwich, CT: Information Age Publishing, 2006, 273–294.

Dewey, John. *The Child and the Curriculum and the School and Society*, Tenth edition. Chicago: University of Chicago Press, 1969. Originally published in 1899 and 1902.

———. *Democracy and Education: An Introduction to Philosophy of Education*. New York: Free Press, 1916.

———. *How We Think*. Mineola, NY: Dover Publications, 1997. Originally published 1910.

———. *Human Nature and Conduct: An Introduction to Social Psychology*. Carbondale: Southern Illinois University Press, 1976.

Dewey, John, and Albion Small. *My Pedagogic Creed and the Demands of Sociology Upon Pedagogy*. New York: E. Kellogg and Co., 1897.

Dewey, John, and James Tufts. *Ethics*. New York: Henry Holt and Co., 1908.

Dixon, Royal. *Americanization*. New York: Macmillan, 1916.

Dodd, Catherine Isabel. *Introduction to the Herbartian Principles of Teaching*. New York: Macmillan Co., 1898.

Dopp, Katherine Elizabeth. "Some Steps in the Evolution of Social Occupations." *The Elementary School Teacher and the Course of Study* 3 (1903): 219–29.

———. *The Tree-Dwellers: Age of Fear*. New York: Rand McNally, 1904.

Dunn, Arthur. *The Community and the Citizen*. New York: Heath and Company, 1907.

Dunning, William Archibald. *Reconstruction: Political and Economic, 1865–1877*. New York: Harper and Brothers, 1907.

Durkheim, Emile. *The Elementary Forms of Religious Life*. London: G. Allen and Unwin, 1915.

Dutton, Samuel Train. *Social Phases of Education in the School and the Home*. New York: Macmillan Co., 1907.

Dyke, Charles Barlett. "Essential Features in the Education of the Child Races." In *Addresses and Proceeding: National Education Association of the United States*. Chicago: University of Chicago Press, 1909, 928–32.

Eliot, Charles William. *Education for Efficiency: And The New Definition of Cultivated Man*. New York: Houghton Mifflin, 1909.

Ellwood, Charles. "Education for Citizenship in a Democracy." *American Journal of Sociology* 26 (July 1920): 73–81.

———. "Our Compulsory Education Laws, and Retardation and Elimination in Our Public Schools." *Education: Devoted to Science, Art, Philosophy and Literature in Education* 34 (May 1914): 572–76.

———. "Primitive Concepts and the Origins of Cultural Patterns." *American Journal of Sociology* 33 (July 1927): 1–13.

———. "Review of The Negro and the Nation: A History of American Slavery from Enfranchisement by George Merriam." *American Journal of Sociology* 12 (September 1906): 275–6.

———. "Review of Social and Mental Traits of the Negro by Howard W. Odum." *International Journal of Ethics* 21 (April 1911): 371.

———. *Sociology and Modern Social Problems*. New York: American Book Company, 1919.

———. *Sociology in Its Psychological Aspects*. New York: D. Appleton & Co., 1912.

———. "A Survey of Recent Literature upon the Negro Problem in the United States." *Weltwirtshcaftliches Archiv* (1913): 399–402.

———. "Theories of Cultural Evolution." *American Journal of Sociology* 23 (May 1918): 779–800.

———. "The Theory of Imitation in Social Psychology." *American Journal of Sociology* 6 (May 1901): 721–41.

Fiske, John. *Darwinism and Other Essays*. New York: Houghton Mifflin, 1902. Originally published 1879.

Foster, Olive Hide. "An Experiment in Education; Professor Dewey's Theories and Methods as Exemplified in a School Conducted by the Pedagogical Department of the University of Chicago." *The Sunday Times-Herald Chicago* (June 3, 1900): 1.

Froebel, Frederich. *Education of Man*. Translated by W. N. Hailman. New York: D. Appleton Press, 1906.

Frye, Alex Everett. *Elements of Geography*. Boston: Ginn and Co., 1990.

Galton, Francis. "Eugenics: Its Definition, Scope and Aims." *The American Journal of Sociology* 10 (July 1904): 1–6.

Giddings, Franklin. *Principles of Sociology: An Analysis of the Phenomenon of Association and of Social Organization*. New York: Macmillan, 1896.

Goldenweiser, A. A. "The Principle of Limited Possibilities in the Development of Culture." *The Journal of American Folklore* 26 (July–September 1913): 259–90.

Haddon, A. C. *The Study of Man*. London: Bliss, Sands, & Co., 1898.

Haeckel, Ernst. *Die Lebenswunder*. Stuttgart, Germany: Kroner, 1904.

Hall, G. Stanley. *Adolescence: Its Psychology and Its Relation to Physiology, Anthropology, Sociology, Sex, Crime, Religion, and Education*. New York: D. Appleton Press, 1905.

———. "How Far Are the Principles of Education along Indigenous Lines Applicable to American Indians?" *Journal of Proceedings and Addresses of the Forty-Sixth Annual Meeting of the National Education Association* 46 (1908): 1161–4.

———. "Moral Education and Will Training." *The Pedagogical Seminary* (1892): 72–89.

———. "The Natural Activities of Children as Determining the Industries in Early Education II." *Journal of Proceedings and Addresses of the Forty-Third Annual Meeting of the National Education Association* (1904): 443–447.

———. "The New Psychology as Basis of Education." *The Forum* 17 (March–August 1894): 710–20.

———. "The Point of View toward the Primitive Races." *The Journal of Race Development* 1 (July 1910): 5–11.

———. "The Underdeveloped Races in Contact with Civilization." *The Bulletin of the Washington University Association*, (1905): 145–53.

Harris, William T. Address Delivered at the Inauguration of the Reverend John Gordon, D.D. Washington, D.C.: Government Printing Office, 1904.

———. "An Educational Policy for Our New Possessions." *Educational Review* 18 (September 1899): 114–5.

———. *Psychologic Foundations of Education: An Attempt to Show the Genesis of the Higher Faculties of the Mind*. New York: D. Appleton and Company, 1902.

Hart, Albert Bushnell. *School History of the United States*. New York: American Book Company, 1918.

Hegel, Georg Wilhelm Frederich. *Hegel as Educator*. Edited by Frederic Ludlow Luqueer. New York: Macmillan, 1896.

Hendricks, Luther V. *James Harvey Robinson: Teacher of History*. New York: King's Crown Press, 1946.

Hill, Howard Copeland. *Community Life and Civic Problems*. New York: Ginn and Company, 1922.
Hodgman, H. M. "A New Departure in Education." *Education* 21 (December 1900): 232.
Howerth, Ira W. "The Social Aim of Education." In *The Fifth Yearbook of the National Herbart Society for the Scientific Study of Teaching*. Edited by Charles McMurry. Chicago: University of Chicago Press, 1899, 69–108.
Hughes, Ray Oswald. *Community Civics*. New York: Allyn and Bacon, 1917.
Huntington, Ellsworth. *Civilization and Climate*. New Haven, CT: Yale University Press, 1915.
Inglis, Alexander James. *Principles of Secondary Education*. New York: Houghton Mifflin, 1918.
Jackman, Wilbur Samuel. *Nature Study and Related Studies for Common Schools*. Chicago: Normal School Publishing, 1898.
James, William. *Principles of Psychology*. New York: Henry Holt and Co., 1890.
Jones, Thomas Jesse. *Social Studies in the Hampton Curriculum*. Hampton, VA: Hampton Institute Press, 1908.
Judd, Charles H. *Genetic Psychology for Teachers*. New York: D. Appleton Press, 1909.
Kelsey, Carl. "The Influence of Heredity and Environment upon Race Improvement: An Introductory Paper upon the Significance of the Problem." *Annals of the American Academy of Political and Social Science* (July 1909): 3–8.
———. *The Physical Basis of Society*. D. Appleton and Co., 1916.
Kemp, Ellwood. *An Outline of Method in History*. Terre Haute, IN: Inland, 1897.
Kidd, Benjamin. *The Control of the Tropics*. New York: Macmillan, 1898.
———. *Social Evolution*. New York: Macmillan, 1894.
Kilpatrick, William Heard. *Foundations of Method: Informal Talks on Teaching*. New York: Macmillan, 1925.
———. "The Project Method." *Teachers College Record* (September 1918): 319–35.
King, Charles Francis. *Elementary Geography: A Textbook for Children*. Boston: Lothrop Publishing Company, 1903.
King, Irving. *Education for Social Efficiency: A Study in the Social Relations of Education*. New York: D. Appleton Press, 1913.
———. *The Psychology of Child Development: With an Introduction by John Dewey*. Chicago: University of Chicago Press, 1903.
———. *Social Aspects of Education: A Book of Sources and Original Discussions with Annotated Bibliographies*. New York: Macmillan, 1912.
Kirkpatick, Edwin Ashbury. *Genetic Psychology: An Introduction to the Objective and Genetic View of Intelligence*. New York: Macmillan, 1910.
Kroeber, A. L. "Eighteen Professions." *American Anthropologist* 17 (April–June 1915): 283–88.
Langley, Elizabeth, and Annette Butler. "Manual Training." *Elementary School Record* 3 (1900): 377–9.
Lasker, Bruno. *Race Prejudice in Children*. New York: Henry Holt, 1929.
Longfellow, Henry Wadsworth. *The Song of Hiawatha*. Boston: Tickner and Fields, 1855.
Marshall, L. C., and Charles Judd. "An Introduction to Social Studies." In *The Twenty Second Yearbook of the National Society for the Study of Education: Part II, The Social Studies in the Elementary and Secondary School*. Edited by G. M. Whipple. Bloomington, IL: Public School Publishing Company, 1923, 77–110.

Mayo, Marion Jacob. *The Mental Capacity of the American Negro.* New York: Science Press, 1913.

McMurry, Charles. *The Elements of General Method: Based on Principles of Herbart.* New York: Macmillan, 1903.

McMurry, Dorothy. *Herbartian Contributions to History Instruction in American Elementary Schools.* New York: Bureau of Publications, Teachers College, 1946.

Mead, Margaret. *Coming of Age in Samoa: A Psychological Study of Primitive Youth for Western Civilization.* New York: HarperCollins, 2001. Originally published in 1928.

Mill, John Stuart. *Principles of Political Economy: With Some of Their Applications to Social Philosophy.* New York: Longmans, Green and Co., 1909. Originally published 1848.

Miller, Kelly. "Eugenics and the Negro Race." *The Scientific Monthly* 5 (July 1917): 57–9.

———. *Out of the House of Bondage.* New York: Neale Publishing, 1914.

Monroe, Walter and Foster, I.O. *The Status of the Social Sciences in High Schools and the North Central Association.* Urbana, IL: University of Illinois Press, 1922.

Montessori, Marie. *The Montessori Method.* Translated by Anne George. New York: Frederick Stokes Co., 1912.

———. *Pedagogical Anthropology.* Translated by Frederic Taber Cooper. New York: Frederick Stokes Co., 1912.

Morgan, Lewis Henry. *Ancient Society: Researchers in the Lines of Human Progress from Savagery through Barbarianism to Civilization.* Chicago: Charles H. Kerr, 1877.

Morgan, Thomas J. "A Plea for the Papoose." *Baptist Home Mission Monthly* 18 (December 1896): 404.

Munsterberg, Hugo. *Psychology and the Teacher.* Baltimore: Review Publishing, 1909.

Muzzey, David Saville. *An American History.* New York: Ginn and Company, 1911.

Myers, Philip Van Ness. *A Short History of Medieval and Modern Times.* New York: Ginn and Company, 1906.

O'Donnell, William Charles. "The Gary System in the Crucible of a Political Campaign." *Educational Foundations* 29 (January 1918): 271.

O'Shea, Michael. *Dynamic Factors in Education.* New York: Macmillan, 1906.

———. *Education as Adjustment: Educational Theory Viewed in Light of Contemporary Thought.* New York: Longman, Green and Co., 1903.

Parker, Francis Wayland. *Talks on Pedagogics: An Outline of the Theory of Concentration.* New York: E. L. Kellogg, 1894.

Rigast, Adolph K. *Industrial Education among the American Negroes.* Master's thesis, University of Wisconsin, 1921.

Ripley, William Z. *The Races of Europe: A Sociological Study.* New York: D. Appleton and Co., 1899.

Robinson, James Harvey. *Medieval and Modern Times.* Ginn and Company, 1916.

———. *New History: Essays Illustrating the Modern Historical Outlook.* New York: Macmillan, 1912.

Roddy, Henry Justin. *Elementary Geography.* New York: American Book Company, 1902.

Ross, Edward A. *Old World in the New: The Significance of Past, Present, Immigration to the American People.* New York: The Century Co., 1914.

———. *Social Control: A Survey of the Foundations of Order.* New York: Macmillan, 1901.

Rousseau, Jean Jacques. *Discourse upon the Origin of the Inequality.* Indianapolis, ID: Hackett Publishing Co., 1992. Originally published 1755.

Ruediger, William Carl. *The Principles of Education.* New York: Houghton Mifflin, 1910.

Rugg, Earl. "How the Current Courses in History, Geography, and Civics Came to Be What They Are." In *Social Studies in the Elementary and Secondary School: 22nd Yearbook for the National Society for the Study of Education*. Bloomington, IL: Public School Publishing Company, 1923, 48–75.

Rugg, Harold. *American Life and the School Curriculum: Next Steps toward Schools of Living*. New York: Ginn and Company, 1936.

———. "A Century of Curriculum-Construction in American Schools." In *Making Past and Present: The 26th Yearbook of the National Society for the Study of Education*. Bloomington, IL: Public School Publishing Company, 1933, 3–116.

———. *Foundations for American Education*. Yonkers-on-Hudson, NY: World Book Company, 1947.

———. "How Shall We Reconstruct the Social Studies Curriculum?" *The Historical Outlook* 12 (May 1921): 184–9.

———. *An Introduction to Problems of American Culture*. New York: Ginn and Company, 1931.

Rugg, Harold, and Ann Shumaker. *The Child-Centered School: An Appraisal of the New Education*. New York: World Book Company, 1928.

Runyon, Laura. "A Day with the New Education." *Chautauquan: Organ of the Chautauqua Literacy and Science Circle* 30 (1900): 589–90.

———. The Teaching of Elementary History in the Dewey School. Master's thesis, University of Chicago, 1906.

Schell, Walter. "The Value of Play in the Development of the Child." *The Inland Educator* 9 (5): 214–5.

Scott, Harriet, and Gertrude Buck. *Organic Education: A Manual for Teachers in Primary and Grammar Grades*. Boston: DC Heath and Co., 1899.

Small, Albion. "Demands of Sociology upon Pedagogy." *Addresses and Proceedings: National Education Association of the United States* (1896): 174–84.

———. *General Sociology: An Exposition of the Main Development in Sociological Theory From Spencer to Ratzenhofer*. Chicago: University of Chicago Press, 1905.

Snedden, David. *Educational Sociology*. New York: The Century Co., 1922.

Spencer, Herbert. *Education: Intellectual, Moral, and Physical*. London: John Childs and Son, 1861.

———. *First Principles*. London: Williams and Norgate, 1864.

———. "Progress: Its Laws and Cause." In *Seven Essays: Selected From the Works of H. Spencer*. London: Watts and Co., 1907, 7–34.

Stimson, John Ward. *The Gate Beautiful: The Philosophy of Beauty*. Trenton, NJ: Albert Brandt, 1903.

Sully, James. "The New Study of Children." In *Mind: Little Masterpieces of Science*. Edited by George Iles. New York: Doubleday, 1902, 21–52.

———. *Studies in Childhood*. New York: D. Appleton, 1895.

Terman, Lewis. *The Intelligence of School Children: How Children Differ in Ability, the Use of Mental Tests in School Grading and the Proper Education of Exceptional Children*. Boston: Houghton Mifflin, 1919.

———. *Intelligence Tests and School Reorganization*. Yonkers-on-Hudson, NY: World Book, 1922.

———. *Measurement of Intelligence: An Explanation and Complete Guide for the Use of the Stanford Revision and Extension of the Binet-Simon Intelligence Scale*. New York: Houghton Mifflin, 1916.

Thomas, William I. "The Gaming Instinct." *American Journal of Sociology* 6 (July–May 1901): 750–763.

———. "The Mind of Woman and the Lower Races." *American Journal of Sociology* 12 (January 1907): 435–69.

———. "The Psychology of Race-Prejudice." *American Journal of Sociology* 9 (March 1904): 593–610.

———. "Race Psychology: Standpoint and Questionnaire, With Particular Reference to the Immigrant and the Negro." *American Journal of Sociology* 17 (May 1912): 725–75.

———. *Source Book for Social Origins: Ethnological Materials, Psychological Standpoint, Classified and Annotated Bibliographies for the Interpretation of Savage Society*. Chicago: University of Chicago Press, 1909.

Thorndike, Edward, and R. S. Woodworth. "Biographical Memoir of Granville Stanley Hall, 1846–1924." *National Academy of Sciences Biographical Memoirs*, 12 (1925): 135–80.

———. "Darwin's Contribution to Psychology." *University of California Chronicle* 12 (1909): 65–80.

———. *Educational Psychology, Vol. III: Mental Work and Fatigue and Individual Differences and Their Causes*. New York: Teachers College Press, 1913.

———. *The Elements of Psychology*. New York: A. J. Seiler, 1905.

———. "The Influence of Improvement in One Mental Function upon the Efficiency of Other Functions." *Psychological Review* (May 1901): 247–260.

———. *Measurement of Twins*. New York: Science Press, 1905.

———. *The Principles of Teaching: Based on Psychology*. New York: A. J. Seiler, 1911.

———. "Review of The Feebly Inhibited: Nomadism, or Wandering Impulse, with Special Reference to Heredity: Inheritance of Temperament by Charles B. Davenport." *Science* 43 (March 1916): 429.

Turner, Frederick Jackson. *The Frontier in American History*. New York: Henry Holt and Company, 1921.

Tylor, Edward Burnett. *Anthropology: An Introduction to the Study of Man and Civilization*. New York: D. Appleton and Co., 1881.

———. *Primitive Culture: Researches into the Development of Mythology, Philosophy, Religion, Language, Art and Custom*. New York: Putnam and Sons, 1871.

Van Liew, C. C. "The Educational Theory of Culture Epochs Viewed Historically and Critically." In *The First Yearbook of the Herbart Society for the Scientific Study of Teaching*. Bloomington, IL: National Herbart Society, 1895, 70–121.

Veblen, Thorstein. *The Theory of the Leisure Class: An Economic Study of Institutions*. New York: Macmillan, 1899.

Vincent, George Edgar. *The Social Mind and Education*. New York: Macmillan Company, 1897.

Ward, Lester Frank. *Dynamic Sociology, or Applied Social Science*. New York: D. Appleton and Co., 1883.

———. *Haeckel's Genesis of Man, or History of the Development of the Human Race*. Philadelphia: Phillip Stern and Company, 1879.

———. *The Psychic Factors of Civilization*, 2nd ed. New York: Ginn and Company, 1906. Originally published in 1893.

Watson, John B. *Behaviorism*. Chicago: University of Chicago Press, 1924.

———. *Psychological Care of Infant and Child*. New York: Norton, 1928.

Wissler, Clark. "The Psychological Aspects of the Culture-Environmental Relation." *American Anthropologist* 14 (April–June 1913): 217–25.

———. "Review of Mental Development in the Child and the Race by James Mark Baldwin and Ethical Interpretation in Mental Development: A Study in Social Psychology by James Mark Baldwin." *American Anthropologist 9* (January–March 1907): 194–6.
Woodson, Carter G. "Negro History Week—The Eleventh Year." *The Journal of Negro History* 21 (April 1936): 105–10.
———. "Negro Life and History in our Schools." *The Journal of Negro History,* 4 (July 1919): 273–80.
Wundt, Wilhelm. *Outlines of Psychology.* Translated by Charles Judd. New York: G. E. Stechert and Co., 1896.
Wyss, Johann David. *The Swiss Family Robinson: Edited for Use in the Schools.* Boston: Ginn and Company, 1885.

PUBLISHED SECONDARY WORKS

Adams, David Wallace. *Education for Extinction: American Indians and the Boarding School Experience.* Lawrence: University Press of Kansas, 1995.
Alridge, Derrick. *The Educational Thought of W.E.B. Du Bois: An Intellectual History.* New York: Teachers College Press, 2008.
Anderson, James D. *The Education of Blacks in the South, 1860–1935.* Chapel Hill: University of North Carolina Press, 1988.
Angulo, A. J. *Empire and Education: A History of Greed and Goodwill from the War of 1898 to the War on Terror.* New York: Palgrave Macmillan, 2012.
Au, Wayne. "Teaching under the New Taylorism: High-stakes Testing and the Standardization of the 21st Century Curriculum." *Journal of Curriculum Studies 43* (2011): 25–45.
Bair, Sarah. "The Early Years of Negro History Week, 1926–1922." In *Histories of Social Studies and Race: 1865–2000.* Edited by Christine Woyshner and Chara Bohan. New York: Palgrave Macmillan, 2012, 57–78.
Baker, Lee D. *From Savage to Negro: Anthropology and the Construction of Race, 1896–1954.* Berkeley: University of California Press, 1998.
Banks, Cherry McGee. *Improving Multicultural Education: Lessons from the Intergroup Education Movement.* New York: Teachers College Press, 2005.
Barkan, Elazar. *The Retreat of Scientific Racism: Changing Conceptions in Britain and the United States between the World Wars.* New York: Cambridge University Press, 1992.
Bloom, Benjamin S. *Compensatory Education for Cultural Deprivation.* New York: Holt, Rinehart, and Winston, 1965.
Bowler, Peter. *The Eclipse of Darwinism: Anti-Darwinian Evolution Theories in the Decades around 1900.* Baltimore: Johns Hopkins Press, 1983.
Brandom, Robert. "When Philosophy Paints Its Blue on Grey: Irony and the Pragmatist Enlightenment." In *Pragmatism, Nation, and Race: Community in the Age of Empire.* Edited by Chad Kautzer and Eduardo Mendieta. Bloomington: Indiana University Press, 2009, 19–45.
Brantlinger, Patrick. *Dark Vanishings: Discourse on Extinction of Primitive Races, 1800–1930.* Ithaca, NY: Cornell University Press, 2003.
Bredo, Eric. "Evolution, Psychology, and John Dewey's Critique of the Reflex Arc Concept." *The Elementary School Journal* 98 (May 1998): 447–66.
Burkholder, Zoe. *Color in the Classroom: How American Schools Taught Race 1900–1954.* New York: Oxford University Press, 2011.
Burks, Ben. "Unity and Diversity through Education: A Comparison of the Thought of W.E.B. Du Bois and John Dewey." *The Journal of Thought* (Spring 1997): 99–110.

Butchart, Ronald. "Race, Social Studies, and Culturally Relevant Curriculum in Social Studies' Prehistory: A Cautionary Meditation." In *Histories of Social Studies and Race, 1865–2000*. Edited by Christine Woyshner and Chara Bohan. New York: Palgrave Macmillan, 2012, 19–36.

Callahan, Raymond. *Education and the Cult of Efficiency*. Chicago: University of Chicago Press, 1962.

Chapman, Paul D. *Schools as Sorters: Lewis M. Terman, Applied Psychology, and the Intelligence Testing Movement, 1890–1930*. New York: New York University Press, 1988.

Church, Robert L., and Michael W. Sedlak. *Education in the United States: An Interpretive History*. New York: Free Press, 1976.

Coloma, Roland Sintos. "Destiny Has Thrown the Negro and Filipino under the Tutelage of America: Race and Curriculum in the Age of Empire." *Curriculum Inquiry* 39 (2009): 495–519.

Cormier, Harvey. "William James on Nation and Race." In *Pragmatism, Nation and Race: Community in the Age of Empire*. Edited by Chad Kautzer and Eduardo Mendieta. Bloomington: Indiana University Press, 2009, 142–162.

Cravens, Hamilton. *The Triumph of Evolution: American Scientists and the Heredity-Environment Controversy 1900–1941*. Philadelphia: University of Pennsylvania Press, 1978.

Cravens, Hamilton, and John C. Burnham. "Psychology and Evolutionary Naturalism in American Thought, 1890–1940." *American Quarterly* 23 (December 1971): 635–57.

Cremin, Lawrence. *Transformation of the School: Progressivism in American Education 1876–1957*. New York: Knopf, 1961.

Curti, Merle. *The Social Ideas of American Educators*. New York: Charles Scribner and Sons, 1935.

Durst, Anne. *Women Educators in the Progressive Era: The Women Behind Dewey's Laboratory School*. New York: Palgrave Macmillan, 2010.

Egan, Kieran. *Getting It Wrong from the Beginning: Our Progressive Inheritance from Herbert Spencer, John Dewey, and Jean Piaget*. New Haven, CT: Yale University Press, 2002.

Fallace, Thomas. *Dewey and the Dilemma of Race: An Intellectual History, 1895–1922*. New York: Teachers College Press, 2012.

———. "Did Social Studies Really Replace History in American Secondary Schools?" *Teachers College Record* 110 (2008): 2245–70.

———. "John Dewey and the Savage Mind: Uniting Anthropological, Psychological and Pedagogical Thought, 1894–1902." *The Journal of the History of Behavioral Sciences*, 44 (Fall 2008): 335–349.

———. "John Dewey's Influence on the Origins of the Social Studies: An Analysis of the Historiography and New Interpretation." *Review of Educational Research*, 79 (2009): 601–624.

———. "'The Mind at Every Stage Has Its Own Logic': John Dewey as Genetic Psychologist." *Educational Theory* 60 (April 2010): 129–146.

———. "Repeating the Race Experience: John Dewey and the History Curriculum at the University of Chicago Laboratory School." *Curriculum Inquiry*, 39 (June 2009): 381–405.

Fallace, Thomas, and Victoria Fantozzi. "Was There Really a Social Efficiency Doctrine? The Uses and Abuses of an Educational Idea." *Educational Researcher* (May 2013): 142–150.

Fass, Paula. "The IQ: A Cultural and Historical Framework." *American Journal of Education* 88 (August 1980): 431–458.

Feinberg, Walter. *Reason and Rhetoric: Intellectual Foundations of Twentieth Century Liberal*

Educational Policy. New York: John Wiley, 1975.
Franklin, Barry. *Building the American Curriculum: The School Curriculum and the Search for Social Control.* Philadelphia: Falmer, 1986.
Fredrickson, George. *Racism: A Short History.* Princeton, NJ: Princeton University Press, 2003.
Garrison, Joshua. "'A Problematic Alliance Colonial Anthropology, Recapitulation Theory, and G. Stanley Hall's Program for the Liberation of America's Youth." *American Educational History Journal* 35 (2008): 131–47.
Goodchild, Lester F. "G. Stanley Hall and an American Social Darwinist Pedagogy: His Progressive Educational Ideas on Gender and Race." *History of Education Quarterly* 52 (Winter 2012): 62–98.
Gossett, Thomas. *Race: The History of an Idea in America.* New York: Schocken Books, 1963.
Gould, Stephen Jay. *Ontogeny and Phylogeny.* Cambridge, MA: Belknap, 1977.
Graham, Patricia Albjerg. *Progressive Education: From Arcady to Academe: A History of the Progressive Education Association, 1919–1955.* New York: Teachers College Press, 1967.
Herrnstein, Richard, and Charles Murray. *The Bell Curve: Intelligence and Class Structure in American Life.* New York: Free Press, 1994.
Hobsbawm, Eric. *The Age of Empire: 1897–1914.* New York: Vintage, 1987.
Hochschild, Adam. *Kind Leopold's Ghost: A Story of Greed, Terror, and Heroism in Colonial Africa.* New York: Houghton Mifflin, 1998.
Hook, Sidney. *John Dewey: An Intellectual Portrait.* New York: John Day Company, 1939.
Howard, Tyrone. *Why Race and Culture Matters in Schools: Closing the Achievement Gap in America's Schools.* New York: Teachers College Press, 2010.
Jacobs, Margaret. *White Mother to a Dark Race: Settler Colonialism, Maternalism, and the Removal of Indigenous Children in the American West and Australia, 1800–1940.* Lincoln, NA: University of Nebraska Press, 2013.
Jacobson, Matthew Frye. *Barbarian Virtues: The United States Encounters Foreign Peoples at Home and Abroad, 1876–1917.* New York: Hill and Wang, 2000.
———. *Whiteness of a Different Color: European Immigrants and the Alchemy of Race.* Cambridge, MA: Harvard University Press, 1998.
Jensen, Arthur A. "How Much Can We Boost IQ and Scholastic Achievement?" *Harvard Educational Review* 39 (1969): 1–123.
Joncich, Geraldine. *The Sane Positivist: A Biography of Edward Thorndike.* Middletown, CT: Wesleyan University Press, 1968.
Katz, Michael B. *The Undeserving Poor: From the War on Poverty to the War on Welfare.* New York: Pantheon, 1990.
Kim, David H. "The Unexamined Frontier: Dewey, Pragmatism, and America Enlarged." In *Pragmatism, Nation and Race.* Edited by Chad Kautzer and Eduardo Mendieta. Bloomington: Indiana University Press, 2009, 46–72.
King, LaGarrett J., Christopher Davis, and Anthony Brown. "African American History, Race and Textbooks: An Examination of the Works of Harold O. Rugg and Carter G. Woodson." *The Journal of Social Studies Research* 36 (4): 359–86.
Kliebard, Herbert. *The Struggle for the American Curriculum 1893–1958,* 2nd ed. New York: Routledge, 1995.
Kloppenberg, James T. *Uncertain Victory: Social Democracy and Progressivism in European and American Thought, 1870–1920.* New York: Oxford University Press, 1986.
Knoll, Michael. "From Kidd to Dewey: The Origin and Meaning of Social Efficiency." *Journal of Curriculum Studies* 41 (2009): 361–391.

———. "I Made a Mistake: William Heard Kilpatrick and the Project Method." *Teachers College Record* (February 2012): 1–45.

Krug, Edward. *The Shaping of the American High School, 1880–1920.* Madison, WI: University of Wisconsin Press, 1964.

Labaree, David. "Progressivism, Schools, and Schools of Education: An American Romance." *Paedagogica Historica* 41 (February 2005): 275–88.

Lagemann, Ellen C. "Experimenting with Education: John Dewey and Ella Flagg Young at the University of Chicago." *American Journal of Education* 104 (1996): 171–185.

———. "The Plural Worlds of Educational Research." *History of Education Quarterly* 29 (Summer 1989): 183–214.

Lasch-Quinn, Anna. *Black Neighbors: Race and the Limits of Reform in the American Settlement House Movement, 1890–1945.* Chapel Hill: University of North Carolina Press, 1993.

Lovejoy, Arthur. *The Great Chain of Being: A Study of the History of an Idea.* Cambridge, MA: Harvard University Press, 1936.

Margonis, Frank. "John Dewey's Racialized Visions of the Student and Classroom Community." *Educational Theory* 59 (2009): 17–39.

Martinez, Sylvia, and John Rury. "From 'Culturally Deprived' to 'At Risk': The Politics of Popular Expression and Educational Inequality in the United States, 1960–1985." *Teachers College Record* 111 (2012): 1–31.

Mayhew, Katherine Camp, and Alice Camp Edwards. *The Dewey School: The Laboratory School of the University of Chicago, 1896–1903.* New York: Appleton-Century, 1936.

McKee, James B. *Sociology and the Race Problem: Failure of a Perspective.* Urbana, IL: University of Illinois Press, 1993.

Meier, August, and Elliot M. Rudwick. "Early Boycotts of Segregated Schools: The Alton, Illinois Case, 1897–1908." *The Journal of Negro History* 36 (Autumn 1967): 394–402.

———. "Early Boycotts of Segregated Schools: The Case of Springfield, Ohio, 1922–23." *American Quarterly* 20 (Winter 1968): 744–58.

———. "Early Boycotts of Segregated Schools: The East Orange, New Jersey, Experience, 1899–1906." *History of Education Quarterly* 7 (Spring 1967): 22–35.

Menand, Louis. *The Metaphysical Club: A Story of Ideas in America.* New York: Farrar, Straus, and Giroux, 2001.

Mills, Charles. *The Racial Contract.* Ithaca, NY: Cornell University Press, 1997.

Mirel, Jeffrey. "Old Educational Ideas, New American Schools: Progressivism and the Rhetoric of Educational Revolution." *Paedagogica Historica* 29 (August 2003): 477–97.

———. *Patriotic Pluralism: Americanization Education and European Immigrants.* Cambridge, MA: Harvard University Press, 2010.

Novick, Peter. *That Noble Dream: The Objectivity Question and the American Historical Profession.* New York: Cambridge University Press, 1988.

O'Donnell, John M. *The Origins of Behaviorism: American Psychology, 1870–1920.* New York: New York University Press, 1985.

Olneck, Michael R. "American Public Schooling and European Immigrants in the Early Twentieth Century: A Post Revisionist Synthesis." In *Rethinking the History of American Education.* Edited by William. J. Reese and John L. Rury. New York: Palgrave Macmillan, 2008, 103–142.

Painter, Nell Irvin. *The History of White People.* New York: Norton and Company, 2010.

Paulet, Anne. "To Change the World: The Use of American Indian Education in the Philippines." *History of Education Quarterly* 47 (May 2007): 173–202.

Provenzo, Eugene F. Jr. *Culture as Curriculum: Education and the International Expositions (1876–1904)*. New York: Peter Lang, 2012.

Ravitch, Diane. *Left Back: A Century of Battles over School Reform*. New York: Touchstone, 2000.

Reese, William J. "The Origins of Progressive Education." *History of Education Quarterly* 41 (Spring 2001): 1–24.

———. *Power and Promise of School Reform: Grassroots Movements during the Progressive Era*. Boston: Routledge and Kegan, 1986.

Richards, Robert. *Darwin and the Emergence of Evolutionary Theories of Mind and Behavior*. Chicago: University of Chicago, 1987.

Riessman, Frank. *The Culturally Deprived Child*. New York: Harper, 1962.

Ritterhouse, Jennifer. *Growing up Jim Crow: How Black and White Children in the South Learned Race*. Chapel Hill: University of North Carolina Press, 2006.

Roberts, Peter. *The Problem of Americanization*. New York: Macmillan, 1920.

Robinson, James Harvey. *New History: Essays Illustrating the Modern Historical Outlook*. New York: Macmillan, 1912.

Roche, Agnes M. "Carter G. Woodson and the Development of Transformative Scholarship." In *Multicultural Education: Transformative Knowledge and Action: Historical and Contemporary Perspectives*. Edited by James A. Banks. New York: Teachers College Press, 1996, 91–114.

Ross, Dorothy. *G. Stanley Hall: The Psychologist as Prophet*. Chicago: University of Chicago Press, 1972.

———. Ed. *Modernist Impulses in the Human Sciences 1870–1930*. Baltimore: Johns Hopkins Press, 1994.

———. *The Origins of American Social Science*. New York: Cambridge University Press, 1991.

Rudwick, Elliott M., and August Meier, "Black Man in the 'White City': Negroes and the Columbian Exposition 1893." *Phylon*, 26 (4th Quarter 1965): 354–361.

Scott, Daryl Michael. *Contempt and Pity: Social Policy and the Image of the Damaged Black Psyche, 1880–1996*. Chapel Hill: University of North Carolina Press, 1997.

Selden, Steven. *Inheriting Shame: The Story of Eugenics and Racism in America*. New York: Teachers College Press, 1999.

Selig, Diana. *Americans All: The Cultural Gifts Movement*. Cambridge, MA: Harvard University Press, 2008.

Semel, Susan F., and Alan R. Sadovnik. *Schools of Tomorrow, Schools of Today: What Happened to Progressive Education?* New York: Peter Lang, 1988.

Skiba, Russell. "'As Nature Has Formed Them': The History and Current Status of Racial Difference Research." *Teachers College Record* 114 (2012): 1–49.

Spack, Ruth. "English, Pedagogy, and Ideology: A Case Study of the Hampton Institute, 1878–1900." *American Indian Culture and Research Journal* 24 (2001): 1–24.

Stack, Sam F. Jr. "John Dewey and the Question of Race: The Fight for Odell Walker." *Education and Culture* 25 (2009): 17–35.

Stocking, George Jr. *Race, Culture and Evolution: Essays in the History of Anthropology*. Chicago: University of Chicago Press, 1968.

———. *Victorian Anthropology*. New York: Free Press, 1987.

Strickland, Charles. "The Child, the Community, and Clio: The Uses of Cultural History in Elementary School Experiments of the Eighteen-Nineties." *History of Education Quarterly* 7 (Winter 1967): 474–92.

Tanner, Daniel, and Laurel Tanner. "Environmentalism in American Pedagogy: The Legacy of Lester Ward." *Teachers College Record* 88, no. 4 (1987): 537–47.

———. *History of the School Curriculum.* New York: Macmillan, 1990.

Tanner, Laurel. *Dewey's Laboratory School: Lessons for Today.* New York: Teachers College Press, 1997.

Thomas, William B. "Black Intellectuals' Critique of Early Mental Testing: A Little Known Saga of the 1920s." *American Journal of Education* 90 (May 1982): 258–92.

Tyack, David. *The One Best System.* Cambridge, MA: Harvard University Press, 1974.

Valencia, Richard R. "Contextualizing 'Rethinking Compensatory Education': The Value of a Temporal Continuity Analysis." *Teachers College Record* 114 (2012): 1–5.

———. *Dismantling Contemporary Deficit Thinking: Educational Thought and Practice.* New York: Routledge, 2010.

———. "Genetic Pathology Model of Deficit Thinking." In *The Evolution of Deficit Thinking: Educational Thought and Practice.* Edited by Richard R. Valencia. Washington, D.C.: Falmer Press, 1997, 41–113.

Voneche, Jacques. "Reflections on Baldwin." *The Cognitive Developmental Psychology of James Mark Baldwin: Current Theory and Research in Genetic Epistemology.* Edited by John M. Broughton and John Freeman-Moir. Norwood, NJ: Ablex Publishing Company, 1982, 80–86.

Walker, Vanessa Siddle. "Organized Resistance and Black Educators' Quest for School Equality, 1878–1938." *Teachers College Record* 107 (March 2005): 355–88.

Watkins, William. *The White Architects of Black Education: Ideology and Power in America, 1865–1954.* New York: Teachers College Press, 2001.

Weiner, Melissa F. *Power, Protest, and the Public Schools: Jewish and African American Struggles in New York City.* New Brunswick, NJ: Rutgers University Press, 2010.

West, Cornell. *The American Evasion of Philosophy: A Genealogy of Pragmatism.* Madison, WI: University of Wisconsin Press, 1989.

Westbrook, Robert. *John Dewey and American Democracy.* Ithaca, NY: Cornell University Press, 1991.

White, Morton. *Social Thought in America: The Revolt against Formalism.* New York: Oxford Press, 1947.

Wiebe, Robert. *The Search for Order, 1877–1920.* New York: Hill and Wang, 1967.

Winfield, Ana G. *Eugenics and Education in America.* New York: Peter Lang, 2007.

Woyshner, Christine, and Chara Bohan, Eds. *Histories of Social Studies and Race: 1865–2000.* New York: Palgrave Macmillan, 2012.

Wraga, William. *Progressive Pioneer: Alexander James Inglis and American Secondary Education, 1879–1924.* New York: Peter Lang, 2007.

Zilversmit, Arthur. *Changing Schools: Progressive Education and Practice, 1930–1960.* Chicago: University of Chicago Press, 1993.

Zimmerman, Jonathan. *Whose America? Culture Wars in the Public Schools.* Cambridge, MA: Harvard University, 2002.

Index

Adams, Herbart Baxter, 29, 33, 77
Addams, Jane, 50
Adolescence, 107–108
Adolescence (Hall), 25, 93, 107
African Americans. *See also* Non-Whites
   capacity for civilization, 39, 40, 82, 133
   capacity for self-government, 40
   curriculum for, 39, 40, 41. *See also* Hampton-Tuskegee model
   depictions of, 43, 100, 122
   disenfranchisement of, 123
   education of, 136–137
   excluded from settlement houses, 50–51
   Hall on, 93–94
   industrial education for, 45, 137
   James's views on, 24
   justification for policy on, 35
   perceived limitations of, 41, 51
   at P.S. 26, 62–63
   studies of intelligence of, 89–91
   study of secondary education for, 138
   in textbooks, 81–82
   Thomas on, 120
   value of education by, 138
Africans, 1, 2, 3, 9, 102
Agassiz, Louis, 18
Akinson, Fred, 44
American History, An (Muzzey), 76, 135
American Indians. *See* Native Americans
Americanization, 80. *See also* Assimilation; Citizenship
Americanization (Dixon), 78–79
American Social Problems (Burch & Patterson), 81–82
Anatomy, and potential, 3
Ancient Society (Morgan), 13–14
Anthropology, 17–19, 22–23, 26, 32, 107, 146
Anthropology (Tylor), 14
Appleton, Francis, 76
Armstrong, Samuel Chapman, 39, 45
Army recruits, 91, 101
Art, 23, 55–56
Assimilation. *See also* African Americans; Immigrants
   alternative to, 142
   challenges to, 110
   Dewey on, 49–50, 113
   Du Bois's rejection of, 109
   melting pot metaphor, 111, 141
   of Native Americans, 38–39
   policy of, 45
   in race relations cycle, 142
   resistance to, 121
   Rugg on, 140–141, 143
Attendance, mandatory, 131
Ayes, Leonard, 129

Bagley, William, 6, 7, 8, 72, 74
   challenges to intelligence testing, 92
   change in views of, 8–9
   Determinism in Education, 96–97
   Educational Values, 95

Bagley, William *(continued)*
   Educative Process, The, 70, 95
   position on race, 94–97
   racial views of, 101–102
   on social efficiency, 70
Baldwin, James Mark, 26, 32,
   71, 85, 114, 115, 147
Ball, Frank H., 46
Barbarians/barbarianism, 8, 14,
   20, 27–28, 32, 64–65
Barrie, James M., 75
Barrows, David Prescott, 44
Behavioral psychology, 121
Behaviorism, 100
Behaviorism (Watson), 141–142
Benedict, Ruth, 123
Benga, Ota, 1, 2, 3, 9
Bennion, Milton, 77–78, 80
Billings, Neal, 140
Biological deficiency, 81–82
Blacks. *See* African Americans
Boas, Franz, 16, 103–108, 124, 131, 143
   challenge to social deficiency
      arguments, 146
   challenge to theory of
      recapitulation, 83
   influence on Dewey, 118–119
   as outsider, 121
Boasians, 108, 122, 139
Bourne, Randolph, 108,
   111, 121, 135, 136
Brandom, Robert, 17
Bredo, Eric, 16
Brigham, Carl C., 88, 91, 102, 124
Brookings Institute, 43
Buck, Gertrude, 34, 56–57
Burch, Henry Reed, 81–82
Burgess, John W., 29

Cephalic index, 37, 88
Chamberlain, Alexander Francis, 53–54

Changing Conceptions of Education
   (Cubberley), 87
Charters, W. W., 73–74, 92
Chicago, University of. *See*
   Laboratory School
Child (Chamberlain), 54
Child-centeredness, 3–4, 38, 125–128
   and belief in sociological
      inferiority, 124
   Chamberlain's proposal for, 53–54
   child-centered progressives,
      125–128, 134, 142–143
   content in, 126
   curriculum in, 128
   justification for, 35
   Parker's curriculum, 37
   persistence of, 147
   race in, 124, 125, 126
   and Rousseau, 36
   and theory of recapitulation, 7, 38
Child-Centered School, The (Rugg &
   Shumaker), 4, 126–127, 140
Child development, 25–26,
   34, 35–36, 48, 54, 74
Child races, 45, 46
Child-savage analogy. *See*
   Savage-child analogy
Child study movement, 25
Chinese, 25, 95, 96
Christianity, 75. *See also* Religion
Citizenship, 77–80, 112, 132.
   See also Assimilation
Civics textbooks, 81
Civilization
   capacity for, 39, 40, 78–79, 82, 133, 134
   defined, 14
   as overcoming biological impulse, 78
   and religion, 32, 75
   Rousseau's view of, 36
Clark, Kate Upson, 80
Class, 4, 27–28

Climate and Civilization (Huntington), 132–133
Collins, Mary, 43
Coming of Age in Samoa (Mead), 107–108
Committee on Social Studies report, 59, 65, 66–69, 79–81, 136, 140
Community and the Citizen (Dunn), 65
Community Civics (Hughes), 81
Community Life and Civic Problems (Hill), 81
"Conservation of Races, The" (Du Bois), 109
Control of the Tropics, The (Kidd), 28
Counts, George, 137–138, 143
Cuba, 44, 45
Cubberley, Ellwood, 87, 90–91
Cultural deficit model, 145–146, 147
Cultural development, 105–106
Cultural gifts movement, 139–140, 141
Cultural pluralism. *See* Pluralism, cultural
Cultural relativity. *See* Relativity, cultural
Culture
  beliefs about, 8
  Dewey's definition of, 53, 113, 119
  Dewey's view of, 111, 114, 115
  Ellwood's approach to, 131
  as learned attribute, 131
  Rugg's definition of, 141
  similarities of, 105
  use of term, 8
  views of, 7
Culture and Democracy in the United States (Kallen), 142
Culture-epoch theory, 55, 56, 57. *See also* Recapitulation, theory of
Culture of poverty model, 145
Cultures, 18, 116, 119

Curriculum. *See also* Educational materials
  and administrative progressives, 129
  for African Americans, 39, 40, 41. *See also* Hampton-Tuskegee model
  in child-centered education, 128
  of innovation schools, 62–63
  of Laboratory School, 60–62
  Rugg's, 140
  savage-child analogy in, 55–58, 61
  and stage theory, 147
  suggested by Dewey, 55
  theory of recapitulation in, 55–57
Curriculum, differentiated, 34–35
Curriculum Construction (Charters), 74
Curriculum utilitarianism, 132
Cyclopedia of Education, 53, 115

Darwin, Charles, 13, 16, 84
Darwin and the Humanities (Baldwin), 26
Darwinism, 84–85, 92, 98–99
Darwinism and Other Essays (Fiske), 29
Davenport, Charles, 87, 101
Deficiency, biological, 81–82
Deficiency, sociological. *See* Sociological deficiency
Deficit model, 145–146, 147
DeGarmo, Charles, 59
"Demands of Sociology upon Pedagogy, The" (Small), 33
Democracy, 29, 30–31, 112, 113, 120–121, 134
Democracy and Education (Dewey), 2, 17, 48, 113, 116, 117, 122–123
Democracy and Social Ethics (Addams), 50
"Democracy Versus the Melting Pot" (Kallen), 110
Descent of Man, The (Darwin), 13
Determinism, 1, 2–3, 19–20, 96–97, 99

Determinism in Education (Bagley), 96–97
Development, child, 25–26, 34, 35–36, 48, 54, 74
Development, cultural, 105–106
Development, human, 14–15, 127
Development, psychological, 3, 26, 48–49. *See also* Recapitulation, theory of
Dewey, Evelyn, 4, 35, 36, 62, 63, 68, 135, 137
Dewey, John, 7, 34. *See also* Laboratory School
   before 1916, 47–53
   after 1916, 112–121
   approach to theory of recapitulation, 58
   on assimilation, 49–50
   on behaviorism, 100
   beliefs about education, 67–68
   Boas's influence on, 118–119
   challenges to intelligence testing, 92
   change in views of, 9, 112–121
   on child development, 48
   compared with Thorndike, 98–100
   and cultural deficit model, 145–146
   cultural relativistic approach of, 143
   on culture, 111, 114, 115
   definition of culture, 53, 113, 119
   Democracy and Education, 2, 17, 48, 113, 116, 117, 122–123
   divergence from Hall, 55
   divergence from Herbartians, 55
   "Education and Culture," 116
   Ethical Principles Underlying Education, 60, 65, 68
   Ethics, 22, 49, 113
   on heredity, 99
   historicism of, 53
   on history, 67–68
   How We Think, 2, 48, 127–128
   Human Nature and Conduct, 121
   on inferior races, 120
   "Influence of Darwinism on Philosophy, The," 16–17
   influence of Thomas on, 118
   influence on child-centered progressives, 125, 126, 127–128
   influence on Kilpatrick, 126
   influence on O'Shea, 71
   "Interpretation of Culture Epoch Theory," 51
   "Interpretation of the Savage Mind," 52, 118, 131, 146
   on King's approach, 71
   "My Pedagogic Creed," 33
   "Nationalizing Education," 113, 116
   and NEA Committee on Social Studies report, 66–68
   on need for diversity, 117
   position on sociological deficiency, 124
   pragmatism of, 2, 63, 114
   on psychological development, 48–49
   on race, 51, 112, 146
   on racial diversity, 49
   "Racial Prejudice and Friction," 119–120
   reference to cultures, 116, 119
   rejection of neo-Lamarckianism, 52
   and religion, 32
   School and Society, The, 48, 60, 65, 67–68, 69, 70
   "School as Social Centre, The," 112
   Schools of To-Morrow, 4, 35, 36, 62, 63, 68, 135, 137
   on significance of social psychology, 99, 100
   on sociological progress, 51
   "Some Stages of Logical Thought," 48, 60
   speech on race, 1–2
   suggested curriculum, 55
   and theory of recapitulation, 32

use of pluralistic language, 115–116
use of savage-child analogy, 49, 51, 61
Dewey School. *See* Laboratory School
Difference, significance of, 100
Diversity, 49, 117
Dixon, Royal, 78–79, 80
Dodd, Catherine Isabel, 57
Dopp, Katherine Elizabeth, 57
Double-consciousness, 109
Douglass, Frederick, 43
DuBois, Rachel Davis, 139
Du Bois, W.E.B., 103, 108, 130
   on African American Schools, 83
   "Conservation of Races, The," 109
   Dusk at Dawn, 76
   education of children, 136
   "Of Our Spiritual Strivings," 109
   as outsider, 121
   Souls of Black Folk, The, 109, 134
Dunn, Arthur, 64–66, 67, 68, 75
Dunning, William, 40
Durkheim, Emile, 22
Dusk at Dawn (Du Bois), 76
Dutton, Samuel Train, 70–71, 72
Dyke, Charles Bartlett, 45–46
Dynamic Factors in Education (O'Shea), 71
Dynamic Sociology (Ward), 20

Economics, 27–29, 32
Education. *See also* Schools
   as college preparation vs. life preparation, 68
   Dewey's beliefs about, 67–68
   and frontier thesis, 30
   vs. heredity, 117
   importance of, 128
   influence of recapitulationist scholars on, 33
   as means of race improvement, 94–95, 96
   and overcoming savage tendencies, 130
   role of in democracy, 112, 113, 120–121
   and social environment, 63
   social nature of, 59
   and sociological stages, 20, 47
Education, progressive
   administrative progressives, 125, 128–134, 142–143
   child-centered progressives, 125–128, 134, 142–143
   described, 3–4
   national scope of, 63, 134
   need to simplify language of, 127
   progenitors of, 35–38
   targets of, 125
   transition to, 63
Educational materials
   race in, 74–82
   textbooks, 74–82, 135–136, 140
   theory of recapitulation in, 54–57
"Educational Policy for our New Possessions, An" (Harris), 46–47
Educational Psychology (Thorndike), 97–98, 100
Educational Sociology (Snedden), 133
Educational Values (Bagley), 95
"Education and Culture" (Dewey), 116
Education as Adjustment (O'Shea), 71
Education for Efficiency (Eliot), 71
Education for Social Efficiency (King), 72
Educative Process, The (Bagley), 70, 95
Efficiency, meaning of, 71
Efficiency, social, 28, 59, 69–74
"Eighteen Professions" (Kroeber), 107
Elementary Forms of Religious Life, The (Durkheim), 22
Elementary Geography (Appleton), 76
Elementary Geography (King), 76
Elementary Geography (Roddy), 76
Elementary School Teacher, The, 57

Elements of General Method (McMurray), 55
Elements of Geography (Frye), 76
Eliot, Charles, 71, 72
Ellwood, Charles, 52, 129–132, 140
  approach to racial problem, 133–134
  on imitation theory, 85
  influence of, 146
  on non-Whites, 143
  Sociology and Modern Social Problems, 81
Elyria High School, 64–65, 77
Emerson, Ralph Waldo, 24
Empires. *See* Imperialism
Enlightenment, second, 17
Environment. *See also* Interaction
  and education, 63
  vs. heredity, 86, 117, 137–138
  James on, 24
  as means of race improvement, 96
  significance of, 30, 96
  Thorndike on, 100
Essays on Child Psychology (Lombroso), 34
Essences, static, 16–17
"Essential Features in the Education of the Child Races" (Dyke), 45–46
Essential types, 51
Ethical Principles Underlying Education (Dewey), 60, 65, 68
Ethics (Dewey & Tufts), 22, 49, 113
Ethnic groups, 27. *See also* Race; Races, White
Ethnicity, evolution of views on, 5–6
Ethnocentrism, persistence of, 147
Eugenicists, 9, 87
Eugenics, 86–91
  Boas's critique of, 105–106
  in child-centered education, 126
  Ellwood's endorsement of, 130
  linked to school administration, 131
  Snedden on, 133
  and social efficiency, 74
  Thorndike's support for, 101
  views of, 102
Evolution, 1, 13, 16, 84–85, 92, 98–99. *See also* Darwin, Charles; Neo-Lamarckianism
Exceptionalism, American, 29, 30, 142

Feeble-minded individuals, 87, 101, 131, 146
Feebly Inhibited, The (Davenport), 101
First Principles (Spencer), 19–20
Fiske, John, 29
Fletcher, Alice, 38, 39
Foundations of Method (Kilpatrick), 126
Frederickson, George, 9, 83, 145
Froebel, Friedrich, 36, 38
Frontier thesis, 30–31, 59, 79
Frye, Alexis Everett, 76

Gary Plan, 4, 134–135, 136
Gary Schools, The (Bourne), 135
General Sociology (Small), 21
Genetic Psychology (Kirkpatrick), 57
Genetic Psychology for Teachers (Hubbard), 25
Genetics, 52, 85, 86. *See also* Neo-Lamarckianism
Geography, race in, 75–76
"German Origin of New England Towns, The" (Adams), 29
Germ theory, 29, 30, 77, 79
Giddings, Franklin, 21, 30, 34, 41, 85
Goddard, H. H., 86, 92, 120, 124
Goldenweiser, Alexander A., 104, 105, 107, 121
Graham, Patricia Albjerg, 4
Grant, Madison, 88
Great Chain of Being, 13, 14, 15, 17, 55

Index

"Great Men and their Environment" (James), 24
Growth, contingent, 16–17

Haddon, Alfred C., 19
Haeckel, Ernst, 1, 2–3, 14, 21, 32
Haeckel's Genesis of Man (Ward), 21
Hall, G. Stanley, 9, 33, 70, 114, 124
   Adolescence, 25, 93, 107
   on African Americans, 93–94
   focus on, 5, 7
   "How Far Are the Principles of Education along Indigenous Lines Applicable to American Indians?," 94
   as pluralist, 94, 101
   "Point of View Toward Primitive Races, The," 47
   and religion, 32
   and savage-child analogy, 22–23, 25–26, 54
   on teaching non-Whites, 44
Hampton Normal and Agricultural Institute, 39, 40, 41, 42, 66. *See also* Hampton-Tuskegee model
Hampton-Tuskegee model, 44, 45, 63, 70–71, 82, 91, 94, 109, 137
Harris, William Torrey, 7, 23, 32, 44, 45, 46–47, 71
Hart, Albert Bushnell, 29–30, 33
Hawaii, 44, 45, 46
Hegel, G. W. F., 23
Herbart, Johann, 5, 36, 71
Herbartians, 55, 56, 57
Heredity, 97–101. *See also* Eugenics
   determinism of, 99
   vs. environment, 86, 137–138
   and potential, 2–3
   significance of, 95, 100
   Thorndike on, 101
   used to explain racial difference, 92
"Hiawatha" (Longfellow), 55, 66, 75

Hierarchy, racial, 1–2, 24, 74–75, 122–123
High schools, 138
Hill, Howard Copeland, 81
Historicism, Dewey's, 17, 53
History. *See also* Social studies
   African American history, 109–110
   African history, 109–110
   Dewey on, 67–68
   in Dewey's curriculum, 65
   Dunn's suggestions for, 65–66
   at Elyria High School, 64–65
   King's suggestions for curriculum, 72
   narrative of Reconstruction, 40
   Robinson on, 66–67
   savage-child analogy in, 31
   textbooks for, 76, 77, 135–136
   theory of recapitulation in, 29–31, 32
History, intellectual, 6
Hobsbawm, Eric, 45
Hobson, John A., 69
Holmes, Oliver Wendell, 87
Howerth, Ira W., 69
"How Far Are the Principles of Education along Indigenous Lines Applicable to American Indians?" (Hall), 94
How We Think (Dewey), 2, 48, 127–128
Hubbard, Charles, 25
Hughes, Ray Oswald, 81
Hull House, 50
Human development, 14–15, 127
Human Nature and Conduct (Dewey), 121
Humans, origins of, 18
Huntington, Ellsworth, 132–133, 134

Ideas, history of, 6
Identity, American, 59
Imitation, 85, 115, 121

Immigrants, 15. *See also*
    Assimilation; Races, White
  alternatives to assimilation, 142
  belief in sociocultural
    inferiority of, 134
  Boas on, 106–107
  Bourne's view of, 111
  capacity for civilization, 51
  in child-centered education, 126
  depiction of in textbooks, 77
  Dewey on, 49–50, 62, 63, 120
  disconnect with intellectual elites, 136
  Dixon on, 78–79
  eugenicists' view of, 87
  and Gary Plan, 4, 135, 136
  need to modernize, 50
  occupations of, 50
  opposition of to textbooks, 135–136
  pluralists' views of, 108
  restriction of, 120, 146
  Ross on, 132
  study of intelligence of, 129
  Thorndike's views of, 101
Imperialism, 6, 9, 15–16, 28, 35, 44–47
Indianapolis, Indiana, 62–63
Individuality, 125. *See also*
    Child-centeredness
Industrial training. *See also* Gary Plan;
    Hampton-Tuskegee model
  for African Americans, 39, 45, 137
  for Native Americans, 39, 45
  at P.S. 26, 63
  in territories, 45, 46
Inequality, social, 20. *See also* Class;
    Socioeconomic status
Inferiority, sociocultural, 6, 124, 134, 146
"Influence of Darwinism on Philosophy,
    The" (Dewey), 16–17
Inglis, Alexander, 125, 127–128
Instincts, 99
Institutions, American, 29

Instructional materials. *See* Educational
    materials; Textbooks
Intellectual capacity, studies on, 101
Intelligence, 89–91, 92
Intelligence testing, 90, 91, 131
  Bagley on, 96–97
  challenges to, 92, 108
  cultural bias in, 102
  Dewey's critique of, 120
  and social efficiency, 74
  Thorndike's support for, 101
Interaction, 24, 30, 100, 119–120.
    See also Environment
"Interpretation of Culture Epoch
    Theory" (Dewey), 51
"Interpretation of the Savage Mind"
    (Dewey), 52, 118, 131, 146
Intolerance, Dewey on, 112–113
*Introduction to American Problems,
    An* (Rugg), 140–141

Jackman, Wilbur Samuel, 55
James, William, 16, 23–25, 26,
    33, 47, 52, 98, 115, 126
Japanese, 95, 96
Jews, 100, 110, 135, 136
Johnson, Marietta, 4, 125
Jones, Thomas Jesse, 40–41, 66, 67, 68
Journal of Negro History, 110, 139
Judd, Charles, 25, 32, 33, 56, 92

Kallen, Horace, 108, 110–111, 121, 142
Kelsey, Carl, 84, 86
Kemp, Ellwood, 78
Kidd, Benjamin, 28, 32, 69
Kilpatrick, William Heard, 125, 126
King, Charles F., 76
King, Irving, 71–72, 74, 92, 102
Kirkpatrick, Edwin Ashbury, 57
Kliebard, Herbert, 4, 125
Klyce, Scudder, 116

Knowledge, 16, 51, 53, 114
Kroeber, A. L., 104, 107, 122

Laboratory School, 59
  curriculum of, 2, 50, 60–62, 65, 114
  lack of cultural intermixing in, 117
  manual training at, 46
  Runyon on, 73
Laggards in Our Schools (Ayes), 129
Lane, Franklin, 136–137
Language, 8–9
Lasker, Bruno, 139
Latent potential, 2, 16, 51, 74, 112
Law of sympathy, 41, 85
Learn by doing, 135
Leisure class, 27–28
Lewis, Oscar, 145
Lippman, Walter, 92, 135
Literature, children's, 74–75
Literature, education, 53–58
Locke, Alain, 110, 121, 141
Lodge, Henry Cabot, 69
Lombroso, Paola, 34
Lovejoy, Arthur, 6, 13

Man and Culture (Wissler), 131
Manual training. *See* Industrial training
Materialism, 22
Mayo, Marion J., 89–90, 91, 128
McGee, W. P., 19, 32
McKee, James, 143
McMurray, Charles, 55, 56
Mead, Margaret, 104, 121, 122
Measurement of Intelligence (Terman), 90–91
Medieval and Modern Times (Robinson), 31
Melting pot metaphor, 111, 141
Mendelian genetics, 52, 85, 86
Mental Capacity of the American Negro, The (Mayo), 89–90

Mental Development in the Race and Child (Baldwin), 26
Methodology, 6–7
Methods of Teaching (Charters), 73
Mill, John Stuart, 27, 28
Miller, Kelly, 88–89, 102, 103, 122, 130
Mind of Primitive Man, The (Boas), 105
"Mind of Woman and the Lower Races, The" (Thomas), 118
Mirel, Jeffrey, 136
Mitchell, John Purroy, 135
Monoculturalism, resistance to, 121
Monogenists, 18
Montessori, Maria, 36–37, 38
Montessori Method, The (Montessori), 36
Morgan, Lewis H., 13–14, 18, 32, 76
Morphology, 128–129
Munsterburg, Hugo, 26, 33
Muzzey, David Saville, 76, 135
Myers, Philip Van Ness, 77
"My Pedagogic Creed" (Dewey), 33

National Association for the Advancement of Colored People (NAACP), 2
National Education Association (NEA)
  Commission on the Reorganization of Secondary Education, 66
  Committee on Social Studies report, 59, 65, 66–69, 79–81, 136, 140
Nationalism, 113
"Nationalizing Education" (Dewey), 113, 116
National Negro Conference, 52
National Origins Act, 87
Native Americans. *See also* Non-Whites
  belief in biological restraints of, 41
  in children's literature, 75
  in civics textbooks, 81
  curriculum for, 38, 39, 41
  depiction of, 42–43, 122

Native Americans *(continued)*
  disenfranchisement of, 123
  education of, 45, 94, 136–137
  Miller on, 89, 122
  policy on, 35, 38–39
  referred to as savages, 30
  removal policy, 38–39, 43
  teaching of culture of, 147
  Thomas on, 120
Natural selection, 84
Nature-nurture debate, 137–138.
  See also Environment
Nature-study movement, 55
NEA Committee on Social
  Studies report, 59, 65,
  66–69, 79–81, 136, 140
"Needs of present growth," 68, 69
Negro History Week, 110, 122
Neo-Lamarckianism, 14, 39, 47, 84–85
  challenges to, 83, 94–95, 114
  rejection of, 52, 86, 92, 93, 99, 101–102
New education. *See* Education, progressive
New History, The (Robinson), 31, 66–67
Non-Whites. *See also* African Americans; Native Americans
  belief in sociocultural inferiority of, 6, 124, 134, 145–146
  challenges to inferiority of, 106
  curriculum for, 35, 45
  Dewey's beliefs about, 48
  education of, 136–137
  head size of, 37
  perceived limitations of, 47
  potential of, 45–46
  resistance of to reform, 132
  teachers of, 45, 46
  theory of recapitulation in education of, 44
Notes on Child Development (Thorndike), 128

Occupations, social, 59, 60–62
"Of Our Spiritual Strivings" (Du Bois), 109
Old World in the New, The (Ross), 132
On the Origins of Species (Darwin), 13, 16
Organic Education (Scott & Buck), 56
Organic School, 4, 125
Organizations, professional, 15
Origins, human, 18
O'Shea, Michael Vincent, 70, 71, 72, 92
Outlines of Psychology (Wundt), 22
Out of the House of Bondage (Miller), 89
Outsiders, scholars as, 121–122

Park, Robert, 142
Parker, Francis W., 37–38, 46
Passing of the Great Race, The (Grant), 88
Patriotism, 79–80
Patterson, S. Howard, 81–82
PEA (Progressive Education Association), 125
Pearson, Karl, 86, 93, 95
Pedagogical Anthropology (Montessori), 37
Pestalozzi, Johann Heinrich, 36, 38
Peter Pan (Barrie), 75
Philippines, 44, 45, 47
"Philippine Tangle, The" (James), 47
Philosophy, 16–17
Piaget, Jean, 147
Platoon system, 4, 134–135, 136
Play, value of, 57
Pluralism, cultural, 104, 108–112, 142
  Dewey's, 112–121
  Hall's, 94
  necessity of, 115
  and sociological deficiency, 134–142
  suggested by Thomas, 118

"Point of View Toward Primitive Races, The" (Hall), 47
Polygenists, 18
Potential, 53
Potential, latent, 2, 16, 51, 74, 112
Pragmatism, 17, 51
    Dewey's, 2, 63, 114
    James's, 23–24
Pratt, Richard Henry, 43, 45
Prejudice, race, 119–120, 138–142
Primitive, use of term, 70
Primitive Culture (Tylor), 18, 19
Primitive peoples, argument for preservation of, 93–94
Principles of Education, The (Ruediger), 92–93
Principles of Political Economy (Mill), 27
Principles of Psychology (James), 24
Principles of Secondary Education, The (Inglis), 127–128
Principles of Sociology (Giddings), 21
Principles of Teaching (Thorndike), 99
Problems of Democracy (course), 80–82
Progressive education. *See* Education, progressive
Progressive Education Association (PEA), 125
Project method, 126
"Project Method, The" (Kilpatrick), 126
Pseudo-science, 9
P.S. 26, 62–63
Psychic Factors of Civilization, The (Ward), 20, 21
Psychological development, 3, 26, 48–49. *See also* Recapitulation, theory of
Psychological stages, 14
    correspondence with sociological stages, 8, 51, 60–62, 68, 73
    Dewey's beliefs about, 48
    Harris's, 23

Psychologic Foundations of Education (Harris), 23
Psychology, 21, 22–27, 32, 97, 98–99, 114, 117
Psychology, behavioral, 121
Psychology, social, 85, 99–100, 115, 116–117
Psychology and the Teacher (Munsterburg), 26
Psychology of Child Development, The (King), 71–72
Puerto Rico, 44, 45, 46
Pygmies, 1, 2, 3, 8, 9, 102

Race. *See also* African Americans; Native Americans; Non-Whites; Races, White; Whites
    cultural aspects of, 103. *See also* Culture
    and democracy, 29
    differences in, origins of, 78
    differences in, scholarship on, 103
    evolution of views on, 5–6, 101
    positions on, 124
    progressives on, 143
    researching views on, 6–7
Race Attitudes in Children (Lasker), 139
Race prejudice, 119–120, 138–142
Race relations, 142
Races, White. *See also* Ethnic groups; Whites
    describing cultural worth of, 76–80
    intelligence of, 91–92
    James on, 24–25
    Ripley on, 27, 87–88, 91
Races of Europe, The (Ripley), 27, 87–88, 91
Race suicide, 132, 133
Racial development, factors in, 105–106
Racial hierarchy, 1–2, 24, 74–75, 122–123

"Racial Prejudice and Friction" (Dewey), 119–120
Racism, 9, 83, 88, 90, 139, 147
Racists, biological, 9
Ravitch, Diane, 4
Reason, 1
Recapitulation, theory of, 14
   and acquired characteristics, 85–86
   in anthropology, 17–19, 32
   in Chamberlain's work, 54
   Charters on, 73–74
   in child-centered education, 7, 126
   described, 3
   and Dewey, 48, 51, 58, 60–62, 71–72
   in economics, 27–29
   in education literature, 53–58
   in education of non-Whites, 44, 45
   Emerson's subscription to, 24
   and Hall's views on race, 94
   in history, 29–31
   influence of, 3, 15, 63
   lack of questioning of, 32
   loosening of, 58
   loss of scientific backing, 86
   methodological justification for, 104
   in Parker's writing, 37–38
   in pedagogical reform, 34
   persistence of, 146–147
   pervasiveness of, 5
   in policy on Native Americans, 39
   and professional knowledge, 32
   in psychology, 22–27
   refutation of, 107
   rejection of, 83, 97–98, 114, 138
   in report of Committee on Social Studies, 68–69
   in science education, 55
   shift toward sociocultural version of, 59, 60
   skepticism about, 85
   and social efficiency, 69, 71, 72–73
   in sociology, 19–22
   as tacitly presupposed, 7
   underlying racial assumptions of, 5
   use of term, 8
Reconstruction, 40, 82
Reel, Estelle, 38–39
Relativity, cultural, 104–108, 124, 139, 143, 146
   rejection of, 124, 134, 141
Religion, 22, 32, 39, 75, 77, 80
Rice, Emily, 56
Rigast, Adolph, 137
Ripley, William Z., 27, 87–88, 91
Robinson, James Harvey, 16, 31, 32, 33, 76
   Medieval and Modern Times, 31
   and NEA Committee on Social Studies report, 66–67, 68–69
   The New History, 31, 66–67
Robinson, Louis, 54
Robinson Crusoe (Defoe), 55, 65, 75
Rockefeller, Steven, 118
Roddy, Henry J., 76
Ross, Edward A., 132, 146
Rousseau, Jean-Jacques, 35–36, 38
Ruediger, William Carl, 92–93, 102
Rugg, Harold, 4, 125, 126–127, 128–129, 139–141, 143
Runyon, Lauren, 61–62, 73
Ryan, Alan, 118

Savage
   in children's literature, 75
   coded meaning of, 38
   Dewey's view of, 52
   in geography textbooks, 76
   Giddings on, 21
   identity of, 32
   meaning of term, 7, 13
   as non-Christian, 32, 39

Rousseau's view of, 36
use of term, 8
Savage-child analogy, 21,
  49, 51, 54, 71, 72
  in curriculum, 55–58, 61
  in history, 31
  in imperialism, 28
  in psychology, 22–23, 25, 26–27
  refutation of, 107
Savagery, defined, 14
Savagery-barbarianism-civilization.
  See Sociological progress
Schell, Walter, 57
School and Society, The (Dewey),
  48, 60, 65, 67–68, 69, 70
"School as Social Centre,
  The" (Dewey), 112
*School History of the United
  States* (Hart), 29–30
Schools. *See also* Education
  African American attendance of, 89
  mandatory attendance, 131
  as social control, 132
  success in and socioeconomic
    status, 137–138, 143
Schools, experimental, 4
Schools of To-Morrow (Dewey & Dewey),
  4, 35, 36, 62, 63, 68, 135, 137
School surveys, 64–65
Science, 23, 134
Science education, 55
Scott, Harriet Maria, 34, 56–57
Segregation, 83
  failure to criticize, 138
  justification for, 35, 90, 91, 123
  Miller's criticism of, 88
*Selective Character of American Secondary
  Education, The* (Counts), 137–138
Settlement houses, 50–51
Shufeldt, R. W., 54
Shumaker, Anna, 4, 126–127, 140

"Significance of the Frontier in American
  History, The" (Turner), 30–31
Slavery, 29–30
Small, Albion, 16, 21, 30, 32, 33, 52
Snedden, David, 77, 132, 133, 134, 146
Social Aspects of Education (King), 72
Social control, 74, 77, 132, 134
Social Control (Ross), 132
Social efficiency, 28, 59, 69–74
Social Evolution (Kidd), 28, 69
Socialization, 128, 139, 141
*Social Mind and Education,
  The* (Vincent), 58
Social occupations, 59, 60–62
*Social Phases of Education in the School
  and Home* (Dutton), 70–71
Social problems, 80–82, 126, 140
Social psychology, 85, 99–100,
  115, 116–117
Social studies, 59, 68. *See also* History
Sociocultural inferiority, 6, 124,
  134, 146
Socioeconomic status, and
  success, 137–138, 143
Sociological deficiency
  basis of, 59
  belief in, 9, 143, 146
  causes of, 3, 21
  challenges to arguments of, 146
  and child-centered education, 124
  and cultural pluralism, 134–142
  culture of poverty model of, 145
  Dewey's position on, 124
  of immigrants, 62, 63
  Inglis on, 128
  philosophical foundations of, 13
  sociologists' views on, 19–22
  in textbooks, 81–82
  use of term, 8
Sociological development, 13, 26,
  35–36. *See also* Sociological stages

Sociological progress, 1, 14, 51, 105, 108, 119, 122. *See also* Barbarians/barbarianism; Civilization; Savage; Sociological stages
Sociological stages. *See also* Sociological progress
   in art and science, 23
   correspondence with psychological stages, 8, 51, 60–62, 68, 73
   and Dewey, 2, 48
   in economics, 27–29
   and education, 20
   Morgan's identification of, 18
   in pedagogical reform, 34
   Ward's, 20
Sociology, 19–22, 32, 81, 146
Sociology, indirect, 68
Sociology and Modern Social Problems (Ellwood), *81*
Sociology in Its Psychological Aspects (Ellwood), 130
Soldiers, 91, 101
"Some Stages of Logical Thought" (Dewey), 48, 60
"Song of Hiawatha, The" (Longfellow), 55, 56, 75
Souls of Black Folk, The (Du Bois), 109, 134
Spencer, Herbert, 6–7, 16, 19–20, 21, 30, 52, 53, 84, 126
Stages, psychological. *See* Psychological stages
Stages, sociological. *See* Sociological stages
Stage theory, 147
Sterilization, 87, 89, 146
Stimson, John Ward, 55–56
Studies in Childhood (Sully), 57
Study of American Intelligence, A (Brigham), 88, 91
Sully, James, 7, 57, 71
Survival of the fittest, 89
Swiss Family Robinson, The (Wyss), 75

Talks in Pedagogics (Parker), 37
Tarde, Gabriel, 85, 115, 121
Teaching the Child Patriotism (Clark), 80
Teaching the Common Branches (Charters), 73
Terman, Lewis, 90–91
Terminology, 8–9
Territories, education of children in, 44–47
Teutonic germ theory, 29, 30, 77, 79
Textbooks, 74–82, 135–136, 140
Theory of the Leisure Class, The (Veblen), 27
Thomas, William I., 52, 85–86, 115, 118, 120
Thorndike, Edward, 97–101, 114
   Educational Psychology, 97–98, 100
   on heredity, 95
   influence on child-centered progressives, 125, 126, 127–128
   position on race, 124
   research on intelligence, 91, 102
Totem group, 22
"Trans-national America" (Bourne), 111, 136
Transnationalism, 108
Tufts, James, 22, 49, 113
Turner, Frederick Jackson, 16, 30–31, 32, 33, 59, 79
Tuskegee Normal and Industrial Institute, 39. *See also* Hampton-Tuskegee model
Tylor, Edward Burnett, 14, 18, 19, 32

United States, social change in, 15. *See also* Immigrants
Urbanization, 126. *See also* Social problems

Valencia, Richard R., 145
Veblen, Thorstein, 16, 27, 28, 32
Viewpoints, diversity of, 115
Vincent, George, 58
Vocational education. *See*
    Industrial training

Ward, Lester Frank, 7, 20, 21, 30, 34
    and cultural deficit model, 145–146
    on evolution, 84
    reliance on recapitulation, 19–21, 32
    on social efficiency, 69
Washington, Booker T., 39, 109, 130
Watson, John, 114, 121, 141–142
Weismann, August, 52, 85, 93
White, Morton, 16
Whites, 24–25, 35, 37. *See*
    also Races, White

White supremacy, 75, 94,
    102, 103, 121, 145
Wiebe, Robert, 15
Wirt, William, 134–135
Wissler, Clark, 104, 131
Women, 118
Woodson, Carter, 108, 109–
    110, 121, 122, 139
Woodworth, Robert, 101, 126
World's Columbian Exposition,
    42–43
Wundt, Wilhelm, 22, 25, 32, 98, 114
Wyss, Johann David, 75

Yerkes, Robert, 91, 101, 124

Zilversmit, Arthur, 3
Zimmerman, Jonathan, 135–136

About the Author

Thomas D. Fallace is an associate professor of social studies education at William Paterson University of New Jersey. He earned a PhD in education, an MA in history, and an MEd, all from the University of Virginia, after receiving a BA in history from Washington and Lee University. In addition to dozens of articles and book chapters on curriculum history, he is the author of *Dewey and the Dilemma of Race* (2012) and *The Emergence of Holocaust Education in American Schools* (2008). He lives in Montclair, New Jersey, with his wife and two children.